MIDLOTHIAN
PUBLIC LIBRARY

UNDERSTANDING YOUR NEIGHBOR'S FAITH

What Christians and Jews Should Know About Each Other

BOOKS BY PHILIP LAZOWSKI

Faith and Destiny
A Home Guide to Jewish Rituals, Holidays and Prayer
From The Depths To Redemption—A Passover Haggadah
Reflections on Faith
Rediscovering the Prayerbook—The Daily Service

UNDERSTANDING YOUR NEIGHBOR'S FAITH
What Christians and Jews Should Know About Each Other

Edited by

Rabbi Dr. Philip Lazowski

KTAV Publishing House, Inc.
Jersey City, NJ

Library of Congress Cataloging-in-Publication Data

Understanding your neighbor's faith : what Christians and Jews should know about each other / [edited by] by Rabbi Dr. Philip Lazowski.
  p. cm.
Includes bibliographical references.
 ISBN 0-88125-810-5 -- ISBN 0-88125-811-3 (pbk.)
 1. Christianity--Miscellanea. 2. Judaism--Miscellanea. I. Lazowski,
Philip.
BR50.Y685 2003
296.3'96--dc22
                           2003021271

Published by
KTAV Publishing House, Inc.
930 Newark Avenue
Jersey City, NJ 07306
Email: info@ktav.com
www.ktav.com
(201) 963-9524
Fax (201) 963-0102

This book is dedicated to my friend and colleague,
the late Rev. John J. Kiely, who had a vision of a world with
religious harmony and ecumenism, and whose efforts to
achieve it have been a source of personal inspiration to me and
to all who knew him. His presence at the Institute of Living
in Hartford, Connecticut, is especially missed.

TABLE OF CONTENTS

ACKNOWLEDGMENTS

My heartfelt appreciation to Bishop LeRoy Bailey, Jr., W. Robert Chapman, Rev. Robert W. Cudworth, Rev. Aidan N. Donahue, Dr. Alvan N. Johnson, Jr., Dr. Frank G. Kirkpatrick, Dr. Andrew Walsh, Rev. Terry Wiles, and Bishop David Williams for their outstanding contributions to this book.

I am indebted to Judy and Dr. Mark Conway for their insightful criticism, indispensable advice, and suggestions, which ensured a tighter manuscript.

I wish to express my gratitude to each of these individuals for their valuable time, advice, and constructive criticism: Dr. Karen Blank, Irene and Dr. Carl Braren, Ms. Lynne Bundesen, Rabbi Stephen Fuchs, Annmary Huckstadt, Dr. Jeffrey and Llyn Kaimowitz, Rabbi Ephraim P. Slepoy, Dr. S. Edward Weinswig, and Moshe Zwang.

To all of them I tender my most profound thanks. May God reward them with eternal blessings.

To my sons and daughters-in-law, Barry and Cynthia, Alan and Marcia, David and Dana, a special thank-you for providing the necessary administrative services and beautiful office, allowing me the setting in which to write my manuscript. May God bless them.

To my devoted assistant, Elaine Dobrutsky, for her patience in typing and retyping the manuscript, Bless her.

Above all, and beyond words, I am eternally grateful to my beloved wife, Ruth, for her patience, understanding, and devotion.

ACKNOWLEDGMENTS

I wish to thank the following people who so graciously made it possible for me to publish this book.

My deepest appreciation to you and your families.

Mitchell & Margo Blutt Family Foundation
Barbara, James, Caitlin, Julie, James, and Jackie Carter
The Cheryl Chase and Stuart Bear Family Foundation, Inc.
The Rhoda and David Chase Family Foundation, Inc.
The Sandra and Arnold Chase Family Foundation, Inc.
Amy and Eric Federman
Vicki, Michael, Rachel, Danielle, Adam, and Benjamin Gross
Elisabet, Michael, Aleksander, and Nikolas Harth
Linda, Mark, and Jeffrey Hatten
Rachel and Max Javit
Diane, Jeff, Perry, Danny, and Katie Kahan
Amy, Ted, Aaron, Ethan, and Alex Kahan
Jill, Jeffrey, Ben, Sam, and Daniel Karp
Angela, Marty, Mallory, Patrick, and Kevin Kenny
Dori, Michael, Connor, and Matthew Kuziak
Marcia, Alan, Jesse, and Jonah Lazowski
Cynthia Lahm, Barry, Alexa, and Elizabeth Lazowski
Dana, David, Mikayla, and Ari Lazowski
Shelly and David Lerman
Julie and Jerry Levy
Deborah and Samuel J. Linder
Linda and Harris Simons
Betsy and Bruce Simons
Maxine and Michael P. Weinstein
Stacy R. Nerenstone, M.D., and Morton L. Weinstein
Jessica, Eric, Ben, Jacob, and Zoë Zachs

INTRODUCTION

As a rabbi living in Bloomfield, Connecticut, serving Beth Hillel Synagogue for the past forty-five years, and as a chaplain in the Hartford Police Department, I have developed a close relationship with members of the clergy in Catholic and Protestant churches. In February 2000, three clergy members, Rev. Alvan N. Johnson, Jr., Rev. John T. Simmons, Jr., Fr. Joseph V. DiSciacca, and I decided to make an ecumenical pilgrimage to Israel. Seventy people signed up and went with us, visiting many holy places. Many questions were asked, but some were not answered. The participants of the tour suggested that there ought to be a book about what Christians should know about Judaism and what Jews should know about Christianity.

In our time, Christians and Jews have reached a unique moment—"ecumenism"—talking to each other, learning from each other, and sharing a hope for the future rooted in a willingness to know more about each other. The aim of this book is to bring Jews and Christians together in a common study enterprise that will inevitably lead to increased knowledge about one another and help to remove the religious misinformation that has been basic to so much intolerance throughout the centuries. Such an effort may spur Jews and Christians to communicate intelligently for the benefit of both religions.

Ironically, the interpretation of scriptural text on which we Jews base our faith and traditions has been a battleground for many, many centuries. This struggle over the "correct" interpretation of the Hebrew Bible and the New Testament had unfortunate results, often leading to the persecution of the Jews and denigrating them to the position of second-class citizens.

History is replete with the ever-present existence of anti-Semitism, which took its diabolic shape during the Second World War, when six million Jews perished under Nazi totalitarianism. Despite and because of this evil and horror, we hope that Christians and Jews can come together in a process of understanding. That is what this book is about. A respectful acceptance of one another and a mutual knowledge of our faith commitments enhance the recognition of our separate but spiritually related identities. This mutual knowledge increases awareness of our traditions and spirituality.

Encounters with another faith raise questions about our own faith, and such questions can be overwhelmingly difficult. We have been and still are, in some respects, in confrontation. One aim of this book is to be enlightened by the questions and answers offered by the respective faiths. It is an invitation to friendship. It is a way to deepen our comprehension of our respective traditions as partners in God's covenant. It is important to learn from others. Before you study other religions, however, you must know your own. "Know thyself." Only by knowing your own can you then enlighten others and learn from them as well.

As the Talmud states: "He is wise who learns from others." Maimonides gratefully acknowledged his debt to Aristotle; Rabbi Joseph Baer Soloveitchik acknowledged the influence of Søren Kierkegaard, the Protestant philosopher. I, too, have read many works by non-Jews (Harry Emerson Fosdick, George Foot Moore, and others).

Jews and Christians who converse and learn with and about each other's religions develop a deeper and firmer grounding in both Judaism and Christianity. Getting Jews and Christians to learn, and to talk with one another, has proven an effective way to increase understanding and reduce prejudice. The outcome may be a deeper sense of self-understanding and a renewed commitment to one's tradition.

For some readers, these questions and answers will be a welcome review; for others they will be an appetizer, a foretaste of a much larger feast or banquet.

By learning from one another, we can maintain a respectful mutual relationship to understand and accept each other and help to "mend the world" (*tikkun olam*).

As I write this introduction, there are reports of the recrudescence of anti-Semitism, principally in Europe. Israel is being used as the platform for anti-Semites to viciously attack the Jewish people and Jewish institutions. It seems as if the devastation of the Holocaust and the loss of six million souls have been forgotten.

Let us hope that this book will make a small contribution, through mutual understanding, to the elimination of the scourge of anti-Semitism, anti-Christian prejudice, and all other forms of religious bigotry and intolerance.

Chapter 1

JUDAISM

By Rabbi Dr. Philip Lazowski

Pope Pius XI emphasized the Judaic roots of Christianity when he declared that Christians are "spiritual Semites." Christianity arose out of Judaism. Jesus, Paul, and the apostles were Jews. The two religions share basic views and values. Both profess faith in a supreme Creator who is revealed in nature and history. Both teach that God judges the world with compassion and justice, and that when His kingdom is ultimately established, righteousness, wisdom, harmony, security, and peace will prevail.

The chief and fundamental difference between Judaism and Christianity is that Judaism is committed to pure and uncompromising monotheism, whereas most Christians subscribe to a belief in the trinitarian nature of the Divine Being.

Trinitarianism, that is to say, the belief in and worship of "God, the Son, and the Holy Spirit," is basic and important to most denominations of Christianity but is contrary to Judaism's beliefs.

Christianity made the salvation of the individual its main goal. Judaism emphasized improvements of the individual by means of God's commandments, called *mitzvot*, good deeds. Judaism teaches that the righteous of all peoples have a share in eternal life. Every person practicing the tenets of his own faith may attain this righteous life. In the words of the prophet, "Let all the peoples walk each in the name of its God, and we will walk in the name of the Lord our God forever and ever" (Micah 4:5).

1

What does God require of man? Micah states: "To do justly, to love mercy, and to walk humbly with God."

Judaism teaches: "Revere God, and keep His commandments; for this is the whole duty of man" (Ecclesiastes 12:13). "Ye shall therefore keep my statutes, and my judgments: which if a man does, he shall live by them: I am the Lord" (Leviticus 18:5).

When learning and studying take place, a shared desire for knowledge will bring about a committed effort to face reality with candor and legitimacy, not to convert each other, but to make this world a better place to live in harmony and peace.

The Jewish prophets, sages, and rabbis throughout the ages, even amid cruel persecutions, have advocated this type of good will.

My own attitude to Christianity and Christians has always been one of respect and appreciation. I have felt and feel a spiritual kinship with truly religious Christians. As a rabbi for forty-five years, I enjoyed a most cordial relationship with members of the Catholic and Protestant clergy. I always had a continuous dialogue with Catholic and Protestant groups that I addressed in their churches or in our synagogue.

What justifies the expression "Judeo-Christian culture"?
Christianity's debt to Judaism and the profound influence of the Hebrew Bible on the New Testament is well known, and "Christian culture has grown up as much around the Hebrew Bible Scripture as around the New Testament."[1]

The link between Judaism and Christianity
The greatest liturgical link between Judaism and Christianity is the Hebrew Bible Scripture, which holds an essential place in both traditions. It is true that Christians differ in their interpretation of the Hebrew Bible, especially concerning messianic prophecy. The

---

[1] I. Graeber and St. N. Britt, eds., *Jews in a Gentile World* (New York: Macmillan, 1942), pp. 7 f.

Hebrew Bible remains the word of God to this day and always, and that is why the Jews revere and honor it.

Can people of different religions be true friends to one another?
There are several Hebrew words meaning "friend," and each illustrates a different aspect of the dynamic process of friendship. One Hebrew word is *yadid*. It can be related to two words: *yad*, meaning "hand," and *dod*, meaning "loved one." It is basic to the process of religion that it involves extending a hand to another in affection and love, to seek good for the benefit of others. Similarly, friendship involves an ongoing process of willingness to reach out for better understanding. Being a friend certainly does not require one to agree to what another's religious issues are. Yet friendship requires one to be tolerant and try to understand other religious beliefs, practices, and habits without necessarily accepting them.

Being a friend requires us at times to seek forgiveness. A good friend requires loyalty. Rabbi Eliezer taught: "Let the honor of your friend be as dear to you as your own."

Friendship is a reciprocal process of understanding one another, encouraging one another, and, above all, respecting one another A fundamental example of this concerns the Ten Commandments.

The Jewish, Protestant, and Catholic versions of the Ten Commandments are based on Exodus 20:1–17.

Jewish Version
I am the Lord your God, who brought you out of the land of Egypt, out of the house of bondage.
You shall have no other gods before me. You shall not make for yourself a graven image . . . you shall not bow down to them nor serve them.
You shall not take the name of the Lord your God in vain.
Remember the Sabbath day, to keep it holy.
Honor your father and your mother.
You shall not murder.

You shall not commit adultery

You shall not steal.

You shall not bear false witness against your neighbor.

You shall not covet your neighbor's house; you shall not covet your neighbor's wife, or his manservant, or his maidservant, or his ox, or his ass, or any thing that is of thy neighbor's.

Protestant Version

I am the Lord your God, who brought you out of the land of Egypt, out of the house of bondage. You shall have no other gods before me.

You shall not make for yourself a graven image . . . you shall not bow down to them nor serve them.

You shall not take the name of the Lord your God in vain.

Remember the Sabbath day, to keep it holy.

Honor your father and your mother.

You shall not kill.

You shall not commit adultery.

You shall not steal.

You shall not bear false witness against your neighbor.

You shall not covet.

The Ten Commandments from the Hebrew Bible (Old Testament) are somewhat different for Catholics. To Jews, "I am the Lord your God" is the first commandment, and the second commandment is, "Have no other gods beside me." Catholics regard the first two commandments as one, and divide the one beginning, "Do not covet," into two commandments.

Roman Catholic Version

I am the Lord your God: You shall not have strange gods before me.

You shall not take the name of the Lord your God in vain.
Remember to keep holy the Lord's Day.
Honor your father and your mother.
You shall not kill.
You shall not commit adultery.
You shall not steal.
You shall not bear false witness against your neighbor.
You shall not covet your neighbor's wife.
You shall not covet your neighbor's goods.

What do Christianity and Judaism have in common?
The two religious traditions have a great many things in common:

The existence of God as Creator and Sustainer is common to Christians and Jews.

Both religions have the Hebrew Bible as a sacred Scripture.

The Psalms are used in the liturgies of both faiths.

Worship as essential to human life is the credo of both religions.

Prayer as an avenue of approach to God is essential to both religions.

The Priestly Blessing is used for Christians and Jews.

Both religions hail God as the Heavenly Father.

Christians and Jews constantly use the words "Amen" and "Hallelujah."

Both religions believe that man was created in the image of God.

Both religions believe in the fatherhood of God and the brotherhood of man.

Both religions believe that man has an immortal soul.

The reality of sin and the need for expiation and forgiveness are of prime importance to both religions.

Confession is a means of facing up to sin and error among Christians and Jews.

The sanctity of marriage is common to both religions.

> Individual responsibility is a need for practicing both Christianity and Judaism.
>
> Both religions advocate concern for one's neighbor in the ministry of love and charity.

The above merely scratches the surface. We have much in common, and this, therefore, should facilitate the development of closer relationships between Jews and Christians. Genuine good will suggests an endeavor to understand and respect each other, and to recognize that each religion has God's work to do. If anything, however, such understanding and respect must be predicated on the knowledge and grasp of the differences that distinguish one's own religion from that of those with whom one wants to live in friendship and harmony.[2]

Even with the differences, we have to try to maintain a harmonious relationship. After all, we are all created in the image of God. Although we hold different beliefs, there is a higher law, God's law, that unites us all, Jew and Christian alike. Man's role in Hebrew is *letaken olam*—to improve the world under the rule of God.

What we need is more knowledge, learning, understanding, compassion, and more meeting places to communicate with each other. What is man's role in this world? Our dialogue must be motivated not by the desire to convert each other, but by a desire to convert a world that is constantly at war to a more peaceful world that is loving, caring, and sharing.

Who is Jesus?

To talk about Jesus requires tremendous sensitivity, especially to those who practice Christianity and regard Jesus as God. We must have great respect when we speak about Jesus, whom so many revere as the Son of God and the Messiah.

---

[2] Trude Weiss-Rosemarin, *Judaism and Christianity*, p. 12.

Jews believe that Jesus was a human being born like all other people and that he was reared by his family as a Jew. When Jesus was asked what the greatest commandment was, he quoted Deuteronomy 6:5, "You shall love the Lord your God with all your heart and with all your soul and with all your might." This verse is also found in the New Testament (Matthew 22:37). Jesus stated, "You shall love your neighbor as yourself," a quotation that came from Leviticus 19:18. "The Lord's Prayer," Matthew 6:9–15, "Our Father who art in Heaven, hallowed be Thy name, Thy Kingdom come," closely resembles the ancient wording of the Kaddish (memorial) prayer, "Hallowed and sanctified is Your great name. May you speedily establish your kingdom of righteousness on earth."

We believe that Jesus was a great teacher who interpreted Judaism as He understood it, helping people in every possible way. Jesus offered help to the needy and the poor whose needs were not being met.

The Jewish definition of a Messiah is that he is human, and when he comes, he will create a social order respected by all nations.

Why did Jews not accept Jesus?

We do not know from any contemporary Jewish sources what the Jews thought about the young carpenter from Galilee who died on a hill overlooking Jerusalem. There is not a single reference to him in any existing Jewish document of that period. Was this a conspiracy of silence? Possibly, but probably not. Those were very turbulent times. The Jews, under the heel of Rome, were seething with discontent. Zealots rose all over the land. To break the spirit of rebellion, Emperor Tiberius sent his most ruthless procurator, Pontius Pilate, to enforce order and obtain obedience from the Jews. The records show that he put thousands of Jews to death for actual or potential rebellion. The names of most of them are unknown. It is quite likely that the crucifixion (which was the common Roman practice of punishment) of a young zealot from Galilee was lost in the troubled sea of unrecorded suffering and multiple crucifixions.

When Paul further developed the nascent Christian sect, Christianity became unrecognizable to the Jews because of its practices, and so Jews rejected Jesus, the Jewish teacher, as the Messiah. There were definite criteria for the advent of the Messiah. He was to usher in the messianic kingdom of justice, truth, and peace—but after Jesus, in Jews' eyes, this did not happen.

Jews have not accepted Christianity because of the concepts with which the Church Fathers buttressed and embellished the new faith as they spread it through the pagan Roman world. Completely alien to Jewish thought were such ideas as immaculate conception, virgin birth, the Trinity, the Holy Spirit, vicarious atonement. The religion *of* Jesus was understandable to them; it was Jewish. The religion *about* Jesus was beyond their recognition. His stature is that of a Hebrew prophet, a fearless fighter for righteousness. As with Isaiah and Amos before him, he did not merely echo his people's convictions. The ancient beliefs were transformed through Jesus. They received the immortal guidance of his luminous, loving personality.

Who crucified Jesus?

The question should really be, "What caused Jesus to be crucified?" Analyzing the trial, the crucifixion, and especially the background times, it becomes evident that the Jewish people were not responsible for the death of Jesus.

The Jewish people were crushed under Roman tyranny. The Roman authorities punished not only the individuals, but also the leaders of the people, especially those who provoked incitement against the Romans. Some of the Jewish leaders were held as hostages to try to force the submission of the Jewish people to the Roman state.

The Jewish people had been in the grip of Rome long before the time of Jesus when the Roman general Pompey had stamped the seal of Rome on the Jewish king Hyrcanus II (63–40 B.C.E.), and procurators like Pontius Pilate (26–36 C.E.) governed as instruments of the Roman imperium. The imperial grip was painful, and the frustration, bitterness, and resentment of the people began to be expressed in strident defiance and violent demonstrations. After Herod the Great's death, Rome dispensed with puppet kings and determined to rule Judea directly through procurators like Pontius Pilate, appointed by the emperor. From that moment on, the Jews were to know no peace, security, or serenity. Thousands lay slain or were exiled to Rome. The tragedy began with the cutting down of the golden eagle from the Temple. The golden eagle was a sensitive issue. Was it equivalent to an image of the emperor or merely a symbol of loyalty to Rome? To the Jews it was a violation of the second commandment. Some wondered whether the Roman eagle was a symbol of loyalty to Rome or an object of worship. Were the Jews merely demanding their religious rights when they equated the golden eagle with busts of the emperor, or did their objection mask a political challenge, thinly veiled by a religious pretext?

The story of the crucifixion will always arouse pain, sorrow, and anger in the hearts of Christians and Jews. It is, therefore, understandable that the disciples of Jesus who witnessed the tragedy were shocked, outraged, embittered, and unforgiving of Pontius Pilate, who was ultimately responsible for the heinous crime.

We should not dodge the question of responsibility. As seekers of truth, we wish to know what truly occurred, why it occurred, and who was responsible for its occurrence. We wish to build this reconciliation on facing the facts rather than holding feelings of hatred. We must shift our focus from the question of who crucified Jesus to the question of what caused Jesus to be crucified. However, where shall we find such a source?

We have only the gospel record, a record penned with faith, written with passion, and bristling with hostility and resentment. What we need is a source that would provide us with the historical Jesus, free of the hostile intensity of the gospel story.

It is true that the Gospel According to John laid the blame for the crucifixion upon the Jews. Nevertheless, we must again be reminded that this gospel was written more than a few decades after the destruction of the Temple. Some New Testament scholars even place it at the end of the first quarter of the second century.

We must not forget that the gospel was written for Gentiles. The animosity between the Jews and the new sect, the Christians, by then, had become very intense.

The Jews were blameless for the death of Jesus. Most of the church fathers never accused the Jews of the crucifixion of Jesus. In their polemics against Judaism, they rarely used this accusation. What the church fathers did charge the Jews with was their delivering Jesus to Pilate. Ignatius, a church father, in his Epistle to the Tralleans, said that Jesus was truly persecuted by Pontius Pilate. Likewise, Tacitus, a pagan historian, confirmed the fact that Pilate put Jesus to death. Jews have never put people to death by crucifixion.

Jesus did not die an ordinary death under ordinary circumstances. His crucifixion was a cruel and inhumane act.

The synoptic gospels, Peter, and the writings of Paul and the church fathers—in a word, the founders of Christianity and the creators of the Church—did not accuse the Jewish people of the death of Jesus of Nazareth.

It emerges with great clarity from the gospels that the culprit was not the Jews but the Roman imperial system. It was the Roman imperial system that was at fault, not the system of Judaism. The Roman emperor appointed the procurator. The procurator appointed the high priest, and the high priest convened his Privy Council. The Roman imperial system exacted harsh tribute. The appointment of the high priest by the Roman emperor had no sanction from the Bet Din (Sanhedrin, the High Court), and the political consequences were devastating indeed. It was not the Jewish people who crucified Jesus for a number of reasons:

The Jews did not use crucifixion as a form of punishment in that or any other period.

Only the Sanhedrin, the High Court, could give a verdict, but the High Court never met before Passover (and at night!). In addition, the Romans had removed the power of capital punishment from the Sanhedrin.

It was also a law that when the verdict was pronounced, the death sentence could not be executed the same day because perhaps, a witness, would dispute the decision of the court. Jesus was tried and executed the same day, which timing was against Jewish law.

The imperial Roman system victimized Jews, Christians, and the spirit of God. Jesus twisted in agony on the cross, lifted his head upward toward God and pleaded, "Father, forgive them, for they know not what they do" (Luke 23:34).

Who are Jews for Jesus?

Jews for Jesus is one of the so-called Hebrew Christian groups that assert that the acceptance of Jesus as the Messiah is consistent with Judaism. However, as mentioned previously, the acceptance of Jesus as the Messiah is not theologically consistent with Jewish belief, and therefore Jews who profess to accept Jesus can no longer be considered practicing Jews.

What is the covenant?

The descendants of Abraham, Isaac, and Jacob (also known as Yisra'el) whom God delivered from Egyptian bondage are bound by a covenant with God to live in accordance with His commandments. Israel, in turn, has accepted those obligations and is confident that the promises will be fulfilled. The promise made by God was that the Jewish people were to be a blessing to all humankind and a light to all nations. The promise of the covenant also can be attributed to the prophet Isaiah's statement that it would remain the eternal legacy of the Jewish people, as quoted in Isaiah 59:20–21: "This is My covenant with them, says the Eternal. My spirit which is upon you, and My word which I have placed in your mouth, shall not depart from your mouth or from the mouths of your children. From now and forevermore."

What is the relationship between Christianity and Judaism concerning the covenant?

The covenant relationship is a little complex and yet it is special and unique. The complexity is the very fact that Judaism does not agree on the identity of Jesus of Nazareth as the Messiah, nor does Judaism agree with Christianity's understanding of the nature of the Messiah as God's lamb, whose blood was necessary for the redemption from sin.

Christianity views her mission, her very religious life, as an "adoption" into the covenant of Israel, and an "extension" of it. Through Abraham, God established a covenant with the people of Israel by which the redemption of the world would begin. The covenant blossomed under Moses and the prophets. To Christians, Jesus, as the Messiah, is the culmination of the covenant and the fulfillment of it. Therefore, actually, Christianity has a kind of "inner Judaism." Deep inside, it has a relationship with the Jewish people as the "root" from which Christianity arose and draws strength. As mentioned before, some Jewish truths are at the very foundation of Christian truths and indeed are inseparable from them.

How do Jews and Christians regard each other's religious beliefs?

Judaism has always believed that the Messiah has not yet arrived. This is a fundamental difference between Jewish and Christian theology.

Christianity believes, as you will read in later chapters, that the Messiah has already come in the form of Jesus Christ, who is designated as the Son of God. The New Testament is a purely Christian "Bible." Some Christians believe that it replaces the Hebrew Bible. Other Christians believe that the New Testament is an addition to the Jewish Bible.

Another fundamental difference between Christian and Jews is the Christian belief that only those who accept Jesus Christ as their savior will find salvation in the next world.

From the Jewish point of view, when the Messiah comes men will no longer be afraid of one another or seek to destroy each other, and wars will be no more. Nowhere in the Book of Isaiah does the prophet specifically mention Jesus by name. Isaiah 7:14 states: "Behold the *almah* has conceived, and she will bear a son." The word *almah* in Hebrew means a "young woman." Christian scholars interpret the word *almah* as "virgin." They have further extended this interpretation to mean the mother of Jesus, although neither Mary nor Jesus is mentioned by name.

Are there signs of change?

There are definite signs of change. In 1965, perhaps the first most fundamental, most miraculous of these world-shattering changes took place. The Roman Catholic Church, reflecting deeply upon her inner consciousness, took a bold, courageous step to put an end to one of the most ancient of human scourges: anti-Semitism.

Some of the changes in certain Protestant denominations took place prior to 1965, notably the removal of blame from the entire Jewish people for the death of Jesus.

For nearly twenty centuries, Jews have suffered unspeakable horrors as they attempted to survive the brutal prejudice of those who professed themselves Christian in name but not in deed. This, however, was not always the case. The earliest Christians were Jews. Jesus' apostles were Jews. Mary was a Jew. Jesus of Nazareth was a Jew. Early Christianity was a movement within Judaism. Christians still honored the traditions of the Jewish fathers. They followed circumcision, kept kosher, obeyed the Torah, and upheld the authority of the sages. They differed only in the belief that Jesus was the Messiah.

With Paul of Tarsus, Saint Paul, a separation began to take place between Jews and followers of Jesus. Paul carried the belief in Jesus' messianic mission outside the confines of ancient Judea, spreading it throughout the world, which was at that time culturally Greco-Roman.

Paul differed significantly in his viewpoint from the other apostles. He felt that it was not necessary for Gentiles to obey the many laws of Judaism in order to become Christians. They only needed to believe in Jesus as the Messiah, accept him "in faith." Paul thought that Judaism was burdensome. Paul's belief held a powerful attraction, and so those Gentiles who accepted the God of Israel were described as "God-fearers." The separation of Jews and Christians came during the time of Hadrian. Pagan Roman persecution had the effect of pitting Jews and Christians against one another, and so the divergence of the two religions took place. Two faiths, two brothers born from the same parents, went two separate ways.

During the fourth century, there was a dramatic change in the character of Christianity. Emperor Constantine embraced Christianity and made it the official religion of the Roman Empire. Jews were viewed and perceived as enemies of Jesus. Jews were seen as "infidels," literally "without faith." Moreover, many Christians blamed Jews for the crucifixion of Jesus. Over the years, this would become the theological justification for untold cruelty and inhumanity. Jews were tortured, massacred, and burned at the stake.

The Inquisition in Spain in 1492, the blood libel, the bubonic plague, economic conditions, political problems—all these and much more became the justification for persecution.

Many honorable Christians were appalled by this behavior. Some Catholic clergy refused to participate in the persecution, and some popes condemned these charges, but the fact remains that anti-Semitism spread like a cancer throughout Christian society.

With the advent of democratic ideas after the age of enlightenment, certain improvements appeared. Jews were still considered outcasts no matter how they tried to integrate into society. In the twentieth century, the most vicious, most incomprehensible form of anti-Semitism emerged. The Nazi Holocaust, mass incarceration, mass extermination, and mass biological experimentation led to the eradication of six million Jews. In addition to Jews, millions of gypsies, Serbs, Slavs, and Poles also received such treatment.

What led to the awakening of Christian conscience was a Jew by the name of Jules Isaac. A survivor of the Holocaust, Isaac made it his sacred mission to study Christian Scripture and the theology of the church fathers. His conclusion was summed up in the title of his important book, *The Teaching of Contempt*. Isaac's work soon caught the attention of well-intentioned Christian scholars and theologians around the world, especially that of a kind, gentle man, Pope John XXIII. He was an extraordinary humanitarian with immeasurable love and warmth. He called the book in Italian an *aggiornamento*, a "bringing up to date." It was the most systematic, thorough, and dramatic change in the Church the world had ever seen. Consequently, a new spirit of openness emerged (April 19, 1965).

Nostra Aetate, the first doctrinal statement of the Church, was the seed of a completely new relationship with the Jews, the end of theologically justified anti-Semitism. *Nostra Aetate* planted what would begin to bear fruit, transforming the relationship of Jews and Catholics permanently. Anti-Semitism had been declared anti-Christian.

In 1986, the world Jewish community witnessed an unprecedented event: the first visit by a pope to a synagogue. At the synagogue in Rome, John Paul II declared the Jews to be the Christians' "elder brothers." The pope personally set a living example for all the Catholic faithful to follow.

Perhaps the most startling and human event of all occurred at a conference in Prague in 1990. Cardinal Edward Cassidy, speaking for the Church, openly and publicly asked forgiveness from the Jewish people for all the suffering the Church had inflicted upon them.

Last, but not least, in 1993, through the initiative of John Paul II, a full diplomatic relationship with the modern State of Israel was established. All these extraordinary events bring a new outlook to a new beginning. *Nostra Aetate* was the seed from which grew all the miraculous events to follow, the beginning of a new world for Jews and Catholics.

After centuries of religious divisiveness and political hostility, the Roman Catholic Church had made the decision to lead the world to a new vision for the future of mutual understanding and of love among all God's children regardless of race, nationality, or religion. Pope John XXIII began the dream, but gradually it was transformed into reality by his successors, Paul VI and then John Paul II.

Jewish History

Summary of Jewish history

Let us take a glimpse at history from the Jewish perspective. An observer of Jewish history cannot but stand in awe of the almost incredible sequence of events as the panorama of Jewish wanderings and persecution unfolds itself. In virtually every corner of the world, the Jewish people have been beset by ruthless oppression, ever-recurring expulsion, interminable exile, and insufferable persecutions. This is the concise history of the incredible perseverance of the Jewish people, which has manifested a spiritual tenacity to survive over four thousand years without a country.

The Bible is the only source for the lives and activities of the patriarchs (Abraham, Isaac, and Jacob). Abraham heard a command from God: "Leave behind the life you know, and I will make you a great nation, and I will bless you; I will make your name great, and you shall be a blessing." (Genesis 12:1–2)

Let us not forget that in addition to being regarded as the father of the Jewish people, Abraham is also revered by Christians and Muslims as patriarch and forebear. The followers of Muhammad speak of Ishmael, son of Abraham and Hagar, as the progenitor of their race.

What are the twelve tribes of Israel?

Reuben was the first-born. Jacob observed that he was the eldest, adding, "My might and the first fruits of my strength" (Genesis 49:3–4).

Simeon is depicted as a *fortress*, a symbol of the strength of the warrior (Genesis 49:5–7).

The men of the tribe of Levi were granted the privilege of a priestly rank. The *levi'im* (Levites) were the custodians of the Temple, acting as assistants to the *kohanim* (priests). Among their duties were keeping the records, opening the gates of the Temple, and serving as musicians, scribes, and teachers. For the maintenance of the Levites, a tenth (tithe) of all yearly produce was set aside for them. They, in turn, were to contribute to the priests a tenth part of that which they had received from the people.

Judah is universally depicted as a *lion* for power and leadership. Many of the kings of Israel were descended from this tribe. "The scepter shall not depart from Judah, nor the ruler's staff from between his feet" (Genesis 49:8–12).

"Zebulon shall dwell at the shore of the sea, and he shall be a shore for ships." This was a seafaring tribe of sailors and anglers (Genesis 49:13).

Issachar "bowed his shoulder, to bear and became a servant under taskwork" (Genesis 49:14–15). This was the laboring tribe.

Dan "shall judge his people," as depicted by the *scales of justice.* "Dan shall be a serpent in the way . . . that biteth the horse's heels, so that his rider falleth backward" (Genesis 49:16–18). Dan's second calling was one of guerrilla warfare.

Gad's militia role as border guard against raiding bands is denoted by *tents* (Genesis 49:19).

Asher means "fortunate." This was to be a prosperous tribe. The *potted plant* is an indication of luxury (Genesis 49:20).

Naphtali "is a hind let loose" (Genesis 49:21), symbolizing swiftness and grace of movement.

Joseph is "a fruitful vine" (Genesis 49:22–26). The mythical *unicorn* has come to be a symbol for this tribe. The traits of strength and majesty ascribed to Joseph are embodied in the unicorn by virtue of its lofty horn.

Benjamin "is a wolf that raveneth" (Genesis 49:27). The tribe was meant to have a warlike character.

Dates in Jewish history

Before the common era (B.C.E.)

1802 Abraham was born.

1712 Isaac was born.

1652 Jacob was born.

1567–1564 The tribes (except Joseph and Benjamin) were born.

1563 Joseph was born.

1498 Enslavement in Egypt began.

1394 Moses was born. He was the emancipator of the people and its lawgiver, who dwarfs the mountain on which he stands.

1312 Exodus of Israel from Egypt.

1312 Passage through the Red Sea.

1312 Torah given on Mount Sinai.

1200 Canaan conquered.

980 First Temple built by Solomon.

930 Kingdom divided.

598 Nathan and Elijah rebuked king for deeds of oppression.

586 Destruction of First Temple, exile of Jews to Babylonia.

560   Amos proclaimed the universality of God and the primacy of justice in His service.

520   Isaiah proclaimed God's Kingdom of universal peace and equity.

510   Return from Babylonian Exile.

500–300   The Men of the Great Assembly, a legislative body consisting of 120 members (Ezra, Nehemiah, Hananiah, Mishael, Azariah, and others), were called together at critical times when matters of national policy were involved. According to tradition, the Great Assembly received the Torah from the prophets and instituted the basic prayers and benedictions. Its main function was to preserve the biblical laws.

Dedicated teachers of the last three centuries B.C.E. and the first five centuries after the beginning of the common era erected treasure houses of piety, idealism, and Jewish lore: the Mishnah, the Talmud, and the Midrash. They enriched young minds to study and practice Judaism and, as a result, exerted a tremendous influence for the masses of Jews and their faith, and enriched their souls.

300   Alexander the Great conquered Judea.

165   The revolt of the Maccabeans. The reign of the Greek ruler Antiochus IV Epiphanes (175–164) proved to be a turning point in the history of the Jewish nation. At the beginning of his reign, he intervened in the internal affairs of Jerusalem, deposed the high priest Onias, and replaced him with Jason, who had Hellenizing tendencies and had promised the king to raise more taxes than his predecessor. After a few years, Antiochus also deposed Jason and appointed Menelaus. Then Antiochus went a step further. He totally prohibited the fulfillment of the *mitzvot* (commandments) of the Jewish religion—observing the Sabbath, circumcision, studying the Torah—and many other laws. Anybody caught practicing *mitzvot* was put to death. Antiochus forced upon the Jewish population idolatrous rites. The Temple was desecrated. Contrary to Antiochus's expectations, various classes showed a readiness to

undergo martyrdom. A revolt began. A large movement or rebellion was speedily forged into a powerful fighting force by the Hasmonean dynasty, a priestly family from Modi'in. For a period of about 130 years, the Hasmonean dynasty was at the center of Jewish life.

Common era (C.E.)

70 Romans destroyed the Second Temple. Part of the wall is still standing in the old section of Jerusalem. This part of the wall, known as the *Kotel Ma'aravi* (Western Wall), has been regarded as sacred ever since the talmudic period. It has served as a place of endless pilgrimage for Jews from all parts of the world. Since about the tenth century, regular services have been held daily near the wall, which is popularly known as the Wailing Wall.

130 Bar Kokhba's revolt against Rome.

200 Mishnah compiled.

The destruction of the Temple constituted a double crisis. Not only were the people cast off the land, but the Divine Presence departed from Jerusalem (Ezekiel 10:19, 11:23).

300–700 The vast majority of the Jewish people were dispersed to different parts of the world: the Persian Empire, Mediterranean countries, and the Roman Empire and Europe. The vast Jewish Diaspora was concentrated in great numbers in Rome, Milan, and Alexandria. The so-called Edict of Milan, issued in June 313, was couched in terms expressing general tolerance and coexistence of religions. The Jewish people were developing a new life of intellectual and social creativity.

325 Rome persecution of Jews.

400 Byzantine period.

450 Talmud compiled.

624–628 Islam appeared. Muhammad turned savagely against the Jews in Arabia for not accepting the new religion.

712 Muslim forces conquered Persia. Soon after, Islam ruled from the borders of India to south of the Pyrenees, thus uniting under its sway more than 90 percent of the world's Jewish population.

638 Arabs captured Jerusalem.

1070 The great sage Rashi.

Tenth and eleventh centuries The Charter of Bishop Ruediger of Speyer (1084) offered the Jews attractive concessions. Emperor Henry IV granted the Jews of Speyer and Worms a charter giving them extensive rights of trade and self-government six years before the First Crusade in 1190.

1171 France's first blood libel. One spring morning in the year 1171, a Christian boy was found drowned in the French town of Blois on the Loire River. The town is called Biblias in a number of Jewish books. Today it is the capital of the Loire-et-Cher department. A Christian wagoner declared that he had seen a Jewish wagoner throw the dead child into the water. Who had killed the Christian boy? A rumor immediately spread that the community's thirty-one Jews had murdered the boy and drained his blood for use at the Passover Seder. The ensuing tragedy turned medieval France into the mother of blood libels in Western Europe. Men, women, and children were accused of the crime and were imprisoned pending the trial. Proof? The only witness was the wagon driver who stated that he had seen a Jew throw the dead body of the boy into the river.

The only means with which the Jews could defend themselves were prayer and money. There was no investigation. Every proof the Jews could bring was turned down, and no plea of mercy was entertained. It was declared, obviously falsely, that the Jews used human blood in their Passover food and crucified Christian children for that purpose. The accusation that blood was used in the wine or the *matzah* for the Seder was added later on May 26, 1171, which has remained a bloody date in Jewish history. Hundreds of communities were slaughtered, especially before Passover.

The Roman Catholic Church, reflecting deeply upon her own inner consciousness, has taken steps to put an end to the most ancient of human scourges: anti-Semitism. Some of the Church's changes regarding Jews and Judaism had already begun to appear in certain Protestant denominations prior to 1965, notably the removal of blame from the entire Jewish people for the death of Jesus.

1180 Maimonides.

1290 Jews expelled from England.

1350 Black Death massacres of German Jews.

1390 Jews in Spain persecuted.

1394 Jews of France expelled.

1475 First Hebrew book printed.

1480 Spanish Inquisition.

1492 Jews of Spain expelled.

1500–1599 The Reformation. During this period, Catholic Europe was at war. As Spanish, French, and Austrian nationalism undercut the Holy Roman Empire, the Dutch revolted against Spain. Civil war occurred in France between the Huguenots and Catholics. German princes withdrew from the empire. The wars worked to the advantage of the Protestant Reformers. The church could not effectively respond to the Protestant challenge. By the time the Council of Trent was called to deal with the problem, Protestantism was well established. Generally, the Protestant countries reflected a previously unknown tolerance. Jews living in solidly Catholic countries were the hardest hit. The ghetto was formally established in Venice. Copies of the Talmud were seized and burned.

Martin Luther, a champion of the Jews against Catholic persecution, hoped that the Jews would convert to his faith. The Jews resisted and Luther became anti-Semitic. Later anti-Semites utilized Luther's anti-Semitic writings. The attitudes and actions against Jews, based on the belief that the Jews were evil scapegoats, may explain some of the medieval anti-Semitism, such as the persecution during the Black Death. The Black Plague killed off a great part of the population in Europe from 1348 to 1349. The Jews were blamed for the catastrophe. The Black Death, that is, bubonic plague, was carried by rat fleas that were infected by biting rats carrying the disease. Both Jews and Christians were afflicted. Jews were massacred when they were accused of causing the plague by poisoning wells. Obviously, this accusation was false.

1512 Ottoman Empire conquered Palestine.

1565 *Shulḥan Arukh* compiled. (See page 33)

1648 Jews of Poland massacred by Bogdan Chmielnicki. He and his savage followers, the Cossacks, destroyed hundreds of Jewish communities.

1654 First settlement of Jews in North America.

Jews settled all over the world. However, the United States would become the center of the Jewish world, the largest, most influential, secure haven in all of Jewish history. On September 22, 1654, the French ship *St. Charles* carried 23 Jews who were former residents of Holland to New Amsterdam. They were refugees fleeing the Inquisition. The Jews were robbed on the way there and therefore could only pay part of the money required for passage. The Dutch magistrate of New Amsterdam gave permission to the captain of the *St. Charles*, Jacques de la Motthe, to hold two of the Jewish passengers, Abraham Israel and Judic De Mereda, as hostages against possible insufficient proceeds from an auction sale of the Jews' possessions. In this rather strange manner, the greatest modern Jewish community outside of Israel was founded. Asher Levy became the first Jewish citizen in America on April 21, 1657. It was not until 1728 that the Jews of New Amsterdam, which later became New York, finally received permission to build a synagogue and to assemble for public worship without fear or molestation. By 1750, the Ashkenazic Jews (European Jews) formed the majority among the 2,500 Jews in the thirteen colonies. The second Jewish settlement in the American colonies was founded in Newport, Rhode Island, and then Pennsylvania and the Carolinas. When the Napoleonic Wars ended, hundreds of poor Jews in quest of freedom or bread began to arrive, principally from Germany.

1880 Wave of pogroms in Russia. The stated policy of the tsarist government was to solve the "Jewish problem" in Russia by starving a third of the Jews to death, forcing a third to emigrate, and absorbing the remainder by conversion to the Orthodox Church. Tens of thousands fled the country. Between 80 and 85 percent of those who left Russia, Lithuania, and Poland crossed the Atlantic to the United States. Conservatively estimated, during the period 1881–1914, about two million Jewish immigrants had found a haven in the United States. During the Russian pogroms, the annual influx greatly exceeded that of previous years.

1899–1914 America absorbed 300,000 Jewish immigrants from Austria-Hungary, and 62,813 from Romania. Hunger and persecution brought them from those countries to begin new lives in the United States. In 1776, there were 2,000 Jews in the United States. In 1840, there were 15,000. In 1861, during the Civil War, there were 150,000 Jews, and in 1900, one million. In 1915, there were three million. Today there are six million Jew in the United States. Half of the Jews in the world live in the United States. Jews have achieved prominence in all fields of endeavor, such as science, medicine, politics, law, business, industry, commerce, the arts, music, literature, the media, and academia.

1900 Dreyfus Affair stirs European Jewry.

1917 Balfour Declaration.

1918 British occupation of Palestine.

1940 The Holocaust.

1947 United Nations partitions Palestine.

1948 Proclamation of the State of Israel.

Holy Books

What is the Torah?

The Torah is the soul of Judaism. Without it, Judaism would be an empty shell. It is the foundation of the Jewish religion, its main content, and its dynamic force.

The word Torah refers explicitly to the Five Books of Moses. In addition to the Five Books of Moses, there are the Prophets (Nevi'im) and the Sacred Writings (Ketuvim).

The Five Books of Moses are Genesis, Exodus, Leviticus, Numbers, and Deuteronomy. These names are descriptive of the contents of the books: *Genesis* ("origin") begins with the story of creation; *Exodus* ("going out") tells of the going out from Egypt; *Leviticus* ("pertaining to Levites") contains laws which relate to the priests, members of the tribe of Levi; *Numbers* derives its title from the census of the Israelites in the wilderness; *Deuteronomy* ("repetition of the law") contains a restatement of the Mosaic laws. God revealed all of it to Moses.

The Torah is the civilization of the Jew, the totality of Jewish history and experience, the beliefs, ethics, morality, culture, literature, and philosophy of our people from the days of Abraham to our own time. It affects and penetrates every phase of Jewish life. The Torah aims to refine our character and personality and helps us discover a noble purpose so that we may strive for justice and honesty in our daily endeavors.

What is the Nevi'im?

The second part of the Hebrew Bible, Nevi'im, or Prophets, is subdivided into the writings of the former prophets and the latter prophets. The former prophets comprise four historical books: Joshua, Judges, Samuel, and Kings. The latter prophets also comprise four books: Isaiah, Jeremiah, Ezekiel, and the twelve minor prophets. Grouped in one volume, the twelve minor prophets are Hosea, Joel, Amos, Obadiah, Jonah, Micah, Nahum, Habakkuk, Zephaniah, Haggai, Zechariah, and Malachi.

What is the Ketuvim?

The third part of the Bible, known as the Hagiographa or Sacred Writings (Ketuvim), consists of the remaining eleven books:

Psalms, Proverbs, Job, Song of Songs, Ruth, Lamentations, Ecclesiastes, Esther, Daniel, Ezra-Nehemiah, and Chronicles.

The five biblical books known as the Five Scrolls are recited in the synagogue as part of the liturgy on the following special occasions: *Song of Songs* on Passover; *Ruth* on Shavuot; *Lamentations* on Tishah be-Av, the fast-day commemorating the destruction of Jerusalem; *Ecclesiastes* on Sukkot, the autumn festival; and *Esther* on Purim (the holiday in winter for merrymaking—it commemorates a smashing victory over suppression of the Jews characteristic of bigots in every country and every age). The Five Scrolls form a class by themselves, and are arranged in the Hebrew Bible according to the sequence of the said occasions.

What is the Oral Torah?

The Oral Torah comprises the customs, interpretations, and regulations that came after the Written Torah, which is the Five Books of Moses. The Oral Torah was transmitted orally by individual scholars, by courts, and by schools from generation to generation. In 200 C.E., Rabbi Judah ha-Nasi (*nasi* means "prince" or "chief") edited and organized the Mishnah. Three centuries later, Rabbi Ashi and many other famous rabbis edited the commentary on the Mishnah known as the Gemara. The Mishnah and Gemara together are known as the Talmud. All three words, Mishnah, Gemara, and Talmud mean "study" or "learning." The Talmud includes and explains the many laws of the Torah, the Mishnah, and moral and ethical teachings and discussions in the schools and individual comments on history, geography, astrology, and other subjects. The Mishnah was created in the Land of Israel. The Talmud (Gemara) was created in Babylonia and Israel, and thus has two versions: the Babylonian Talmud and the Jerusalemite Talmud.

The oral and written laws transmitted by the authoritative teachers of every generation comprise the teachings and customs that were handed down from generation to generation. A people cannot live on a written Torah alone without explicit interpretation. Every age, every generation brings certain new applications and interpretations. A closed book would result in a stagnant life, whereas Judaism, by its very nature, represents a stream of *mayim ḥayyim*, "living waters."

The Torah cannot be defined in a brief statement. It actually represents "the accumulated literary and spiritual heritage of the Jewish people throughout the centuries." Torah is not merely law, but also the aggregate wisdom of Judaism, its spiritual teachings, its philosophy, its way of life, its practices, and beliefs, in short, its religious civilization.

What Torah means to Judaism has manifested itself by the devotion of the Jew to its preservation even during times of persecution when study of the Torah was forbidden. Rabbis would rather suffer the penalty of death for teaching it to their disciples rather than surrender their birthright. The Jews are rightfully called "people of the book." The book is the Torah, their preeminent contribution to the culture and civilization of the human race. Judaism has always believed in the aristocracy of learning, and its love for learning has always been so great that the *talmud ḥakham* (a person learned in Torah) was the most highly regarded personage in the Jewish community. It was not the aristocracy of wealth and possessions that counted but the distinction of learning and scholarship.

How is the Torah written?

The 613th commandment in the Torah, Deuteronomy 31:19, bids us each to write a scroll of the Torah with our own hand or to cause one to be written. Every Torah scroll must be handwritten, and the scribe must not only be a calligrapher, he must be learned in the biblical laws as to how the Torah must be written and an observant Jew as well. Only a kosher animal skin, prepared specially for the making of a Sefer Torah, may be used as for the parchment scroll. The scribe must demonstrate great reverence for the written word and must be well versed in the text. The scribe copies from an existing *tikkun*, or perfect text. The letters can be very beautiful especially when the scribe is a talented calligrapher. It takes a year to write a Torah scroll, working six days a week, eight to ten hours a day.

What is the sidrah or parashah?

The Five Books of Moses are transcribed by a *sofer* (devout scribe) on a single scroll of parchment, with four blank lines between each book. There are 54 written portions, called *sidrot* or *parashiyyot*, though there is no special marking to indicate the start or finish of each. Every Sabbath morning, another *sidrah* (order) is read in the synagogue. They are read consecutively, so that in the course of a year the public reading of all five books of the Torah is completed.

The *sidrah*, or portion, is divided into seven *parashiyyot* (sections). As each of the seven sections is read, a different worshipper is called up to the *bimah* (platform). This is known as receiving an *aliyah* (ascending). The first *aliyah* is given to a *kohen* (one of priestly descent); the second to a descendant of the tribe of Levi, and the remaining *aliyot* are given to other members of the congregation. Originally, each person who was honored with an *aliyah* read his particular portion. Later, however, a *ba'al keri'ah* (special reader) was designated to do all the reading. Today, those who are honored with an *aliyah*—men and women in Conservative and Reform synagogues, men only in Orthodox synagogues—only recite the appropriate benediction before and after each *parashah* is read. The two blessings contain 40 words, which symbolize the 40 days Moses spent on Mount Sinai.

What is the Haftarah?

The Haftarah is the portion of the Prophets that is recited immediately after the reading of the Torah on Sabbaths and festivals. The custom of concluding the reading of the Torah with a selection from the Prophets dates back over 2000 years to the period of persecution preceding the Maccabean revolt. At that time, Antiochus Epiphanes, king of Syria and Palestine, forbade the reading of the Torah under penalty of death. The scribes therefore instituted the chanting of a chapter of the Prophets relevant to the portion of the Torah that would have been read. Some authorities suggest that the reason for the readings from the Prophets was to emphasize the great value of these books.

What is the Book of Psalms?

The Book of Psalms is the most widely read biblical book. The psalms have been a true, steadfast friend and companion for thousands of years. There is hardly an occasion in the religious life of a Jew at which an appropriate psalm is not read.

The psalms are generally referred to as the Psalms of David, even though some claim that King David was not the author of all of them; Psalm 90 is ascribed to Moses; Psalm 72 to Solomon. The Talmud claims that David wrote the psalms with the assistance of ten elders.

The primary reason why the psalms were and are read on so many occasions is that they reflect almost every conceivable mood of the individual or group and reflect every mood ranging from the heights of ecstatic joy to the depths of depression. Psalm 23 ("The Lord is my Shepherd") is a reverential, touching, and consoling psalm. It is an expression of dependence on God and faith in Him. When the tide of life is at its lowest ebb, when we are emotionally insecure and need strength to overcome our perplexities, our faith in a divine source will sustain us. Then will we realize that it is not sufficient to know the psalm; we must know the Shepherd. The book contains 150 psalms. The psalms have been adroitly woven into the fabric of prayer not only by Jews but by Christians as well.

The psalms are so popular that there are special "psalm groups" that recite psalms every day. The psalms are consolation for troubled souls. They offer ethical and moral guidance for those who have strayed off the right path. On can find fulfillment by reading psalms.

What is the Mishnah?

The term Mishnah, from the Hebrew root *shanah* (to repeat), refers to the study of the law (Halakhah).

At the beginning of the third century, Rabbi Judah ha-Nasi compiled and edited the Mishnah, and the Oral Law was written down, the most important rabbinic work of the tannaitic period. The combined Written and Oral Law is the source of all the legal, moral, ethical, and religious precepts that govern and guide our lives as Jews. It is a compilation of Jewish material on a huge variety of subjects—ritual, civil, priestly, and everyday—in fact anything subject to rabbinic debate. Conflicting opinions are frequently cited. It contains occasional stories and legends about the rabbis. It is about 800 pages in English translation. The Mishnah is divided into six separate sections (orders), and 63 smaller divisions (tractates).

What is the Talmud?

The name Talmud literally means "learning," or "study." As mentioned previously, there are actually two Talmuds, the Jerusalem Talmud and the Babylonian Talmud, in which are collected the decisions and discussions based on biblical law, but expanded and extended by the rabbis to include all the areas of Jewish life that the Bible does not specifically discuss.

In the year 200, Rabbi Judah ha-Nasi edited and organized the Mishnah. Three centuries later, Rabbi Ashi among other famous rabbis, edited the commentary on the Mishnah known as the Gemara. The Mishnah and Gemara together are known as the Talmud.

Since the middle of the sixth century, the Babylonian Talmud has been the chief source of education for Jews in many lands; its vastness has given rise to the expressive phrase, "the ocean of the Talmud." The whole gamut of human life is covered in this encyclopedic work, which is now available in English translation.

THE TORAH

According to tradition, the Torah ("The Written Law") was given by God to Moses on Mt. Sinai. It was then transmitted to Joshua who transmitted it to the elders who transmitted it to the prophets and eventually to the Sanhedrin.

THE MISHNAH

The Oral Law was transmitted by word of mouth for generations. It was collected and compiled by Rabbi Judah the Prince and his court in Palestine around 160 to 200 C.E.

THE BABYLONIAN TALMUD

The scholars in the academies during the Babylonian exile compiled the commentary on the Mishnah, ending in the year 589. This version is the larger and more authoritative of the two versions.

THE JERUSALEM TALMUD

This was compiled together with the Mishnah with commentary by the amoraim in Palestine in approximately the fourth century.

MIDRASH

The name is derived from the root of the word *derash*: to seek, to search, to examine.

An anthology and compilation of rabbinic literature and homilies forming a running commentary on specific books on the Bible. Early period, fifth and sixth centuries; middle period, sixth to tenth century; late period, 1000 to 1200.

Comments and decisions of the gaonic period ending 1038.

Commentaries by Rashi, France, eleventh century.

Mishneh Torah by Maimonides, the Rambam, Egypt, twelfth century.

Tosafot: commentaries by descendants of Rashi, France and Germany, twelfth and thirteen centuries.

Shulḥan Arukh by Yosef Karo Palestine, sixteenth century.

Responsa literature

Various codes and commentaries

The Talmud is one of the great masterpieces of world literature and next to the Bible is the most important literary creation of the Jewish people. It has molded Jewish life and thought to this day.

What is the Midrash?

The Midrash consists of rabbinical commentaries on the Bible and contains a wealth of moral readings, legends, and parables. Much of it represents a type of popular homiletics or short sermonic messages. The name Midrash means "inquiry," an important section of Jewish literature which dates as late as the tenth or eleventh century of the present era, and as early as when Ezra the Scribe led the people back to Israel from Babylonia in 444 B.C.E. The name Midrash derives from the root *d-r-sh*, which means to "search, seek, examine, investigate" (Leviticus 10:16, Deuteronomy 13:15, Isaiah 55:6).

For centuries, the Midrash has represented the foremost medium of expression for Jewish thought and teachings. It contains ethical teachings and legal discussions which the rabbis sought to impress upon their readers. The literature represents in miniature the religious wisdom of the Jewish people. It is written in a popular and impressive style. The Midrash has proved an unfailing spring with the power to sustain and strengthen the Jewish thirst for the word of the living God.

The most important of the many midrashim is known as *Midrash Rabbah*. It covers the entire Five Books of Moses (Pentateuch) and the Five Scrolls (Song of Songs, Ruth, Lamentations, Ecclesiastes, and Esther) which are read during the synagogue services in the course of the year.

Scholars consider that the earliest midrashim were edited not later than the sixth century. *Exodus Rabbah* dates from the eleventh century. *Leviticus Rabbah* or *Va-Yikrah Rabbah* dates from the sixth century and thus is one of the oldest midrashim.

The midrashim have wonderful maxims and aphorisms. Here some examples:

Man enters the world with closed hands, as if to say, "The world is mine." When he departs with open hands, it is as if to say, "I take nothing with me."

It is easy to acquire an enemy, but difficult to win a friend. He who turns his enemy into a friend is the bravest hero. He who hates a man is as if he hated God.

What is the Shulḥan Arukh?

The *Shulḥan Arukh* (lit. "Prepared Table") by Rabbi Joseph Karo (1488–1575) serves as a practical guide in the observance of traditional Judaism throughout the world. The title itself suggests that the table is prepared. One just has to sit down and get nourishment. Joseph Karo arranged the book with a system that is easily accessible in a concise way to all the laws a Jew should live by.

This material is summarized in an abridged book by Rabbi Solomon Ganzfried (1804–1886) that has been reprinted many times under the name *Kiẓẓur Shulḥan Arukh*. This book remains the standard source of information for traditional observance of Judaism.

There are a number of commentaries on the *Shulḥan Arukh* written by great rabbis. One is the *Mishnah Berurah* by Rabbi Israel Meir ha-Kohen (1838–1932). Another, in eight volumes, is the *Arukh ha-Shulḥan* by Rabbi Jehiel Epstein (1835–1905).

What does the Jew believe?

The first prerequisite and the first requirement for living as a Jew is to know and believe that there is a God—one God, the creator and ruler of the universe, who rules and guides the world in justice and in love.

The Jew does not serve God for the sake of reward; rather he possesses deep religious convictions that run like golden threads through all Jewish history. The most sacred and precious jewel of Judaism is the Torah.

What is the Zohar?

The name Zohar literally means "shining, brightness, splendor." The Zohar is the major work of the Jewish mystical tradition, or Kabbalah. It is written partly in Hebrew but mostly in Aramaic, the language used in Babylon when the Jews were exiled from Palestine. The book is traditionally attributed to the second-century sage Simeon Bar Yoḥai. It is an allegorical and mystical commentary on the Pentateuch. The Zohar became known through its publication by Moses de Leon of Spain toward the end of the thirteenth century. In the Zohar, homiletical passages of striking beauty alternate with discoveries about the nature of God, the nature and destiny of the soul, rich with deep religious inspiration and containing many mystical interpretations of the Torah that have been in existence for centuries.

According to the Zohar, everything in the Torah has threefold significance: the outward, the inner, and the innermost, which is the most important and the most to be desired. The highest goal of the religious person is to penetrate into the innermost purpose of the precepts and practices. It is with this in view that the Zohar deals with ethical duties and problems. The Zohar tries to show the inner worth and the marvelous nature of human beings.

The stories in the Zohar have fascinated many readers. They represent comradeship, love of learning, and the spirit of adventure. The Zohar stresses that every human act has its effect upon the universal and spiritual forces in the world.

What is a genizah?

The word *genizah* refers to a storage place where old, used, and torn pages from Torah scrolls, old prayer books, and any writing with the name of God are kept. Thanks to this law, many valuable manuscripts have been preserved and later found.

Why the Bible?

When I was teaching Hebrew at the University of Hartford, a number of priests, ministers, and nuns registered for the course. I was surprised to see them, so I asked, "Why are you here?" They answered, "We are here to learn the original text."

It is difficult, although not impossible, to approach the Bible and other rabbinic texts without knowledge of Hebrew. Any translation is at best an approximation. In translating Hebrew texts, where often the idioms are very far from those naturally used in English, a literal translation can be very difficult to follow, while a free translation adds something by way of explanation. An example of this would be the famous sculpture of Moses by Michelangelo, which depicts two horns of light emanating from his forehead. These have given corroboration to the ridiculous theory among the ignorant that Jews have horns.

The artistic misconception was due to an accidental or premeditated error in the Aquila (Greek) and Vulgate (Latin) translations of the Bible in which the phrase *keren or panav* ("the skin of his face shone") (Exodus 34:29) was mistranslated as "his head had horns." The Hebrew words for "shone" and "horn" are identical except that "shone" is a verb in the past tense and "horn" is a noun. Also, the word *or* in Hebrew means both "light" and "skin," and although they sound alike, they are spelled differently. It is important for Christians and Jews to understand both the root, the Hebrew Bible (Torah), and the branches that sprang from it.

Jewish Prayer and Holidays

What is the Jewish calendar?

Samson Raphael Hirsh, a nineteenth-century German rabbi, said, "One can learn more spirituality from the cycle of year-round observance through the calendar than from any formal statement of faith."

The mainspring of the Jew's spirituality can be learned from the cycle of year-round observance. Every month brings historical memories and spiritual uplift that teach us patterns of religious conduct and behavior.

The Jewish calendar is lunar-solar. A lunar calendar is based on the moon's orbit around the earth—approximately 29 days. Each cycle is called a month, and 12 months contain 354 days. In contrast the solar calendar, also known as the Gregorian calendar, measures the year by the period it takes for the earth to complete one orbit around the sun—slightly less than 365 days and 6 hours. For convenience, each year is counted as 365 days, with an extra (intercalary) day added every fourth year (leap year) to account for the accumulated partial days that were ignored during the other three years. The difference between the solar and lunar years is approximately 11 days compared with the solar calendar (365 days). A strictly lunar calendar (354 days) would lose 11 days each year. In three years, more than a month would be lost. The Jewish calendar has a complicated method, adjusting itself so that the holidays and festivals fall at approximately the same time each year. If not for the adjustments, we might find Passover in mid-August and Ḥanukkah in June.

When does the Jewish day begin?

According to Jewish law, a day consisting of 24 hours begins at sunset. Sabbath and holidays begin with sunset and continue until three stars appear the following night. The reason, "And there was evening and there was morning, a first day" (Genesis 1:5). Evening is mentioned first.

The Jewish months must be determined by the cycles of the moon (Exodus 12:2). A genius by the name of Rabbi Hillel II offered a nineteen-year cycle in which he was able to insert seven leap years in the third, sixth, eighth, eleventh, fourteenth, seventeenth, and nineteenth years. Each leap year, an entire month is added to the calendar, closing the gap between the 354 lunar days and the 365 solar days in ordinary years.

One of the strangest phenomena of the Jewish calendar is that the year does not begin with the first month but with the seventh. This anomaly is based on two Torah verses: (a) "Nissan is the first of the months" (Exodus 12:2); and (b) "Tishri is the turn of the year" (Exodus 34:22). Thus, the first of Tishri—the day traditionally accepted as the sixth day of creation, the day on which Adam and Eve were created—is "the turn of the year" and is called Rosh ha-Shanah, the beginning of the year. The Jews count by a traditional calendar based on the Bible.

The distinction between the Hebrew calendar and the Gregorian calendar, which is in use throughout the world, is that the Hebrew calendar commences with the creation of the world by God. The Gregorian dates everything in relation to the birth of Jesus.

Jews use the abbreviation B.C.E. (before the common era) and C.E. (common era) instead of the Christian abbreviations B.C. (Before Christ) and A.D. (Anno Domini, "The Year of Our Lord") because the Jewish abbreviation avoids incorporating the name of Jesus.

The first day of the new moon, when the crescent appears, begins a new month and is called Rosh Ḥodesh.

What is Rosh Ḥodesh?
The word *rosh* means "head" and *ḥodesh* means "month," or the beginning of the month. In ancient Israel, the day after the crescent of the new moon was first sighted in the sky was celebrated as a festival with special offerings in the sanctuary (1 Samuel 20:18–34). The prescribed offerings on the new moon festival are enumerated in Numbers 28:11–15. Rosh Ḥodesh is a minor holiday.

Why the Sabbath?
"Remember the Sabbath day to keep it holy" (Exodus 20:8). The fourth commandment is engraved in fiery letters in the Book of Books: "For in six days the Lord made heaven and earth, and He rested on the seventh day."

"Therefore, the Lord blessed the Sabbath day and hallowed it" is the very soul and the mainstay of Judaism. The Sabbath day, through the ages, has been the great solidifying force that has welded the Jewish people and united them in their belief that they are destined to exist to the end of generations.

The Sabbath is designed to raise man's life to a higher level by affording him a day of rest, the most precious of all days

"He who makes the Sabbath pleasurable is rewarded with his heart's desires" (Talmud, Shabbat 118a).

Traditionally, the Sabbath day is designated as *Shabbat Kodesh*—Holy Sabbath. It is also known as *Shabbat Malkah*—Queen Sabbath. On this day, the poorest of the poor, the meek, and the lonely are transformed into kings and princes. The Sabbath has served as a beacon of light, shielding the people from darkness and national despair.

The Sabbath is not another day; it is a day like no other. It is the day of contentment and of holiness.

By observing the Sabbath, as is stated in Exodus 20:8–11, we testify to the fact that God created heaven and earth. However, in Deuteronomy 5:15, the Torah gives a historical reason: "And you shall remember that thou wast a servant in the land of Egypt, and that the Lord thy God brought thee out thence through a mighty hand and by a stretched-out arm; therefore the Lord thy God commanded thee to keep the Sabbath day." Here the Torah says that the observance of the Sabbath reminds us that God is the Lord of history who determines human destiny and delivered us from Egyptian bondage.

The Sabbath is the day to restore your connections to your family, to your community, and above all to God.

Judaism is a religion of time aiming at the sanctification of time. Tradition tells us that on the Sabbath an extra soul (the *neshamah yeterah*) descends from heaven to join each Jew. It is as if a new strength were added so that we can observe the Sabbath in greater holiness. Before the Sabbath, as the sun is about to set, the woman kindles the Sabbath candles officially welcoming the Sabbath with a prayer. After the services, the man makes *Kiddush* (a blessing) over wine. It mentions the observance of the Sabbath; "Thou hast sanctified us with the commandments and have graciously given the holy Sabbath as a heritage in remembrance of creation."

Then the entire family recites the blessings over the *hallah* (a twisted loaf of bread made from wheat). The meal is served, and after and during the meal, we sing *zemirot* (songs.) Grace after meals is then said. Traditionally it is customary for the father to bless the children and grandchildren. Other than breakfast, it is customary to eat three meals during the Sabbath. One meal is on Friday evening, another on Sabbath afternoon after the services, and the third before the Sabbath ends. When twilight comes on Saturday, when you see three stars, it is time to pray for the next week. During this service, we recite the *Havdalah,* the separation between the Sabbath that has just ended and the weekday. We are reluctant to leave the Sabbath, as the day is so serene and spiritual, and we sing the songs of Elijah the Prophet. *Shavuah Tov* ("a good week") is our greeting as we hope to see each other again next week.

The traditional Sabbath celebration has introduced many beautiful home customs to Jewish families. To perpetuate the togetherness and unity of the family, the rabbis instituted the requirement for families to spend time together.

"More than Israel has kept the Sabbath, it is the Sabbath that has kept Israel." Thus did the brilliant Hebrew essayist Aḥad ha-Am epitomize the historical significance of the Sabbath for the Jewish people. Nor is Aḥad ha-Am alone in his exalted opinion of the role the Sabbath has played in the history of the Jews. He reflects the universal regard for the Sabbath as revealed in the life and literature of the Jew.

"The meaning of the Sabbath is to celebrate time rather than space," declared the late Abraham Joshua Heschel, noted Jewish theologian and philosopher. He continues, "Six days a week we live under the tyranny of things of space; on the Sabbath we try to become attuned to holiness in time. It is a day on which we are called upon to share in what is eternal in time, turn from the results of creation to the mystery; from the world of creation to the creation of the world."

The Sabbath is the most precious gift humanity has received from the treasure house of God.

The Sabbath is a delight, a delight to the soul and a delight to the body. Comfort and pleasure are an integral part of the Sabbath observance. The Sabbath is tranquility, serenity, peace, and repose.

The Sabbath is the great contribution of Judaism to our welfare. That man was to pause one day in seven for rest and recreation was—in its day—a revolutionary idea. The Torah specifies two reasons for Sabbath observance. It is, first, a reminder that the world was created in six days and that God rested on the seventh. The Sabbath in its own way, then, should be a day of introspection and meditation that enables us to pause from our daily activities of work and think about our lives and our accomplishments. It is the day to ask the question, "Am I really doing something worthwhile with my life?"

For Jews, over the centuries, the precious gift of Sabbath has been very important. When life was hard and the world was frightening or unfriendly, they turned their minds away from the outside world and drew closer to their families and to God.

Why do we cover two ḥallot for the Sabbath meal?

When the Jewish people were wandering in the desert, the Almighty provided them with food that was called manna. This name derived from the puzzled expression *man hu?* ("What is it?") (Exodus 16:15). The Midrash tells us its taste was whatever you imagined it to be. The *ḥallot* are covered while reciting the *Kiddush* prayer to recall that the manna was covered with a layer of dew. Two *ḥallot* are used because on Friday, the day before the Sabbath, enough manna for two days was collected.

What is prayer?

Prayer is a two-way communication between man and God in manifold ways: petition, praise, thanksgiving, self-examination, confession, contemplation. It is an outpouring of one's inner self. It is, in truth, the language of the soul, for the deepest feelings of man can be best expressed in words of prayer. It is a means of obtaining the highest joy in life, which can only come through a feeling of the nearness of God. It leads to the feeling of closeness to the Almighty that forms the highest experience of a human being. A person should identify himself with his prayer and become "a praying being."

What symbols are important in the synagogue?

God cannot be represented by any symbol. The Torah scroll is the book of law and a symbol in the service. When the scroll is carried around the synagogue, people will touch and kiss it. It evokes reverence and feelings of love. Another symbol is the *Ner Tamid*. The *Ner Tamid* is usually referred to as the "Eternal Light," a lamp that burns continuously in front or on top of the Ark in the synagogue. It symbolizes the continuous presence of God. This custom is traced back to the injunction in the Bible that a lamp burn continuously in the sanctuary (Exodus 27:20–21). The *Ner Tamid* has become a notable symbol in the synagogue.

What are the inscriptions above the Ark?

The inscriptions above the Ark vary from synagogue to synagogue. The most common are:

Hear O Israel, the Lord our God, the Lord is one.

Know before whom you stand.

The world is maintained by Torah, worship, and deeds of loving-kindness.

The world stands on three things: truth, justice, and peace.

This is none other than the House of God, and this is the Heavenly Gate.

Do you have music at your service?
Music was used in the Temple services and was performed by the Levites. After the destruction of the Temple, rabbinic laws forbade music. Today only Reform Jews and some Conservatives use organ music during the Sabbath service. However, during weddings, music is encouraged, since they are celebrated only on weekdays.

Why do men and women sit separately during the services?
Philo, the first-century historian, tells that Essenes separated men and women at worship. The arrangement separating the sexes allows both to concentrate on prayer without distractions, and supports a higher level of modesty. The separator was usually a wall 5 to 7 feet high; in some synagogues, the upper level was for women. Only Orthodox synagogues follow this procedure today. Conservative and Reform synagogues do not adhere to this practice.

What is the Selihot service?
The concept of a midnight service originated in the verse "At midnight I rise to praise you." (Psalm 119:62) This service, called *Selihot* (Penitential Prayers), is based on a passage from the Book of Jeremiah: "Arise and sing into the night at the beginning of the watches." This is the time we pour out our hearts and ask for forgiveness.

The word *selihah*, "forgiveness," is a prayer for pardon in the strict sense of the term, for it gives a feeling of upliftedness to the worshiper who repents and pleads for mercy from God.

What is the origin of the word "amen"?

The Hebrew word *amen* has entered almost every language in the world. *Amen* is translated "so be it." It originated in the Hebrew Bible Scripture as a response of affirmation. In Deuteronomy 27:15–26, we find a series of pronouncements by the Levites to which the people respond "Amen." First Chronicles (16:36) clearly indicates that in 1000 B.C.E., the time of King David, the second king of Israel, the people responded with "Amen" upon hearing the blessing "Blessed be the Lord God of Israel from now and unto all eternity." When a person says "Amen," he indicates his endorsement of the words that he has just heard and affirms his belief in the truth of what has been said. By so doing, he acknowledges his identification with the prayer or the blessing as though he himself had said it.

The Hebrew word *amen* comes from the same root as *emunah* ("trust") and is found in the Pentateuch (Numbers 5:22). When we say "Amen," we are in fact affirming our faith in God. The word "Amen" was never translated or changed to Latin or Greek from the Hebrew word. It is familiar to Christians and Muslims, and is now found in more than a hundred languages.

What is Rosh ha-Shanah?

The different aspects of Rosh ha-Shanah are revealed in the four Hebrew names of the holy day:

> *Rosh ha-Shanah,* "the Beginning of the Year." God is proclaimed Creator, Lord of the Universe, and Ruler of man and nation. Leviticus (23:24) Numbers (29:1)
> *Yom ha-Din,* "the Day of Judgment." Man confronts his Maker face to face in judgment.
> *Yom Teru'ah,* "the Day of Sounding the *shofar.*"
> *Yom ha-Zikkaron,* "the Day of Remembrance." "When mankind passes before the Divine throne to give account of deeds committed."[3]

---

[3] Joseph H. Hertz, *Authorized Daily Prayer Book.*

Rosh ha-Shanah marks the beginning of the Jewish religious year. To the Jew it is a period of deep religious significance. It is celebrated with two days of special solemnity and spiritual renewal.

The Talmud teaches us that there are two kinds of wrongdoing: wrongdoings between a person and God, and between one person and another (Mishnah, *Yoma* 8a). Between God and man: God will hear our prayers and forgive us our wrongdoings if we are sincere. However, between man and man, we must ask forgiveness from the person we have wronged.

The Bible tells us that God does not delight in the death of the wicked. Rather God desires that they turn from their evil ways and live (Ezekiel 33:11).

Rosh ha-Shanah is a serious day, one on which to contemplate the meaning of life and ask ourselves where we are heading. Yet, by the same token, it is a holiday of joy, of hope, especially when family and friends gather together and wish one another a good year (*Le-shanah tovah tikkatevu ve-teḥatemu*, "May you be written and inscribed for a good year").

Rosh ha-Shanah is the Day of Judgment, when every person passes before the Almighty God for judgment, for Him to decree who shall live and who shall die.

Rosh ha-Shanah is also called Yom ha-Zikkaron, the Day of Remembrance, when God remembers his covenant and one is obligated to hear the *shofar*. This commemorates the time when Abraham was ready to sacrifice his only son, Isaac, for the love of God.

In the month of Elul, prior to the Holy Day of Rosh ha-Shanah, the *shofar* (ram's horn) is sounded at the synagogue's morning services to announce the approaching holy season. The *shofar* was sounded in ancient times to proclaim the start of the jubilee year, when slaves went free, the anointing of a king, or to warn of the approach of an enemy. The man who is trained to sound the *shofar*

is called the *ba'al teki'ah*, "the man, or master of the sounding."
There are three distinct sounds of the *shofar*:

1) *Teki'ah*: a long drawn-out sound
2) *Shevarim*: a broken sound
3) *Teru'ah*: a sharp, staccato sound

It is customary to visit the cemetery before Rosh ha-Shanah and during the ten days of repentance, "in order that the dead shall intercede for mercy on our behalf." (Talmud, *Ta'anit* 16a). It is customary to give charity, to visit the graves of family and friends before the holy days, and to pray to God to harken to our prayers because of the merit of the departed. Rabbi Israel Meir ha-Kohen, known as the Ḥafeẓ Ḥayyim (a famous twentieth-century rabbi) explained that since the cemetery is holy, our prayers will be more readily acceptable.

At sunset on the eve of the first and second days of Rosh ha-Shanah, candles are lit. These candles are symbolic of light, happiness, and the purity of the home.

What are the foods for the holiday?
Among the special foods for Rosh ha-Shanah are:

Two round *ḥallot* symbolizing the roundness and smoothness of an unending life-cycle. In various communities *ḥallot* were made in different forms.

Apples dipped in honey so that the Lord will send a sweet year.

Carrots (Yiddish *mern*), pumpkin, beets, and dates, serving as a good omen because of their fertility and growth patterns.

When the sense of holiness fills the room, the prayer over the *ḥallot* is chanted, followed by dipping the *ḥallot* and then apples into the honey, and we say: "May it be the Lord's will to renew for us a year that will be good and sweet."

The spirit of the holiday is felt in the atmosphere around the dining table. The tablecloth is white (for purity), polished candlesticks shine brightly, polished *Kiddush* cups are prepared for every person, and the *hallah* cover reinforces the symbols of the holiday and includes a *shofar*—the symbol of revelation and redemption, the heralder of freedom. It is customary to sing *zemirot*, traditional songs, at the table. The meal ends with the *Birkat ha-Mazon*, grace after meals.

What is Tashlikh? A Ceremony of Repentance.

Tashlikh, originating in the Middle Ages, is a ceremony of repentance and symbolic self-purification. On the afternoon of the first day of Rosh ha-Shanah (or the second day if the first is Shabbat), worshippers gather at a body of running water, the banks of a river or an ocean. They recite several biblical verses, including Micah 7:19, which declares God's commitment to "cast all their sins into the depths of the sea," and recalls the devotion of Abraham, who braved raging floodwaters to serve his Maker.

Tashlikh is a prayer for divine mercy and forgiveness symbolizing self-purification, new beginnings, and a yearly rebirth of the spirit. Man's link with nature is recalled by this ritual, which gives communal support for those admitting transgressions and admits the need to support one another in the process of repentance. There is the optimistic hope that God does, indeed, forgive and we can begin anew.

During the recitation of the prayers, the participants shake out their pockets, symbolically ridding themselves of all sins by casting them into the water.

What is Aseret Yemei Teshuvah?

During these Ten Days of Penitence, we are given the opportunity to repent, regret, and resolve our sins from the past year. On Rosh ha-Shanah, it is written and on Yom Kippur, it is sealed, "who shall live and who shall die."

What is Yom Kippur?

Yom Kippur, the holiest day of the Jewish year, is the final day of the Ten Days of Penitence, which start with Rosh ha-Shanah. It is a day of reconciliation of God and man, a day of atonement, a day of fasting, praying, repentance, soul searching, and communion with God. The judgment of every man, woman, and child is finally decided on this day—"who shall live and who shall die."

There are five services in all, beginning with *Kol Nidrei* evening service asking for absolution of vows. Before leaving the house for the synagogue on *Kol Nidrei* night, the family gathers and it is customary for the parents to bless their children. They pray, in this blessing, for their offspring to be sealed in the Book of Life for health and happiness, and for their hearts to be steadfast in their love of God.

Memorial candles and *yom tov* candles are lit before leaving for the *Kol Nidrei* service. The memorial candles commemorate the souls of our beloved, and the *yom tov* candles are in honor of this most holy day.

Kol Nidrei must be recited before darkness sets in. This is the only night service of the year that we cover ourselves with the *tallit,* or prayer shawl, that is normally worn over the shoulders only during morning prayers. The *tallit* is rectangular in form, adorned with fringes (*zizit*) in keeping with the command to put fringes on the corners of the garment, the sight of which is to remind us to observe all the commandments (Numbers 15:38–39). All the Torah scrolls are taken out from the Ark. The *Kol Nidrei* chant is repeated three times by the cantor, after which the first of the five services of the Day of Atonement commences. *Yizkor* (a memorial service named for the prayer "May God remember the departed") is usually chanted with great solemnity during the service. The *Yizkor* service is conducted on four occasions: Yom Kippur, Shemini Azeret, Passover, and Shavuot. It is recited in the morning service in memory of our departed, and throughout the day we confess our sins and ask for forgiveness. The final service of the day is *Ne'ilah.*

What is Ne'ilah?

The final dramatic service on Yom Kippur is called *Ne'ilah*, meaning "closing," either to recall the Temple gates that were usually closed at the end of the day or because the Gates of Heaven are said to be closing, thus reminding the worshippers to seek God's forgiveness while there is still time. One of the most moving prayers of the *Ne'ilah* service refers to this allegorical interpretation of the closing of the gates: Ta'anith 4:1

> Open for us the gate
> At the time of the gate's closing.
> The day is done,
> The sun is setting, soon to be gone,
> Let us enter Your gates.

What is unique about Ne'ilah?

Several distinguishing features the *Ne'ilah* service help to create an aura of special urgency and solemnity. In many synagogues, the Ark remains open and the worshipers stand during the entire service. The *Kaddish* introducing the Silent Devotion, or *Amidah*, is especially moving and is frequently intoned by congregation and cantor. The congregation, for the first time, now asks to be sealed in the Book of Life instead of the usual petition during the High Holy Days to be inscribed in it. At the conclusion of the service the cantor and congregation chant the three professions of faith: The *Shema*, "Hear, O Israel, the Lord our God, the Lord is One" (Deuteronomy 6:4) is recited once, the phrase "Blessed be the Name of His kingdom forever and ever" is recited three times, and "The Lord, He is God" is said seven times. Finally, the *shofar* is blown, reminding the worshipers that the Day of Atonement is concluded and they may return to their homes and break their fast.

At the conclusion of the *Ne'ilah* service, the congregation exclaims: "Hear, O Israel, the Lord our God, the Lord is one!"

The roar (of the congregation) dwindles to a solemn silence. Then the ram's horn shrills—a stern long-drawn-out note that rises at last into a mighty peal of sacred jubilation. The atonement is complete.

What are the three pilgrimage festivals?

In ancient Palestine, our ancestors would make a pilgrimage three times a year to the Temple in Jerusalem, bringing their offerings to God.

The first pilgrimage was in the spring planting season: Passover, the sacrifice of the paschal lamb.

The second pilgrimage was seven weeks later when the first harvest had been reaped: Shavuot.

The third pilgrimage came at the very end of the summer when the final harvest had been gathered: Sukkot.

Thus, Passover, Shavuot, and Sukkot are called the three pilgrim festivals.

What is Passover?

Passover (Pesach), the first of the three pilgrimage festivals, is the oldest festival of liberty in the annals of civilization and is one of the most beloved holidays of the Jewish people. Thirty-five hundred years ago, the enslaved Hebrews revolted against the tyranny of their Egyptian taskmasters, escaped from slavery, blazed a trail across the wilderness, crossed the river Jordan, and settled in Palestine, the Promised Land. Passover has always been a heartfelt testimonial of joy and appreciation. It is a celebration of freedom that has had profound meaning for all humankind.

Passover is a holiday celebrated mainly in the home. The focal point is the Seder, where family and friends gather to retell the story of the exodus in the *Haggadah*, a special book prepared for the home service.

The word *seder* means "order." The Seder has been characterized as a symbolic trip through Jewish history told through the

Haggadah, the text used during the Seder. The essence of the holiday is simple; the Seder is to involve all present at the Seder table, and especially the youngsters, to stimulate them into awareness of our history.

The Torah informs us that our departure from Egyptian slavery came about so hastily that our ancestors had no time to prepare their bread in the usual manner but were compelled to bake it in the desert before it became leavened. Thus, as they set out on their march to freedom, they ate *matzah* (unleavened bread). In order to relive their experience, we are commanded to neither eat nor have in our possession any form of leavened bread (*ḥamez*) during the eight days of Passover. Foods about which there is even a suspicion of *ḥamez* may not be eaten, for even the smallest amount of *ḥamez* renders an entire product unsuited for Passover use.

A complete Seder plate contains many symbolic foods, such as

Roasted shank bone. This commemorates the paschal sacrifice that our ancestors brought to the Temple on Pesach in ancient times.

Roasted egg. This symbolizes the *ḥagigah*, or festival sacrifice, that was always brought to the Temple on festivals and on Pesach supplemented the paschal lamb.

Bitter herbs. These symbolize the bitterness of Israel's bondage in Egypt. Horseradish is usually used.

Ḥaroset. This symbolizes the mortar that the Israelites used in building the treasure cities for Pharaoh. The *ḥaroset* is a mixture of grated apples, chopped nuts, cinnamon, and a little wine.

Salt water. This symbolizes the tears of bondage and the hardships of slavery.

Green herbs. These symbolize the coming of spring. They suggest the perpetual renewal of life and thus the ever-sustaining hope of human redemption. Parsley, lettuce, watercress, or any other green herb may be used; they are dipped into a dish of salt water before they are eaten.

Four cups of wine are drunk at the Seder. These symbolize the fourfold promise of redemption which, according to the Bible, God pledged to Israel:

"I will free you from the labors of the Egyptians" (Exodus 6:6).
"I will deliver you from their bondage" (Exodus 6:6).
"I will redeem you with an outstretched arm" (Exodus 6:6).
"I will take you to be my people" (Exodus 6:7).

What is the cup of Elijah?
A special cup known as the cup of Elijah is placed on the center of the table. This cup should remain unfilled until the conclusion of the meal, when it is filled with wine and left untouched. Although some rabbis hold that there should be only four cups, others contend that there should be a fifth cup because of a fifth promise made to our ancestors: "I will bring you to the Promised land." Therefore, the fifth cup of wine was provided as a symbol of the hope of redemption which Elijah the prophet will herald. What better time than Passover, the festival of freedom, for such redemption to occur? Since this question could not be settled definitively, the prevailing opinion was to postpone the question until the coming of the Messiah, at which time all unanswered questions could be settled.

A second plate containing three pieces of unleavened bread called matzah is placed on the table. The three matzot represent the three groups into which the Jewish people are divided. The upper matzah represents the *kohanim*, those who trace their descent from Aaron, brother of Moses. The middle matzah represents the Levites, descendents of Levi, the third son of Jacob. The lower matzah represents the Israelites, those who are neither *kohanim* nor Levites.

At the Seder meal, one of the three pieces of matzah is broken in half and hidden. This piece will be the *afikoman*. *Afikoman* is a Greek word meaning "dessert," and this piece will be shared by all at the conclusion of the meal. It has become customary for a child to find the *afikoman* and ask a ransom for its return. This custom enlivens the closing parts of the Seder.

Passover is a happy but serious time. It reminds us of how important it is for people to be free from all kinds of slavery. It is also a time of hospitality. The *Haggadah* teaches, "Let all who are hungry come and eat."

The annual retelling of the story of the Exodus is dominated by the central theme of liberty and freedom. Its importance was so great that the episode of the Exodus from Egypt has been included in our daily prayers and in the *Kiddush* for the Sabbath and holidays. It is also mentioned in the first of the Ten Commandments. The Liberty Bell in Independence Hall in Philadelphia is engraved with the words of the Bible: "Proclaim liberty throughout the land, unto all the inhabitants thereof" (Leviticus 25:10).

As we enjoy the beautiful Seder service, surrounded by our family and friends, blessed with the good things of life, living in the wonderful country of America, we must also remember our oppressed brethren in other parts of the world.

What is Shavuot?

Shavuot (Pentecost) is the second of the three pilgrimage festivals of the Jewish year. This is the time of the receiving of the Torah (*zeman matan toratenu*). Shavuot is the anniversary of that monumental day in the history of humanity; the day the Torah and the Ten Commandments were given to Moses on Mount Sinai. God revealed Himself to humankind and spoke to them, making Judaism unique among all other religions. No religious document has exercised a greater influence on the moral and social life of man than the divine summary of human duty known as the Ten

Commandments, or Decalogue—a summary unequalled in simplicity, comprehensiveness, and solemnity, a summary that bears divinity on its face and cannot become antiquated as the world endures.

Shavuot is intimately linked to the festival of Passover. Its name means "weeks," referring to the *sefirah*—the counting of seven weeks, or forty-nine days, from the second day of Passover. The fiftieth day is Shavuot.

The festival of Shavuot has several names:

Ḥag ha-Shavuot because the festival is celebrated seven weeks from the second day of Passover. It is also reflected to "Shevua, taking a vow."

Yom ha-Bikkurim because it was the time of the ripening of the first fruits, which were brought to the Temple in Jerusalem in appreciation of God's bountiful blessings.

Ḥag ha-Katzir, to commemorate the climax of the grain festival, which commenced with the gathering of the early barley crop at Passover and ended with the harvesting of the barley produce at Shavuot.

Azeret, because it is the closing festival of Passover (*azeret shel pesaḥ*). This name emphasizes that Shavuot completes the harvest that began at Passover time. (Exodus 23:16)

More important, Shavuot is linked to Passover because the freedom from Egypt is connected to the receiving of the divine teachings at Mount Sinai. In other words, freedom and law go hand in hand. This momentous event is celebrated with a two-day holiday on the sixth and seventh days of the Jewish month of Sivan.

On Shavuot, it is customary to eat dairy foods. Since Shavuot is associated with flowers and foliage, it is customary to decorate the home and the synagogue with flowers, plants, and greens. God decorated the barren Mount Sinai with greenery. Flowers symbolize the beauty with which the divine has filled the earth. Branches also symbolize the Torah as a tree of life. Shavuot is an appropriate time to thank the Almighty for the fruits, crops, and food of the earth, which sustains us in life. It is a time to extend gratitude and appreciation to the Lord.

The Book of Ruth is read in the synagogue on Shavuot, manifesting the right of all men and women to come under the sanctity of our Torah through conversion. In the Book of Ruth we find the following words of faith: "Entreat me not to leave you, for whither thou goest, I will go, and whither thou lodge, I will lodge; Thy people shall be my people, and thy God my God." (Ruth 1:16)

What is Sukkot?

Sukkot (Tabernacles), the third pilgrimage festival, is the festival of thanksgiving. It is interesting to note that the Pilgrims of American history, steeped in knowledge of the Bible, set aside a day of Thanksgiving based upon our festival of Tabernacles. "You shall dwell in a booth, that your generations may know that I made the children of Israel to dwell in booths when I brought them out of the Land of Egypt" (Leviticus 23:42–43). These booths are reminders of the temporary houses in which the Israelites lived while traveling in the desert after their escape from Egypt.

In the Bible, Sukkot is called the Feast of Ingathering because it marked the ingathering of the fruits of the orchards and the grapes of the vineyards. In building the *sukkah* hut (tabernacle), the plants or leaves that form the roof are not to be laid on too thickly, to make sure that the heavens and the stars remain visible, for "the heavens declare the glory of God" (Psalm 19:2).

Tabernacles begins five days after Yom Kippur and lasts for seven days. The eighth and ninth days, known as Shemini Azeret and Simhat Torah, are separate holidays. In celebrating Tabernacles, we wave a sweet-smelling *etrog*, or citron, which looks like a lemon, and a *lulav* containing three plants (myrtle, willow, and palm branch) to the heavens above and in every direction to remind us that our blessings come from one God, who is everywhere. A special blessing is said over the four species.

The seventh day of Sukkot is known as Hoshanah Rabbah, the "Great Petition" for abundant rain. Seven processions are held in the synagogue, and a distinctive ritual connected with the willow branches is carried out while praying.

The eighth day of Sukkot is Shemini Azeret, the "Eighth Day of Assembly," observed as a separate festival. It concludes the holiday season that began with Rosh ha-Shanah. At the morning services, *Yizkor* memorial prayers are read and a special prayer for rain is recited.

The ninth day of Sukkot is Simhat Torah, literally "Rejoicing in the Torah." The holiday celebrates the annual conclusion of the reading of the entire Pentateuch (Torah) in the course of the year. It is observed on the day following Shemini Azeret; in Israel, both festivals are celebrated together on the eighth day of Sukkot.

Scrolls of the Torah are carried seven times or more around the synagogue during the evening and morning services, accompanied by dancing and singing. The processions of the scrolls (known as *hakkafot*) are followed by children bearing flags. During the morning service, everyone in the synagogue is called up to recite the blessings for a reading of the Torah. It is customary to call up the new students in the religious school to be consecrated as pilgrims of the Torah. Simhat Torah is a day of rejoicing in every sense of the word.

What is Hanukkah?

Hanukkah, the festival of light, is one of the most meaningful and colorful days of rejoicing in the Jewish calendar. The festival reminds us of the first occasion in human history when a group found it necessary to wage a struggle for religious beliefs.

This is the holiday that commemorates the successful struggle of the Maccabees for religious freedom against the Syrian-Greeks, who sought to prevent the practice of Judaism in the year 165 B.C.E.

The eight-day festival celebrates the rededication of the Temple in Jerusalem following the victory of Judas Maccabeus over the Syrian-Greeks. We light candles for eight days as a reminder of the miracle of the cruse of oil that had enough oil to burn for one day, but instead burned for eight.

The distinctive ceremony of the holiday is the kindling of lights, formerly of oil, for eight nights. Today, special Ḥanukkah candles are used, one candle being lit on the first night, and one more candle being added and lit on each successive night. The candleholder is called a *menorah* (or *ḥanukkiyyah*). Other features of the festival are the singing of the hymn *Ma'oz Ẓur* ("Rock of Ages"), which recounts many wonders of Jewish redemption in Egypt, Babylonia, Persia, and Syria. It is sung after the kindling of the Ḥanukkah light. It was composed by a thirteenth-century poet whose name was Mordechai ben Isaac, as is revealed in the acrostic of the initial letters of the five stanzas. Songs extolling bravery and courage, festive family meals, and the exchange of gifts, particularly within the family, are also part of the festival. A game is played with a spinning top called a *dreidl*, which has four Hebrew letters written on it sides. The letters remind us of the Maccabean victory for religious freedom: *nes gadol hayah sham* "A great miracle happened there."

The festival of Ḥanukkah teaches us about the struggle of the few against the many, of the weak against the strong, and of passion against indifference. The war was not only against oppression from without, but also equally against corruption and complacency within. Its symbol is appropriate: a small light kindled when the shadows fall.

What is Tu bi-Shevat?

Tu bi-Shevat, the Jewish Arbor Day, also known as Rosh ha-Shanah le-Ilanot, the New Year of Trees, occurs on the fifteenth day of the month of Shevat. It is explained in the Talmud (*Rosh ha-Shanah*

14a) that the rains have already departed by this time of the year in Israel. Buds have begun to rise in the trees, and fruit has begun to bloom.

The planting season in Israel starts on the fifteenth of Shevat. Tu bi-Shevat is a symbol of spring and hope, rebirth and joy in nature. It brings with it beautiful thoughts as well as beautiful deeds. Tu bi-Shevat is the festival when Israel is reborn. It is a time to plant trees and plow the soil.

The planting of trees is considered a great *mitzvah*. The word *mitzvah* means divine commandment. We learn from this holiday that we must treat with care and consideration not only the people who live around us but also the trees, the fruits and flowers, the fields and the orchards. "Just as others planted for you, so shall you plant for the sake of your children."

For the people of Israel, Tu bi-Shevat symbolizes the deep bond between them and nature. It is a bond existing throughout the Diaspora and continuing today. Tu bi-Shevat, as a symbol of spring and hope, rebirth and joy, makes us realize how rich and bountiful the world is, and how grateful we should be for all the wonderful growing things that surround us.

What is Purim?

The Feast of Lots is known as Purim in Hebrew. Purim commemorates the deliverance of the Jews of Persia from the threat of destruction planned against them by Haman, a wicked person, as narrated in the Book of Esther. It is a *mitzvah* to read the Book of Esther in the evening and morning of the holiday and to eat a sumptuous meal. The story unfolds with Queen Esther, a Jewish girl who was beautiful and lovely, and the wise Mordecai, her cousin, who adopted her and brought her up as his own daughter. Esther was chosen as queen by King Ahasuerus, who ruled over Persia. Esther used her influence to save her people from a general massacre that Haman had plotted against the Jews. The story is told in the Book of Esther, one of the most cherished books in Jewish literature. It is the last of the five *megillot* (scrolls) or the third division of the Bible, known as Ketuvim (Sacred Writings). Purim, however, is more than just an interesting story. This holiday teaches that other people's religious customs and laws should not be used as excuses to hate, hurt, or destroy them.

On the Sabbath before Purim, a special reading from the Torah (Deuteronomy 25:16) relates: "Remember what Amalek did to you." The Amalekites were the first people to attack the Israelites when they came out of Egypt, and we have always remembered them as the typical example of our enemies and oppressors. Haman was a descendant of Amalek. Purim is a holiday that brings with it the memory of divine intervention on behalf of Israel, the righting of a great injustice, the averting of a terrible calamity, and the punishment of an evil instigator.

In times of persecution, Purim provided an occasion wherein each Jew, identifying himself with Mordecai of old, could surmount despair by recalling triumph over peril. Esther was able to intercede at the last moment and save the Jewish community from genocide. On the gallows that Haman had prepared for Mordecai, he himself was hanged. The Jews of Persia were spared, and judgments were executed on their enemies.

Purim is the merriest festival of the Jewish year, with celebrations in schools featuring plays based on the story of Esther and carnivals in synagogues. Gifts (*shelakh manot*) are sent to friends, and money is given to the poor. Children masquerade in fancy dress and masks, and a huge carnival (Adloyada) is held in synagogues and Jewish community centers.

Purim is a reminder of the painful trials and bitter struggles, torment of body and agony of mind, that have too often been our portion. This day brings to mind the darkness and gloom we have experienced in many generations.

What are Tishah be-Av and Shivah asar be-Tammuz?

Tishah be-Av, the ninth day in the Jewish month of Av, is a tragic day in Jewish history and is observed by mourning and fasting. It is the saddest day in the Jewish calendar and usually occurs in late July or August, beginning before sundown and extending through the day. Why do we fast on Tishah be-Av? Although we thank God that we have returned to our Holy Land and that Jerusalem is reunited, fasting is a tangible symbol of mourning, suffering, and grief. Tishah be-Av is a date in history that can never be forgotten.

It was on the ninth day of Av in the year 586 B.C.E. that Nebuchadnezzar, king of Babylon, destroyed Jerusalem, burned Solomon's Temple, and abolished the first Jewish kingdom in Palestine. On the same day about 650 years later in 70 C.E., the Romans destroyed the Second Holy Temple and brought to an end the Second Jewish Commonwealth. By amazing coincidence, even the great tragedies of the expulsion of the Jews from Spain and the beginning of World War I occurred on the ninth day of Av in the years 1492 and 1914, respectively. Most of the pogroms in Russia and the Ukraine took place on the 9th of Av.

Jews have a commitment to memory. When we remember, we retell, we relive, we feel the pain of hurt, we feel the pain of sadness, of mourning, of crying out; we feel a void in the crevices of our heart.

The three weeks preceding Tishah be-Av are considered a period of preparation. Weddings are not celebrated during this time, and a gradual change of mood ensues. There are special prophetic readings for the three Sabbaths in advance of the ninth of Av. The mood of the day is filled with anguish over the destruction of the Temple; therefore, it is customary to visit the cemetery and pray at the graves of close family members.

On the evening of Tishah be-Av, Jews gather in synagogues and recite the mournful Book of Lamentations, or *Eikhah*, ascribed by tradition to the prophet Jeremiah, an eyewitness to the terrible destruction of the First Temple.

Tradition tells us that the Messiah will be born on Tishah be-Av and that the *Bet ha-Mikdash shel Ma'alah*, the Heavenly Temple of God, will descend to the Holy City of Jerusalem. We pray fervently for the coming of the Great Redeemer who will redeem Israel and all humankind.

Jewish Values, Beliefs, Opinions, and Traditions

Knowing God

Many people today refuse to accept God. People do not want to go to the trouble of seeking God. "Seek and you shall find Him." To know God, you must feel His presence. You must be able to penetrate the hidden, mysterious realms of your deepest heart and soul. "Only the fool says in his heart, there is no God" (Psalms 14:1, 53:2).

Most people are spiritually attuned to feel God. Some accept God or faith. Some cannot fathom His existence so they deny God. I am reminded of a beautiful tale told by the Ba'al Shem Tov, the founder of Hasidism. There once was a wedding in a house. The musicians played the instruments; the guests danced to the music and enjoyed themselves tremendously. A deaf man looked through a window as he passed by. He saw people dancing, leaping, shaking, bending, and throwing their feet and arms about. The deaf man cried out, "Madmen!" because he could not hear the music to which they were dancing.[4] Some people are deaf to the heavenly music that gives such joy and bliss to those whose ears and souls are divinely attuned. Some are soul-deaf; some are ear-deaf. Judaism's God is One! His Oneness is also uniqueness.

One Chronicles 28:9 states: "And you, Solomon, my son, know the God of your father." It is the crowning glory of our faith, our Torah that commands us to *know*. God appeared to Solomon and said to him, "Ask what I shall give you." Solomon said: "Give me

---

[4] Meyer Levin, "Golden Mountain," p. 86.

wisdom and knowledge." God said to Solomon: "Because this was in your heart, and you have not asked for riches, wealth, or honor but for wisdom and knowledge, I will give you riches, wealth, and honor as well" (2 Chronicles 1:7–12). With knowledge we are affected not only physically by the outside world, but also, and this is more important, intellectually and spiritually as well.

What do Jews believe about God?

God is called *Ribbono Shel Olam*. He is the creator, Master of the Universe, and therein lies his distinctiveness. He is the essence of all morality and righteousness. He is the supreme ideal of moral conduct. "The heavens declare the glory of God, and the law of the Lord is perfect, restoring the soul" (Psalm 19:2, 8).

God is called *Ha-Kadosh Barukh Hu*, "The Holy One, blessed be He," to emphasize the moral qualities of His essence. The Jewish people are called *goy kadosh*, "a holy people," because their lives are to be in *imitatio dei*, such as to become God-like (*Shabbat* 86a). God is thus the essence of the Jewish soul, the supreme ideal of the Jewish way of life. Walking in the ways of God, as God is merciful and gracious, so be you. As God is righteous and just, so be you. As God is holy, so be you.

How would you describe God? Maimonides states: "If I could describe God, He would not be God!" (*Guide for the Perplexed* 1:59, 88). Judaism is concerned only with what God wills and demands. It is not for the human eye to penetrate the essence of God. "Man shall not see me and live." (Exodus 33:18–20).

"Show me thy ways that I may know thee." This request was granted to Moses (Exodus 33:13–19).

When the Jews crossed the Red Sea, he apotheosized God. "This is my God, *ve-anvehu*—and I shall glorify Him." Read not *ve-anvehu*, they say, but *ani ve-hu*, "I and He"—"We!" Yea, this is the story of the spiritual "We" of history. God and Jew, the Jew and God. God is the soul, the very life of the Jew, and the Jew, by his life, tries to exemplify, in the highest measure, the glory, the beauty, and the very essence of God!

The Ḥafez Ḥayyim, Rabbi Israel Meir ha-Kohen said: "In the final analysis, for the believer there are no questions, and for the nonbeliever there are no answers."

Trust in God?

The Hebrew word for "trust" is *emunah*. It comes from the same root as *amen*, "It is so," "So be it." Trust implies an experience of higher dimension above nature, as occurred during the Exodus and the miracle of the Red Sea. It means complete trust in the Almighty, whose power is beyond nature. Our everyday life should be nurtured and sustained by faith. It means an unquestioned acceptance of God. Trust denotes absolute belief in divine Providence, in God's unfailing goodness. This is expressed in Jewish hopefulness for a better world and optimistic outlook on life.

Yigdal and *Ani Ma'amin*, both of which embody the Thirteen Principles of Faith formulated by Moses Maimonides (1135–1204), exemplify what we mean by "trust." The principles are summed up in our daily prayer book as follows. Thirteen is reminiscent of the numerical value of the Hebrew word "Echod" one. These are the thirteen attributes of God:

He exists; His existence transcends time.

He is one—there is no oneness like His.

He is bodiless beyond comparison in His holiness.

He is Eternal.

He is the Eternal Lord; every creature must declare His greatness and His Kingship.

His abundant prophecy He granted to the men of his choice and His glory.

Moses was the greatest of all prophets.

The Torah of Truth God gave to His people through his prophet [Moses], His faithful servant.

God will never amend nor ever change His eternal law for any
  other law.

God knows all the acts and thoughts of man.

He rewards the goodly man. He punishes the evil.

Messiah will come.

God will revive the dead [resurrection]. Blessed be His glorious
  name.

Martin Buber described religious faith as a dialogue between
man and God. Buber developed the idea of an "I–Thou" relationship between man and God, enabling man to know God. When
there is no dialogue between man and God, or between man and
man, society breaks down and humanity disappears.

Who is God?

The most significant Jewish contribution to the world is monotheism. The concept of one God has universal and cosmic implica-
tions, as the unifier of the entire universe, the creator of every
human being.

The Hebrew name for God comes from the verb *hayah*, which
means "to be." God is existence. As the song *Adon Olam* states:
"God was, God is, and God will be with glory." The statement that
there is only one God in the world is the indispensable prerequisite
for our faith in the oneness of humankind.

For a Jew, God is an indivisible unity. God cannot be fully
grasped by the human mind or even be defined fully. God is the "I"
of the first commandment, "I am the Lord your God, who took you
out of the land of Egypt, the house of bondage." He is the God of
every man, woman, and child (*Yalkut Shimoni* 286) .Those "who
seek will find Him." Knowing God depends on you.

Judaism emphasizes that God is God, and man is man. Judaism
through the ages has been uncompromisingly faithful to the very
letter of the second commandment, which prohibits the making of
images of God.

The evidence of God's existence is very difficult to prove or disprove. As you live, learn, and experience, you begin to think and feel. You either believe or disbelieve. The world cannot be without a creator, just as a building cannot be built without an architect and a builder.

Why different names of God?

Since Jews have one God, why different names? According to the rabbis, the various names of God represent different conceptions of the divine.

It is true that God is one, but He is called by different names according to how He is perceived.

> *Elohim* emphasizes the God who dispenses justice. It is found in all semitic languages.
> *Jehovah* is the God who displays mercy and compassion.
> *Shaddai* is the God of power and might, and protector.
> *El Shaddai* is the God who rules the universe.

Last, in the world that is to be—in that glorious future that is yet to come, not only will God be one, His name, too, will then be one (Talmud, *Pesaḥim* 50a)

The Jew concludes every prayer service with these words: "The Lord shall be king over all the earth; in that day the Lord be one and His name one" (Zechariah 14:9).

Rabbi, as a Holocaust survivor how can you believe in God?

I wish that I had the infinite wisdom necessary to give a satisfactory answer, but I do not. Yet, from my teaching and my experience as a survivor, I will comment on my own personal view. As I know, God created good and evil in every human being. We have the animal element or instinct, and the human instinct, the evil and the good. At times, evil overpowers good, and at times, good overpowers evil.

Imitatio Dei (imitating God), we must live by the *standards* that God set for us. I do not blame God. I blame people. It is unreasonable to blame God for all the evil that exists in this world. A Hasidic rabbi was asked, "Where is God?" He answered, "Wherever you let him in."

What are the principal tenets of Judaism?

The principal tenets are to be compassionate, to be just, to be tolerant in judgment, to love learning, and to perform good deeds to God and man. The prophet Micah stated: "What does the Lord require of thee? Only to act justly, to love mercy, and to walk humbly with your God" (Micah 6:8).

Psalm 145:8–9. The Lord is gracious, and full of compassion; Slow to anger, and of great mercy. The Lord is good to all; And His tender mercies are over all His works.

Isaiah 55:6–7. Seek ye the Lord while He may be found, call ye upon Him while He is near; Let the wicked forsake his way, and the man of iniquity his thoughts; and let him return unto the Lord, and He will have compassion upon him, and to our God, for He will abundantly pardon.

Psalm 103:13. Like as a father hath compassion upon his children, so hath the Lord compassion upon them that fear Him.

Isaiah 45:22. Look unto Me, and be ye saved, all the ends of the earth; for I am God, and there is none else.

Psalm 145:18. The Lord is nigh unto all them that call upon Him, to all that call upon Him in truth.

Psalm 121:1–2. I will lift up mine eyes unto the mountains: From whence shall my help come? My help cometh from the Lord, who made heaven and earth.

Psalm 121:7–8. The Lord shall keep thee from all evil; He shall keep thy soul. The Lord shall guard thy going out and thy coming in, From this time forth and forever.

Psalm 126:3. The Lord hath done great things with us; We are rejoiced. If other nations acknowledge the miracles, we should rejoice even more.

God cares for man.

Psalm 55:23. Cast thy burden upon the Lord, and He will sustain thee; He will never suffer the righteous to be moved. God does not remove the load but supports the bearer of it.

Psalm 46:2. God is our refuge and strength, a very present help in trouble.

Joshua 1:9. Have not I commanded thee? Be strong and of good courage; be not afraid, neither be thou dismayed: for the Lord thy God is with thee withersoever thou goest.

Psalm 48:15. For such is God, our God, forever and ever; He will guide us eternally.

How would you explain an "eye for an eye"?

The term "eye for an eye" has been misinterpreted throughout the ages. The true meaning of the term is that when there is deliberate damage done to another person's body or property, there are rules for compensation, as indicated in the Book of Exodus 21:22–37. Also, in the Talmud, *Bava Kamma* 83b, it states that the person or persons inflicting the deliberate damage must fully compensate the injured party or parties. The Bible emphasizes mercy and compassion. "As God is merciful and gracious, so must you be as well" (Exodus 34:6). An example: in case of an accident or unintended killing, the killer was provided a refuge city to protect him from an avenging relative of the victim (Numbers 35:9–34).

Why are the Jews referred to as a chosen people?
The concept that Israel is the chosen people is one that is most problematic and emotional, yet most grossly misunderstood.

> O ye seed of Israel His servant,
> Ye children of Jacob His chosen ones.
> He is the Lord our God;
> His judgments are in all the earth.
> Remember His covenant forever,
> The word which He commanded to a thousand genera-
> tions;
> (The covenant) which He made with Abraham,
> And His oath unto Isaac;
> And He established it unto Jacob for a statute,
> To Israel for an everlasting covenant;
> Saying: "Unto thee will I give the land of Canaan,
> The lot of your inheritance."
>
> I Chronicles 16:15, 16, 17, 18

The term "chosen" expresses the idea that God chose the Jewish people to receive the Torah and to proclaim His truths among all peoples. The term "chosen" does not imply any claim of superiority over other peoples or nations, but a superior duty and responsibility.

Jewish chosenness means chosen by God to spread ethical monotheism to the world and to live as a moral "light unto the nations" (Isaiah 49:6).

Every nation is equal before God. God chose the Jews, "not because you are big. Indeed you are the smallest nation" (Deuteronomy 7:7), "but simply because you are the offspring of Abraham," the first ethical monotheist (Genesis 18:19). That is their single merit.

God has given occasion to the Israelites to say that they were His treasured people, as in Exodus 19:5,6. "Now therefore, if you will hearken unto My voice indeed, and keep My covenant, then you shall be Mine own treasure from among all peoples, for all the earth is Mine." The Jewish people have maintained their individuality and identity, their way of life and civilization. They have a record of suffering and persecution greater than any other people suffered, and they have outlived their persecutors. Surely, they are a people chosen for a purpose.

When Abraham was ninety-nine years old, the Lord appeared to Abraham and said to him, 'I am El Shaddai [God Almighty]. Walk in My ways and be blameless. And I will establish My covenant between Me and you' " (Genesis 17:1–2).

God reminded Isaac and Jacob of the Covenant he made with Abraham and that the descendants of Abraham had a special covenantal relationship. The creator of the universe bestowed His blessings upon the patriarchs as a reward for their faithfulness and love, and God promised that their children and all succeeding generations would continue to receive His blessings because of "the merits of their fathers." Israel became a chosen people because of the merits of its ancestors, Abraham, Isaac, and Jacob (Deuteronomy 4:37).

Then Moses came, summoned the elders of the people, and set before them all the words that the Lord had commanded him. And all the people answered as one, saying, "All that the Lord has spoken we will do!" (Exodus 19:5–8).

According to the traditional understanding of our Bible, God made known His will at Sinai. And He chose Israel, the Jewish people, as the instrument for making His will known to the rest of the world. Moreover, the covenant between God and Israel was not solely for Moses' generation: "I will make this covenant . . . not with you alone, but both with those who are standing here with us this day before the Lord our God and with those who are not with us here this day" (Deuteronomy 29:13–14).

The covenant is thus an everlasting agreement between God and the children of Israel. God chose Israel as the vehicle through which to reveal His will to all humankind.

Being chosen conferred upon Israel responsibility, not privilege. Our people were chosen to show how God's righteousness could be made the basis of everyday life.

The Jewish people were chosen as an example, not an exception. The Jew is covenanted to give witness by his words and his deeds, by his way of life, to the ultimate realization of God's kingdom on earth. Being chosen is not a claim but an obligation, not a divine title for rights but a divine mandate for duties. The obligation that God set before Israel was to become a "kingdom of priests and a holy nation"—to serve God in thought and act, to sanctify life and render it significant, to avoid cruelty, diminish evil, and purify man's hands and heart.

And finally, "For the mountains may depart and the hills be removed, but My kindness shall not depart from thee, neither shall My covenant of peace be removed, saith the Lord that hath compassion on thee. (Isaiah 54:10)

How is man judged?

In Judaism, God judges man by his deeds (*mitzvot*). One of the most distinctive features of Judaism is its great variety of rites and ceremonies—rituals that cover every aspect of life from cradle to the grave. Every human relation, every human aspiration is covered by laws. At every juncture in our lives we are touched by holiness. There is no single book that embodies all the religious laws binding upon Jews. The closest anyone has come to compiling a single legal code is the *Shulḥan Arukh*, a sixteenth-century work by Joseph Karo. This book contains the basic law that today guides most Orthodox Jews in the Western world. But it does not contain the full body of Jewish law with the changing of times and circumstances. Even the Bible cannot be considered the unchanging standard for religious practice. The biblical laws concerning polygamy, interest, tithing, slavery, and other subjects have been reinterpreted out of existence. In this sense, rabbinical law and the Bible are not identical.

King Solomon wrote in Ecclesiastes 7:20, "There is no man so righteous who does only good and never sins." In other words, no one is perfect; only angels are. Moses sinned; David sinned, and after repenting and returning to observance of the law that they violated, they were restored to God's graces. Judaism judges a person by his actions rather than by his faith. As the Talmud attests, through observance of the laws "they will return to God." (Jerusalem Talmud, *Ḥagigah* 1:7).

What is the Bet Din?

In Temple times, the *Bet Din Gadol* (Supreme Court) in Jerusalem comprised seventy-one members and was known as the Great Sanhedrin. It exercised final authority on religious problems and appointed judges for the lower courts, consisting of twenty-three members each, to sit in judgment on criminal cases. The local courts, comprising at least three members each, had jurisdiction over civil cases. In the Diaspora, Jewish courts continued to exist in centers of Jewish population. Presided over by rabbinic authorities called *dayyanim* (judges), the Jewish courts had jurisdiction over the internal communal affairs. After the breakdown of communal autonomy in the nineteenth century, they were limited to ritual matters and voluntary arbitration. In the State of Israel, rabbinical courts have jurisdiction in such matters as marriage and divorce.

What are the various forms of Judaism?

Even though Judaism is monotheistic, it is not monolithic. There are major disagreements about a host of fundamental issues that have led to different movements within Judaism.

What is Reconstructionism?

Reconstructionism is a modern religious movement in America. The principles and theory were formulated by Rabbi Mordecai M. Kaplan. He conceived the idea of Judaism as being a "religious civilization" and not a religion exclusively. To be a positive Jew one must identify oneself with all aspects of Jewish life and be an active participant in work for the survival of the Jewish community. Reconstructionism denies Judaism's supernatural God and the chosenness of the Jews.

The Reconstructionists maintain that Judaism must undergo constant change. Jewish life in America must thus be "reconstructed." The program of Reconstructionist Judaism calls for a strong Jewish community based on democratic organization, the importance of the State of Israel as a Jewish homeland, an intensive and effective Jewish educational system, and the need for a cooperative society. Its press publishes books, journals, and numerous pamphlets.

Kaplan argued for what he called an "organic community" in which the synagogue functions as a Jewish center where the individual can find expression for virtually all Jewish and related activities. The Reconstructionist *Sabbath Prayer Book* appeared in 1945. A ban (*ḥerem*) was then proclaimed by the Orthodox rabbis because in accordance with Kaplan's ideology, it excised references to the Jews as a chosen people, and to such concepts as God's revelation of the Torah to Moses and a personal Messiah. The movement has not been successful in recruiting a mass following.

What is Reform Judaism?

Reform Judaism is a religious movement among Jews that began in 1810 in Germany. Its main development has been in the United States, and it has become a most influential religious movement in American Jewry.

Reform Judaism came about in opposition to some of the basic doctrines and practices of what is now known as Orthodox Judaism. Reform Jews believe that modern Jews should reject the belief in revelation. It is inconceivable that God spoke directly to the people or that the Torah is God-given in the strictest sense of the word. The Torah is a creation of the Jewish people, who were inspired by God to make laws of righteousness.

The Torah was conceived by divinely inspired men and was not God-given. Therefore, every generation has the right to accept only those laws of the Torah and those practices which are essential, and to reject those which are no longer necessary or practicable, or are too difficult.

In accordance with the above principles, Reform Judaism emphasizes the ethical teachings of the Torah, the Talmud, and the other sacred writings, and the ritual is given secondary importance. Some Reform Jews do not adhere to the tradition of a prayer shawl (*tallit*) worn in the synagogue, phylacteries, or the wearing of a *kippah* (covering of the head). Reform Judaism does not obligate its adherents to refrain from work on the Sabbath and holidays.

To assure greater participation of the worshiper, the prayer book used in Reform congregations includes more English than Hebrew, and many traditional prayers have been omitted. Reform Jews believe that the traditional dietary laws (*kashrut*) as well as many of the practices and ceremonies in the home and the synagogue have outgrown their purposes and are no longer essential.

What is Orthodox Judaism?

Orthodox Judaism is the religion followed by strict adherents of traditional Judaism, which is a total commitment to God's Written and

Oral Law. The foundation of Orthodox Judaism rests on the teachings of the Torah (Five Books of Moses) and the Oral Law as represented by the Mishnah and Talmud and the codes of legal authority (e.g., the *Shulḥan Arukh*). Orthodox Jews believe in the literal doctrine of revelation that the Torah, both written and oral, was given to Moses by God on Mount Sinai and is, therefore, everlasting, and the only true guide of Jewish conduct. Its premise is that religion dare not be changed by the times. Orthodox Jews advocate unswerving loyalty to Jewish traditions, chief among which are devoted study of the Torah, daily prayer (three times a day), strict observance of the Sabbath, the holidays, the dietary laws, and the laws of family purity. As with other movements in Judaism, Orthodox Judaism requires every Jew to lead a pious, righteous, and charitable life.

In an Orthodox synagogue, you will find a *meḥiẓah*, which is a divider to separate men and women into different sections. This ensures that men and women will not be able to see each other during prayer. Visual contact between the sexes distracts from concentration for prayer. The abolition of the *meḥiẓah* took place by the Reform movement in Europe in the early part of the nineteenth century. In most Conservative synagogues in the United States, the *meḥiẓah* has been abolished. These modern trends have met with vigorous opposition from the Orthodox rabbinate.

What is Neo-Orthodoxy?
Neo-Orthodoxy is identified with Rabbi Samson Raphael Hirsch (1808–1888). This "new" or more modern expression of traditional Judaism finds itself within the freedom and the challenges of an open society, Hirsch taught that it was time to reopen Jewish minds to the dual sources of wisdom. In the ghettos, the Jews were restricted to Jewish culture. Hirsch encouraged study at the universities and considered secular writings to be to an even stronger and more intense religious commitment. Even the synagogue service was modernized with sermons in German—a daring innovation that

went against tradition, but helped to keep many Jews from drifting from their faith.

What is Conservative Judaism?

The Conservative movement came into being in the middle of the nineteenth century in both Europe and the United States because of dissatisfaction with the Orthodox synagogue service and as an opposition to the extreme departures of Reform religious services and practices. Conservative Judaism seeks the middle ground between maintaining the authority of Jewish law and accepting the need for growth and change. Conservative leaders accept the doctrine of divine inspiration, but a number of rabbis hesitate about affirming a literal revelation of the Torah by God at Sinai. However, the laws of the Torah and the Jewish customs transmitted from generation to generation are kept sacred by the Conservative movement. They may not be discarded, but rather are changed and adapted, if necessary, to modern conditions of Jewish life; but only by proper scholars and authoritative bodies. The Sabbath and *kashrut* are sacred traditions to be observed as fully as possible. The Conservative movement made a few changes in the traditional prayer book. A new edition of the Torah, *Etz Hayim,* with commentaries by a Conservative rabbi was published in the year 2001.

What is Hasidism?

Hasidism is a religious movement that originated among the Jews in Poland in the eighteenth century. Israel Ben Eliezer, known by his disciples as Ba'al Shem Tov ("Master of the Good Name," 1700–60) was somehow able to accomplish what nobody had ever before succeeded in doing. A man who never wrote a book was able to translate the spiritual discoveries of his soul to all the generations that followed. It is difficult to do justice to the genius of the Ba'al Shem Tov and the revolutionary nature of his movement. Hasidism came about as a result of the spiritual and economic depression resulting from the Cossack massacres of the Jews in Ukraine in the seventeenth century and the frustration among the Jewish masses resulting from the collapse of the messianic movement initiated by Shabbetai Ẓevi (who in 1626, in Turkey, proclaimed himself Messiah). Talmudic scholarship and the intellectualism of the tal-mudist were inaccessible, incomprehensible, and unsatisfying to the uninformed Jewish masses.

Hasidism brought the uneducated Jew back to a place of honor at a table where he had been unable to sit before. Hasidism stressed the heart over the head, such as vigorous swaying and dancing in order to attain a state of ecstasy during the service. Hasidism emphasized the fervor over the deed itself. Hasidism thought that sincere devotion, zeal, and heartfelt prayers are more acceptable to God than great learning, and that He can best be served through deep-seated joy rather than solemnity and intellectualism.

The Hasidic movement spread rapidly. The Hasidic rebbe, or *zaddik* ("righteous man," was almost an intermediary between God and man. As the Hasidic movement grew, the talmudists began to oppose and even persecute Hasidism. They were called Mitnaggedim ("opponents"). The great talmudist Elijah, known as the Gaon of Vilna, issued a ban against Hasidim. Later the rift diminished. The Hasidic movement today is quite popular. The rebbe sends Hasidic rabbis to all parts of the world, and their work is to spread their philosophy to anybody who is interested. They are now observant and educated.

What is Zionism?

Zionism is both a religious and a political movement. The key to understanding Zionism is in its name. The easternmost of the two hills of ancient Jerusalem during the tenth century B.C.E. was called Zion (2 Samuel 5:7). In fact, the name Zion, referring to Jerusalem, appears 152 times in the Hebrew Bible. The name is overwhelmingly a poetic and prophetic designation. The religious and emotional qualities of the name arise from the importance of Jerusalem as the royal city and the city of the Temple. Mount Zion is the place where God dwells (Isaiah 8:18; Psalm 74:2).

Jerusalem, or Zion, is a place where the Lord is king, and where He has installed His king, David (Psalm 2:6).

King David made Jerusalem the capital of Israel almost 3,000 years ago, and Jerusalem has remained the capital every since. Over the centuries, the term "Zion" grew and expanded to mean the whole of the Land of Israel. The Israelites in exile could not forget Zion. The Hebrew psalmist sat by the waters of Babylon, weeping when he remembered Zion, and swore: "If I forget thee, O Jerusalem, let my right hand forget her cunning" (Psalm 137:5). This oath has been repeated for thousands of years by Jews throughout the world.

Three times a day in worship, Jews have prayed ceaselessly for the rebirth of their homeland, asking God to rebuild Zion. In the marriage ceremony, as well as at the Passover Seder, Jews prayed and hoped for a Jewish state to become a reality. Politically, Zionism is a movement for the reestablishment of an autonomous Jewish community in the Land of Israel. The objective of Zionism was defined by the Basle Program adopted in 1897, at the first Zionist Congress, convened by Theodor Herzl. In his famous pamphlet *Der Judenstaat* ("The Jewish State"), he ardently believed that the Jewish state would bring peace and happiness to the rest of the Jewish people in the Diaspora. By introducing political and social ideals of the modern world to Jews, it prepared the way for Zionism.

The poem *Hatikvah* (literally, "The Hope"), composed by Naphtali H. Imber (1856–1909), became the official song of the Zionist movement and is now, with a slight change in the refrain, the national anthem of the State of Israel. The poem expressed the hope and longing of the Jew to return to Zion.

Zionism is one of the world's oldest movements. It aims at securing for the Jewish people the rights possessed by other nations. It harbors malice toward none. It seeks cooperation and understanding with other peoples and with their national movements. Zionism is the Jewish people's liberation movement, the quest for freedom and equality with other nations. Zionism is the love of Zion.

Zionism is more than a political platform. It is a spiritual credo. A prerequisite is psychological reconditioning in equating personal needs with national goals.

Rabbi Emanuel Rackman wrote: "I am a Jew and a Zionist. For me the two commitments are one. Furthermore, I hold this to be the position of historic Judaism."[5]

What are the 613 commandments?

The 613 commandments were imparted to Moses: 365 of them are prohibitions, answering to the number of the days of the year, and 248 are positive precepts, corresponding to the number of organs or limbs in the human body.

David reduced them to eleven principles (Psalms 15):

Lord, who shall sojourn in Thy tabernacle?
Who shall dwell on Thy holy mountain?
He that walketh uprightly,
Worketh righteousness,
Speaketh truth in his heart,
Hath no slander upon his tongue,
Nor doeth evil to his fellowman,
Nor taketh up a reproach against his neighbor;
In whose eyes an evil [vile] person is despised,
But he honoreth them that fear the Lord.
He that sweareth to his own hurt and breaketh not his word,
He that putteth not out his money on interest,
Nor taketh a bribe against the innocent;
He that doeth these things shall never be moved.

---

[5] *American Zionist*, March 1971.

Isaiah came and reduced them to six principles (Isaiah 33:15–16):

He that walketh righteously,
Speaketh uprightly,
He that despiseth the gain of oppressions,
That shaketh clear his hands from laying hold on bribes,
That stoppeth his ears from hearing of blood,
And shutteth his eyes from looking upon evil.
He shall dwell on high!

Then came Micah, who reduced them to three principles (Micah 6:8):

It hath been told thee, O man, what is good,
And what the Lord doth require of thee:
Only to do justly,
To love mercy,
To walk humbly with thy God.

Then Isaiah came once more and reduced them to two principles (Isaiah 56:1):

Thus saith the Lord: — A call from God.
Keep ye justice,
Do righteousness. — In the observance of the laws.

Then Amos came and reduced them to one principle (Amos 5:4):

Seek ye Me, and live. — A nation to survive must live by just laws.

Habakkuk came and reduced the commandments to one principle (Habakkuk 2:4):

The righteous shall live by his faith. — Without laws man will swallow each other and perish from this world.

The foregoing commandments were not the only attempts in Jewish history to distill and crystallize the essence of Judaism. They are, however, representative and sufficient to establish that basic to Judaism is a twofold affirmation concerning God, on the one hand, and man, on the other; the former being that a man shall seek to know God, love Him, revere Him, and do His will; the latter, that a man shall love his fellow men.

One good deed shall follow another. Zeal for the commandments increases the number of good deeds.

What is the soul?
The soul is the divine spark in man that makes him a responsible, moral being, that bids him to strive for spiritual growth and for intellectual advancement. The soul of man does not die. As God's spirit in man, it is immortal.

All beliefs about the soul are related to the doctrine of the revivification of the dead: "The souls of all generations are said to have been created at the beginning of the world and kept until the time of their birth in a heavenly repository called a body." One of the daily morning prayers, borrowed from the Talmud, *Berakhot* 60b, reads as follows:

Even as the soul is pure entering this world, so let man return it pure to the maker.

My God, the soul which you have given me is pure. You created it. You formed it. You breathed it into me. You keep body and soul together. One day you will take my soul from me, to restore it to me in life eternal. So long as the soul is within me, I offer thanks before you, Master of all creations, Lord of all souls. Praised are you, Lord, who restores the soul to the dead. The doctrine of immortality of the soul is affirmed. The dust returned to the earth as it was, but the spirit returned to God who gave it. (Ecclesiastes 12:7)

Judaism does not view the relationship of the soul and the body as a union of conflict, but rather as a union of cooperativeness. The body cannot function without the soul, nor can the soul fulfill itself without the body. Each plays its role without overstepping the boundaries of the other.

The role of the body is to facilitate the journey and fulfillment of the soul in this life. The role of the soul is to overcome the glaring distractions of this life so that they do not distort its purpose and reality.

According to the mystical teachings in the Zohar, "The destiny of every soul is to return to the source it came from. Those who in their earthly existence failed to develop the purity of perfection necessary for gaining access to their heavenly source above must undergo incarnation in another body and even repeat that experience more than once until they are permitted to return to the celestial region in a purified form."

The process of the soul's faculties is by no means limited to the Jew alone. Jewish tradition teaches that one need not become Jewish to attain even the spiritual level of consciousness required for prophecy (*Tanna de-Vei Eliyahu,* chap. 9).

I call heaven and earth as witnesses, that anyone, Jew or Gentile, man or woman, slave or maidservant, can, depending upon their deeds, attain divine inspiration. Those who are not Jewish can also realize the potential of the faculties of their souls and can, through their deeds, merit the world-to-come (Talmud, *Sanhedrin* 105a; Tosefta; *Sanhedrin* 13; *Pirkei de-Rabbi Eliezer* 34).

Judaism encourages every human being to grow within the structure into which he was born. The Torah is a blueprint for all life (Maharal in *Netivot Olam,* Netiv Ahavat Reya, chap. 1).

What is soul-searching?

Ḥeshbon ha-nefesh, or self-examination, as a deterrent to sin is implied throughout the Bible. One of the functions of prayer is to search the inner recesses of the soul. To pray means to judge oneself. Self-appraisal cultivates humility, and through humility one becomes aware of oneself or the company one keeps.

Soul-searching also cultivates a sense of gratitude. We should thank God every day that we are alive and that He has granted us the power of perception and the intellect to be able to reason, act, and enjoy what we are doing or not doing.

Do Jews believe in the Messiah?

It is interesting that in the entire Bible we do not find the word Messiah, or *Mashiaḥ*, in the sense in which it has come to be understood. In the Bible the word only has its original meaning, signifying "anointed." Thus it is used in connection with the priest, *ha-kohen ha-mashiaḥ*, who was anointed for his office (Leviticus 4:3, 5; 16:6–15). It is frequently used, too, in the constructive state, joined to the name of God: *Mashiaḥ Adonai*, the "anointed of the Lord," especially when it refers to the kings of the Jewish people, who were divinely anointed for their exalted office (1 Samuel 10:6, 24:6, 26:9; 2 Samuel 1:14, 19:22; Lamentations 4:20).

Because of what it meant to the Jew, the messianic idea was fostered by the rabbis and incorporated in the prayer book, thus enabling it to take deep root in the collective and individual Jewish soul, planting within him the hope of the perfectibility of Israel and of all humankind. This hope and dream became for him his sole recompense in a world that was for him a vale of tears!

In the appearance of numerous false Messiahs, Jewish families were uprooted and suffered even more hardship. Norman Cohn, a great philosopher of our times, said, "If the Jewish religion had done nothing more for mankind than proclaim the Messianic idea of the Hebrew Scriptures, it could have claimed to be the bedrock of the entire world's ethical culture. I should say the majority believes that Messiah will come and will establish an invincible and just regime whose law will enlighten the world. The Jews still await the coming of that Messiah."

Who is the Messiah?

Originally, the term Messiah was applied to any person anointed with the holy oil to become king or high priest. This fact cannot be ignored, for it reveals most strikingly the truth that the entire conception of Messiah underwent an interesting development in the life and thought of the Jew.

While every king was the anointed of the Lord, King David won the hearts of all his people as the anointed *par excellence.* His reign represented the consummation of centuries of formative existence. He brought victory over internal and external destructive forces. He was indeed the beloved ruler of his people. The word "anointed" in his case assumed added meaning; he was the savior, the redeemer of his people, who brought glory to his people's name and fame.

When David received the divine promise that the throne would remain in his family forever (2 Samuel 7:13), the title acquired a special reference to be identified with the restoration of Israel under the leadership of the Messiah, the Lord's anointed. The Messiah, who will be a descendant of King David, will be a righteous person endowed with the spirit of the Lord. He will restore the people of Israel, and he will bring about the spiritual regeneration of humanity when all will blend into one unity to perform righteousness with a perfect heart. He will also usher in an era of lasting peace for everyone who acknowledges the oneness of God. The unity of humanity under one God, the father of all, will become a reality during the messianic age, which will happen in God's own time.

"And I will plant them upon their land, and they shall no more be uprooted out of their land which I have given them, saith the Lord the God" (Amos 9:14–15).

To the Jew, the Messiah has not yet appeared. The world's civilization is yet in its infancy; humanity must patiently, hopefully, heroically aspire to reach the heights of that blessed life pictured in the coming of the Messiah, which, the Jew believes, is the time when nations will live in peaceful coexistence.

It would be a mistake, however, to say that this was the only feature of the Jewish Messiah idea. It represents but one side of the picture. There is yet another side on which we behold a second aspect—beautiful and majestic in its grandeur and sweep of vision. The one we might term national, political; the other, universal and religious. The one spoke in terms of Israel's own happiness, the other in terms of all humanity's happiness. One was interrelated with the other. Both had to develop simultaneously, because otherwise it would have been false to the Jewish character, which could think of its own bliss only if bliss was the lot of the whole world.

Israel, according to this twofold picture of the messianic concept, was to be under the sovereignty of a good and wise king, who would bring his people peace, prosperity, happiness, and freedom from all oppression. But he was to achieve more—all the nations of the world were to be influenced by his wisdom and righteousness. They would turn to Zion for light and inspiration; peace would reign supreme; all would be ready to worship the One God as a token of Zion's spiritual sovereignty. There is a classic passage in the Bible, that reveals both of these elements in their clearest light:

Describing the glories of the Messianic age.
And it shall come to pass in the end of days, that the mountain of the Lord's house shall be established as the top of the mountains, and it shall be exalted above the hills; and all peoples shall flow unto it. And many nations shall go and say: "Come ye, and let us go up to the mountain of the Lord and to the house of the God of Jacob; and He will teach us of His ways, and we will walk in His paths. For out of Zion shall go

forth the law, and the word of the Lord from Jerusalem. And He shall judge between many peoples, and shall decide concerning mighty nations afar off; and they shall beat their swords into plowshares, and their spears into pruning hooks; nation shall not lift up sword against nation, neither shall they learn war any more. (Isaiah 2:2–4; Micah 4:1–7)

The prophets preached this exalted vision, which took root in the consciousness of the people. The messianic idea assumed vast dimensions, and the word grew in meaning until it comprised the highest hopes of the nation.

In the dark moment in Jewish history when Rome destroyed the Holy Temple, the Messiah idea took on a new momentum. The Jew found the need for the messianic hope more than ever before. The rabbis said: "On the day on which the Temple was destroyed, the Messiah was born."[6] In that day of utter darkness, when, all hope seemed to be lost, the idea of the Messiah was born in the heart of the Jew to give him new strength and courage to carry on the "battle of the Lord." Indeed, the gloomier the background of reality became, the brighter became the colors with which the future stood out against it. But as the days darkened and the Jews' misery increased, they began to realize more and more that the hope for that day would be long distanced, and that not in their day would the Messiah appear. The people as a whole, however, did not give up hope. "Even though he tarries, yet will I wait daily for His coming," was the determined feeling of every Jew.

Some of the rabbis tried to dampen some of the exaggerated hope to make the people rely more upon themselves and their own will to live, rather than upon a miraculous savior. However, most of the rabbis taught just the contrary, and their words sustained the faith in the redeemer's early appearance. The darker the scene, the brighter became the hope in the miraculous work of the Messiah.

---

[6] Midrash Lamentations Rabbah 1:57 (Warsaw ed., 1867).

"Wait for Him," said Rabbi Johanan. "When you see the generations of Israel growing smaller, and many troubles coming upon them, then he will appear" (*Sanhedrin* 98a).

The prophet Malachi was the first to develop the thought that Elijah would appear first to announce the approach of the great Day of the Lord (Malachi 3:23). So strongly had the Messiah-hope embedded itself in the consciousness of the people that many of them were soon tempted to try all sorts of reckoning and tricks to discover the time of his coming. One sage went so far as to say, "May the curse of heaven fall upon those who calculate the date of the advent of the Messiah, and thus create political and social unrest among the people" (*Sanhedrin* 97b).

The same tendency resulted, too, in the appearance of numerous false Messiahs: Jewish families were uprooted and suffered even more hardship. The most notorious false Messiah was Shabbetai Ẓevi (1626–1676), who in 1648 proclaimed himself as the Messiah and won wide acceptance. He was arrested by the Turkish government and given the alternative of Islam or death. He chose Islam.

Most Jews believe that Messiah will come and establish an invincible and just regime whose law will enlighten the world. The Messiah is not the bearer of individual salvation and the kingdom of heaven, but the harbinger of a new day—a blessed and glorious life to be enjoyed by all the peoples of the world here on earth. This is in keeping with the whole religious ideology of the Jew. To the Jew, as was well said, "Religion was not individualistic in the sense of making the salvation of the soul its sole aim and purpose. Its main object must be the salvation of humanity, the welfare and happiness of the entire social life of men."[7]

What is the Jewish view of afterlife and resurrection?
When I was eleven years old in 1941, I witnessed a Nazi take a Jewish child from the bosom of its mother and thrust a bayonet into

---

[7] Kaufmann Kohler, *Heaven and Hell*, p. 156.

and through the child's heart. Ever since that incident, I have thought to myself about what happens to the soul. Nobody has ever come back from there to tell!

As I grow older, having lost my mother, sister, and brothers in the Holocaust, and having witnessed horrible deaths, I have thought more and more about an afterlife. Studying the Five Books of Moses, I did not find any sources dealing with a belief in a heavenly afterlife in which blessed and vindicated souls abide. However, the doctrine of resurrection is often considered to be connected with the doctrine of Israel's messianic redemption. It is supported by the following prophetic passages:

> I will open your graves and bring you out of your graves (Ezekiel 37:12). Israel's redemption is illustrated in the most graphic manner by a vision of rebirth of Israel.

> Your dead shall live. Their corpses shall rise; awake and sing, you who lie in the dust (Isaiah 26:19). The resurrection of the dead will lead to a new spiritual life.

These verses have been interpreted as Ezekiel and Isaiah predicting that the dead will come to life again. In a striking and beautiful vision, Ezekiel is transported into a valley full of dry bones. As he prophesies to them, they come together into complete skeletons that become covered with flesh and skin. Then the wind blows upon the inanimate bodies and they come to life. The prophecy refers to a revival of the dead nation of which the exiles seemed to be scattered remains.

In biblical times, the concept of afterlife had apparently not taken hold. However, in the later writings and the talmudic period, the writers developed various beliefs about afterlife. In the Middle Ages and the Renaissance, especially after the publication of the Zohar, the book of mysticism, new ideas of afterlife made their appearance.

During the Second Commonwealth, the belief in the resurrection of the body became a fundamental doctrine of the Pharisees; they held that the soul and the body would be reunited in the future world (when the Messiah came), reconstructing the original person who would stand in judgment before God and receive reward or punishment according to his behavior, good or bad, during his or her life.

According to talmudic-midrashic statements, the righteous buried in other lands will roll through to the Land of Israel, where God will breathe into them a spirit of life and they will arise (*Ketubbot* 11a).

It was argued that if a grain of wheat, buried naked, sprouts forth in many robes, how much more so the righteous! (*Sanhedrin* 90b)

According to Mishnah, *Sanhedrin* 10:1, he who says that there is no resurrection of the dead must be counted among those who have no share in the future world.

The whole concept of resurrection is interwoven with the idea of heaven and hell. The teaching of heaven and hell has been fashioned into a firm doctrine by Christians, whereas in Judaism, the teachings on this theme were regarded simply as free expressions of individuals, allowing for wide diversity of opinion and interpretation.[8]

The most dramatic case of contact with the dead concerns the distraught King Saul, who faced an impending battle with the Philistines and lacked confidence. The king himself had banned access to mediums who could summon the dead. He broke his own prohibition by going disguised to ask a woman necromancer at En-Dor to call Samuel back from death (1 Samuel 28:7)

The poetical adaptation of the Thirteen Principles of Faith, namely the *Yigdal* by Maimonides (1135–1204), states categorically: "There will be a resurrection of the dead."

---

[8] Israel Abrahams, *Judaism*, p. 90.

The idea of resurrection is expressed in the *Amidah* prayer recited thrice daily: "Thou revivest the dead . . . Thou causest the wind to blow and the rain to fall." Rain is considered as great a manifestation of the divine power as the resurrection of the dead (*Ta'anit* 2a).

In the preliminary morning service, the following passage is to be found: "My God, may the soul which Thou hast placed within me be pure. Thou hast created it; Thou hast formed it; Thou hast breathed it into me; Thou preservest it within me; Thou will take it from me and restore it to me in the hereafter. Blessed art Thou, O Lord, who restorest the souls to the dead" (*Berakhot* 60b).

This prayer is interpreted as an expression of gratitude for awakening from sleep to new life.

Traditional Jews do believe in resurrection.

After serving in the rabbinate for forty-five years, and after officiating at hundreds and hundreds of funerals, my interest increased in the concept of the world-to-come. Encounters with death have led me into the depths of spiritual despair and personal agony. Suffering the grief that I went through, and observing and learning from others, I know that the death of a loved one can be very cruel, painful, and agonizing. *And yet in my own life, suffering through the Holocaust, death has been a catalyst for genuine spiritual growth, faith, and belief in the Almighty.*

Throughout history, human beings have tried to unravel the mystery of life beyond the grave. The body returns to the earth, but the spirit returns unto God who gave it. The resurrection of the dead is one of the principles of Judaism, to be accepted by us just as we accept the belief in the Messiah and the hereafter.

Studying various sources, I would conclude that Judaism does uphold a belief in life after death, and in resurrection following the coming of the Messiah.

In the life of a Jew, there is a conviction that physical death is not the last act in the drama of life. By the period of the Maccabees, the concept of resurrection of the dead had become a firm doctrine.

Later there arose two other concepts that were held by most Jews until modern times: Paradise, or Gan Eden (literally, the Garden of Eden), where the righteous will be rewarded, and Gehinnom (Gehenna), or hell (a term derived from the Hebrew name of the Valley of Hinnom, near Jerusalem), where the wicked will be punished. This place became detestable because Canaanite children were sacrificed there to Moloch. Paradise and hell are not exclusively for the Jew. A righteous Christian also deserves Paradise, and an evil one deserves hell.

From the twelfth century B.C.E., onward, new concepts of life after death began to emerge among the Israelites, developing slowly and in successive stages forming the historical basis for the afterlife.

Every man who ennobles his soul with excellent morals and wisdom, based on faith in God, certainly belongs to the men of the world-to-come (letter of Maimonides to Ḥasdai Halevi).

I believe with perfect faith that there will be a time of resurrection when it shall please the creator, praised be He, and exalted be His fame for ever and ever (Thirteen Principles of Faith, from the commentary of Maimonides to Mishnah, *Sanhedrin* 10:1).

And there shall be a time of trouble, such as never was since there was a nation *even* to that same time; and at that time Thy people shall be delivered, every one that shall be found written in the book. And many of them that sleep in the dust of the earth shall awake, some to everlasting life, and some to shame *and* everlasting contempt (Daniel 12:1–2).

The reason why man was created and distinguished above all other creatures is that he might serve God, and the reward for his service is life eternal in the world of recompense. Finally, there is the belief of the masses of the Jewish nation that the resurrection of the dead would take place at the time of the redemption (Saadiah Gaon, *Sefer ha-Emunot ve-Deot* 7:1).

Do Jews have baptism?

There is no formal baptism as there is in Christianity. The Torah (Leviticus 12–15) prescribed immersion in water for a variety of purifications. In the first pre-Christian century, the Essenes, the sect to which John the Baptist and Jesus probably belonged, bathed regularly in the Jordan, especially before morning prayers. The Jewish mystics of the Middle Ages bathed frequently, especially on the eve of the Sabbath and holidays. Judaism requires immersion for women a week after their menstrual cycle, during which time the couple abstains from marital relations. Immersion is required for men and women who convert to Judaism.

Who is Satan?

In Jewish tradition Satan is the name of the archangel whose functions are to tempt man to sin, test their loyalty, and inflict punishment upon the sinner. Satan is an adversary who opposes and obstructs. The term is applied to human adversaries in 1 Samuel 29:4, "Lest in the battle he became an adversary to us." This is also found in 2 Samuel 19:23, "And David said: 'What have I to do with you, ye sons of Zeruah, that you should this day be adversaries unto me?' " In the Book of Job, the character of Satan was very real. He was an adversary who begrudged man's contentment and well-being, and he was the indirect cause of Job's misery.

The angel who was sent to distract Balaam (Numbers 22:32) was evidently chosen as Satan, namely to "oppose and obstruct." Satan tries to arouse God's punitive power by his accusations. The sages expressly said that Satan is the evil urge. He is the angel of death (*Bava Batra* 16a).

Satan's name in Jewish literature alludes to the principle of death. There is a well-known phrase during the High Holy day prayers: "Open not your mouth to Satan." The preliminary prayer before the morning service states: "Spare me from the corrupting Satan."

I should mention that in the prayer book, Satan is mostly identified with the evil impulse. The man's spirit, or evil impulse, seduces us to do wrong.

What is hell?

Jewish thought includes various viewpoints about hell—viewpoints that range from the most simple to the most sophisticated. Despite the extreme differences in opinion about the meaning of hell, it is nowhere considered a dogma or a doctrine of faith that Jews are required to profess. Even those sages who delighted in describing the torments of hell were usually aware that they were permitting their imaginations to roam freely.

Judaism does not presume to know in any detail what is in store for man beyond the grave. Rabbi Simon Greenberg noted that "Jewish literature furnishes a wealth of widely varying interpretations on the nature of life and death. But one thing on which rabbinic literature is unanimous and unequivocal is that the grave is not the end."

The Hebrew term for hell, Gehenna, dates from the biblical period and refers to a valley south of Jerusalem called Gebon Hinnom. Gehenna was seen primarily as a place of punishment, a purgatory. "And they have built the high places of Topheth, which is in the Valley of the son of Hinnon, to burn their sons and their daughters in the fire; which I commanded not, neither came it to my mind" (Jeremiah 7:31). The valley was the site of a heathen cult whose rituals included the burning of children. "And he defiled Topheth, which is the valley of the Son of Hinnon, that no man might make his son or his daughter to pass through the fire of Moloch" (2 Kings 23:10).

In Judaism, the name Gehenna is generally used metaphorically as an appellation for the place of torment reserved for the wicked after death. In 2 Kings 16:1, 16–17, it states that when King Ahaz fell under the influence of neighboring peoples to the extent of following their religion, the people offered their sons and daughters as sacrifices to the god Moloch in Gehinnom. The place Gehinnom was associated with burning, shame, and wickedness. Jeremiah 2:23 castigates the people of Israel because they were performing human sacrifice in the Valley of Hinnom.

A widely held view was that the wicked would be punished in Gehenna for 12 months only. After having atoned for their sins, they would join the righteous in Gan Eden. The severity of Gehenna was mitigated in rabbinic thought. It was widely believed that all Israel, except for a few arch sinners, would have a share in the world-to-come and so could not be unconditionally doomed to hell (*Sanhedrin* 10).

Wrongdoers who sin go to Gehinnon and are punished there (*Rosh ha-Shanah* 17a).

What is most significant, however, is that regardless of the manner in which the masses or the scholars interpreted the concept of hell, all agreed that God's world is basically just, providing reward for goodness and punishment for wickedness.

God's love and grace reach beyond the grave. The Jewish belief in life after death strengthened, fortified, and enabled them to undergo martyrdom and served as a powerful motive for the avoidance of sin.

What is Paradise?

Paradise (Gan Eden) is the garden planted by God for Adam and Eve (Genesis 2–3) The location is unknown. According to the rabbis, God will reveal it to Israel during the messianic period. It is viewed as a place of bliss and blessing.

The terms Paradise and Gan Eden have been used synonymously to designate the abode of sanctified souls after death. Because the Garden of Eden was the abode of man in his state of innocence, it became the dwelling place of the upright in the hereafter.

Eden signifies delight and pleasantness and, because of its connection in tradition as the eternal home of bliss, is reserved for the souls of the righteous.

Abravanel, in his commentary on 1 Samuel 25:29 writes: "The reward of the souls in the world beyond is their ability to attain the true concept of God which is a source of the most wonderful feeling, an attainment impossible for man in this earthly life."

The Talmud describes Gan Eden (Paradise) as follows: "In the world-to-come there is no eating, no drinking, no begetting of children, no commerce, no envy, no hatred, no competition; there is only this—that the righteous sit with crowns on their heads and take delight of God's splendor" (*Berakhot* 17a).

Contemporary Jews are not as preoccupied with thoughts of heaven or hell as their ancestors were. Their thoughts are more centered on achieving the blessings that God offers in this world. However, there are many who believe in Paradise.

What is the Jewish attitude toward sin?

The most common terms for sin in Judaism are *het* and *averah*. The first is usually translated as "sin" and the second as "transgression." Literally, however, *het* is a term from archery for missing the mark, and *averah* means crossing over the line. In both cases, it seems to me, the implication is that one should overcome these shortcomings and improve oneself. Any man who departs from the right path commits a sin. There are three different terms for sin. Any transgression, biblical or rabbinical, is a sin. These terms are found in the Bible:

> The sin called *het* is a straying from the right path. Missing the mark. (Exodus 34:7)
> The sin called *avon* is a sin committed knowingly. Sometimes distorted and twisted.

The sin called *pesha* is a rebellious act committed in defiance of
   God and man.
The greatest of all sins is desecrating the name of God.

Judaism teaches that everyone is born without sin, and no one is
under the bondage of sin. No Jew feels the need to be "saved" from
sin in order for life to be intact. Every sin brings with it punishment.

Judaism also distinguishes between intentional sins and uninten-
tional ones. In both cases, it is possible to seek forgiveness and to
achieve atonement. Our annual High Holy Day season focuses on
the possibility of atonement. "God does not desire the death of the
sinner," our prayer book states, "but his return from his way that he
may live." Repentance (*teshuvah*) is always available to the sinner.
One need not wait for the High Holy Days to change one's ways.
Our emphasis is on God's mercy and forgiveness. He is seen as
waiting for us to return to Him. The Bible teaches us that there is
no man on earth who does not sin, so we have no expectation of
perfection. One does the best one is capable of doing, but should be
reassured that we have a forgiving God who is merciful with His
human children.

What is the Jewish attitude toward bad thoughts?

Judaism clearly distinguishes between thoughts and deeds. One
cannot be punished for one's thoughts, only for acting upon them.

Are there certain prayers to cancel bad thoughts or bad dreams?
Admittedly, there is a ritual for reversing a bad dream (it appears in
very traditional prayer books), but I do not know of prayers to cancel out bad thoughts. The closest we come to that are bedtime
prayers which ask, "Let my sleep be undisturbed by troubling
thoughts, bad dreams, and wicked schemes." In the Yom Kippur
liturgy, one also finds prayers asking for forgiveness for any sins
committed before God "by sinful thoughts."

Miracles

A miracle is a marvelous happening that is an exception to the laws of nature or extraordinary phenomena, distinguished from normal and usual events. In the Bible, such extraordinary occurrences are called wonders and signs performed by God in times of great crisis. For example:

The splitting of the Red Sea. (Exodus 14:21)
By Joshua's command, the sun and the moon halt in their path. (Joshua 10:13)
The lions do not hurt Daniel. (Daniel 6:21)
The fish spit out Jonah. (Jonah 3:3.4)
The mouth of the earth opened up to swallow Korah and his followers. (Numbers 16:32, 26:10)
The mouth of the well that provided water for Israelites in the desert. (Exodus 15:25)
The mouth of Balaam's remarkable talking ass. (Numbers 22:28)
The rainbow. (Genesis 9:16)
The manna. (Exodus 16:15)
Moses' rod. (Exodus 7:19)
Ḥanukkah and the oil. (Shabbat 21B)
Purim: Esther saves the Jews. (Book of Esther 7:3)

What is religion from the Jewish point of view?

The Jewish religion is a divine system of beliefs and practices that serve to guide the individual in his relationship with his fellow man, his God, his natural environment, and himself.

Religion is faith in God. Religion is a constant challenge to man's intellect. Religion can bring great comfort when sorrow overwhelms us. The real purpose and goal of religion is to express a relationship between man and God.

The function of religion is to relate man to God and to bring man to a state of God-consciousness each day of his life. Since man is neither only soul nor only body but both joined together, these two constituent elements within man should be related to God. Through good deeds (*mitzvot*), the body unifies the soul in a relationship with the will of God. The observances and laws of Judaism serve to enable the Jew to fulfill the words of the psalmist: "I have set the Lord before me at all times" (Psalm 16:8). God's laws enable one to live in God's presence.

Religion is concerned with the relationships—

Between man and God:
 acceptance of the sovereignty of God—Man is a partner with God.
 adherence to religious law (Zechariah 14:9)
 prayer, study of Torah (Deuteronomy 10:12)
Between man and self:
 self-respect and self-actualization (Genesis 1:27– 28)
Between man and man:
 ethical living and communal involvement (Deuteronomy 6:18)
Between man and nature:
 life of sanctity and holiness (Leviticus 19:2). The capacity for holiness is not restricted to gifted people only, anyone can attain holiness.

The essence of religion is not fear but courage. The first monotheist on earth was Abraham, who was cautioned about fear. "Fear not," said God to Abraham, "for I am a shield unto thee" (Genesis 15:1).

Religion is based on laws by which human conduct may be regulated. Jews regard Judaism as the only true religion for Jews. We respect every other religion, especially when the worshiper is devout, honest, and just. Every great religion must have basic ethical and moral concepts, such as justice, integrity, decency, and kindness toward humanity. We are all creatures of God.

The Talmud tells us that "the righteous of all nations are worthy of immortality."

Are the Jewish people a race?

Judaism is a religion. It is not a race but rather a religious group made up of many diverse people. The word "race" has been contaminated by political extremists and has many different meanings. It would be fair to regard Jews as not only belonging to a religion but also to exist as a nation. Anyone who adopted Judaism became a full member of the Jewish people regardless of origin. King David was a descendant of a Moabite convert named Ruth, born a Moabite (a pagan), who chose to become a Jew and is so highly regarded that Jewish tradition has awarded her the distinction that the future Messiah will come from her family. The incorporation of the Book of Ruth in the Bible demonstrates how unethnic Judaism and chosenness are. According to the Talmud, great teachers of Judaism were descended from converts. Among them was Onkelos, whose commentary on the Bible is outstanding.

Who are the Jews?

The Jews as a people are unified by a common destiny, and, in spite of variations in practices, rituals, and concepts, a common belief in one God as the source of their being and the motivating factor in their lives.

After the death of King Solomon in the tenth century B.C.E., the Hebrew nation split into two parts: the Northern Kingdom (Samaria) and the Southern Kingdom (Judah). The Northern Kingdom disappeared completely, and is now remembered as the Ten Lost Tribes.

The Southern Kingdom never lost its identity. It consisted of the tribe of Judah, the tribe of Benjamin, and part of Levi. Soon the tribe of Judah absorbed the latter and became the only surviving tribe.

The English contraction of "Judah" became "Jew." The period when these biblical events occurred antedated the time when "Judean," "Hebrew," and "Israelite" became equivalent terms.

The word "Jew" is derived from the name of Leah's fourth son, Yehudah (Judah). This word contains the four-letter name of God, which means, "He shall exalt." To exalt God is to reveal His very aspect or existence, spiritually, morally, and intellectually.

One of the world's great writers, the Russian novelist and Christian philosopher Leo Tolstoy, gave this answer to the age-old question, "What is a Jew?"[9]

> This question is not at all as odd as it seems. Let us see what kind of peculiar creature the Jew is, which all the rulers and all nations have together and separately abused and molested, oppressed and persecuted, trampled and butchered, burned and hanged—and in spite of all this is yet alive? What is a Jew, who has never allowed himself to be led astray by all the earthly possessions which his oppressors and persecutors constantly offered him in order that he should change his faith and forsake his own Jewish religion?
>
> The Jew is the emblem of eternity. He whom neither slaughter nor torture of thousands of years could destroy; he whom neither fire nor sword, nor inquisition was able to wipe off from the face of the earth; he who was the first to produce the oracle of God; he who has been for so long the guardian of prophecy and who transmitted it to the rest of the world— a nation of such people cannot be destroyed. The Jew is everlasting, as is eternity itself.

Mark Twain, the distinguished American writer, said:

> If the statistics are right, the Jews constitute but one percent of the human race. It suggests a nebulous dim puff of stardust

---

[9] Tolstoy, *What is a Jew?* American Hebrew, April 22, 1921, p. 658–659.

lost in the blaze of the Milky Way. Properly the Jew ought hardly to be heard of; but he is heard of, has always been heard of. He is as prominent on the planet as any other people, and his commercial importance is extravagantly out of proportion to the smallness of his bulk. His contributions to the world's list of great names in literature, science, art, music, finance, medicine, and abstruse learning are also way out of proportion to the scarcity of his numbers. He has made a marvelous fight in this world, in all the ages; and has done it with his hands tied behind him. He could be vain of himself and be excused for it.

The Egyptian, the Babylonian, and the Persian rose, filled the planet with sound and splendor, then faded to dream-stuff and passed away; the Greek and the Roman followed, and made a vast noise, and they are gone; other peoples have sprung up and held their torch high for a time, but it burned out, and they sit in twilight now or have vanished. The Jew saw them all, beat them all, and is now what he always was, exhibiting no decadence, no infirmities of age, no weakening of his parts, no slowing of his energies, no dulling of his alert and aggressive mind.

All things are mortal but the Jew; all other forces pass, but he remains. What is the secret of his immortality?[10]

The Hebrew language

It is a miraculous surprise that the Hebrew language was able to survive throughout the centuries. Because the Jews had to live in exile, in countries where other languages were spoken for everyday purposes the Hebrew language became a language of prayer and study only. It was known as *Lashon ha-Kodesh*, the holy language, or the holy tongue. Many Hebrew words, idioms, and expressions

---

[10] Twain, "Concerning the Jews," *Harper's Magazine*, 1899, reprinted in *The Complete Essays of Mark Twain* (Garden City, N.Y.: Doubleday, 1963), p. 249.

were preserved in the Jewish vernacular in Yiddish. Because of Torah, they survived.

What is a mitzvah?

Mitzvah is the Hebrew word for "commandment" and refers to a commandment of God. It is a deed unifying body and soul in relating life in its entirety to God.

The observances and laws of Judaism enable the Jew to fulfill the words of the psalmist: "I have set the Lord before me at all times" (Psalm 16:8). God's laws enable us to lie in God's presence in each of the relationships given to man:

Every sphere of life is governed by *mitzvot* (good deeds). (Deut. 16:11; Exodus 15:2)

man and self: self-respect, self-actualization

man and man: ethical living

man and nature: a life of *kedushah*, dignified living; ecology

man and God: acceptance of the sovereignty of God, adherence to His laws, prayer, study of Torah (Deut. 6:5–7)

By observance of the *mitzvot*, God becomes an ever-present reality. The Torah teaches that God makes demands on us spiritually, ethically, and ritually. Every aspect of our lives, even eating, is bound up with God. We can make God present in our lives by doing good deeds. One good deed follows another good deed (*mizvah goreret mizvah*).

What is monotheism?

"Mono" means one; "theism" is the study of a belief in a divine creation, or the belief in one God. The concept of one God originated in Judaism with Abraham. Judaism sees God as the one unifying creator of the universe. The belief in God's oneness in Judaism is simply expressed in the six-word prayer, "Hear, O Israel, the Lord our God, the Lord is one" (Deuteronomy 6:4).

In the Bible, Deuteronomy 4:35 states: "He is God. There is none else beside Him." The second commandment prohibits worshipping other gods.

Deuteronomy 4:39 says: "That the Lord, He is God in heaven above and upon the earth beneath. There is none else."

Deuteronomy 4:4, a verse chanted by the congregation just before the reading of the Torah, says: "But you that did cleave unto the Lord your God are alive today." "Cleaving" describes the closeness of husband and wife in Genesis 2:24. It is not enough to believe in God intellectually. We must cleave to God as one cleaves to a spouse, to a lover, in response to our soul's deepest needs. Only then will our relationship to God be a source of life.

Deuteronomy 7:9 says: "Know therefore that the Lord thy God, He is God, the faithful God, etc." This phrase does not only mean to know God, but to feel the force of God by reverence or by sense of duty.

Deuteronomy 10:17 says: "For the Lord your God is God supreme and Lord supreme, the great, the mighty, and that awesome God who shows no favor and takes no bribe."

Literally, God is the most powerful ruler.

Why anti-Semitism?

When I was a little boy, every Sabbath my mother, of blessed memory, and I walked to visit my grandfather. He lived on the other side of a little town called Bielica in Poland. We walked in the street, which had manure from the horses on it. I asked my mother why I could not walk on the sidewalk and she said that it was because I was a Jew, and a Jew was not permitted to walk on the sidewalk. I asked why. She said, "You will soon learn."

This question bothered me, so I asked my teacher who taught me Bible. He said that Exodus 1:15–22 was the beginning source of anti-Semitism. Pharaoh proposes infanticide, a cruel form of hostility toward the first-born male. Another source of anti-Semitism is found in the Book of Esther. Here Haman wants to destroy all the

Jewish people. Psalms 83:5 states: "They have said, 'Come, and let us cut them off from being a nation; that the name of Israel may be no more in remembrance.' "

My revered teacher said that this was ancient history, and that you must learn medieval and modern history about why the world hates the Jew. It did not take long. When I was eleven and a half years old, I began to experience what Nazism was all about and its relationship to the Holocaust.

During the Holocaust, I saw children pierced with bayonets and thrown like balls from one corner to another. I experienced the unanswered cry of mothers who were holding their babies to their bosoms, only to see them torn apart with laughter and slaughtered in front of their eyes. These were not the only horrors I witnessed.

Jews have been perceived in a way that is incomprehensible. Japan, for instance, has few Jews living there, and yet the venom of anti-Semitic writings, including Hitler's book *Mein Kampf*, was translated into Japanese, along with other writings of an anti-Semitic nature. Even Shakespeare, who never saw a Jew in his life, because the Jews had been expelled from England 300 years before him, reflects anti-Semitism in *The Merchant of Venice*. Other learned people suggested some of the issues that may have exacerbated anti-Semitism: economics, professional success, Jewish affluence, religious bigotry.

The real question is:

What causes anti-Semitism and why?
The "chosen people" has been a major cause of anti-Semitism. Jewish chosenness confers neither privilege nor superiority, only obligation. Attacks on Jewish chosenness continue to the present day. "It is not surprising that Hitler retaliated against the chosen race by decreeing that it was not the Jewish but the Aryan race that was chosen."[11]

---

[11] *Religion in Life*, Summer 1971, p. 279.

The pariah status assigned to Jews and Judaism in the first few centuries of the Christian era discouraged curiosity, interest, and other efforts to know Jews. This helped to create a climate of cultural and religious ignorance on the topic of Jews and Judaism, giving way to hatred and distorted feelings and knowledge that led to pogroms and persecution. The Dark Ages added new techniques to anti-Semitic practices to shun the Jews in every possible way.

The Inquisition in Spain in the fifteenth century had its roots in the Crusades, and the struggle for political and economic supremacy between Christianity and Islam was accompanied by the slaughter of Jewish communities. Many Jews were forcibly converted in order to escape persecution or extermination but continued covertly true to Judaism.

The Jew is looked upon as a stranger toward whom there exists among people an instinctive hatred. The Jew is often the scapegoat for the evils befalling a country.

The consequences of anti-Semitism range from restrictive laws against Jews, denial of civil liberties, social and physical isolation of Jewish groups, to pogroms and the vicious physical destruction of entire Jewish communities.

The Protocols of the Elders of Zion, perhaps the most widely distributed forgery in history and the best-known modern work of anti-Semitism, was based on this portrayal of chosenness. The story of this document, which claims to outline the program of a Jewish world conspiracy, is recounted in an important work of scholarship, *Warrant for Genocide: The Jewish World Conspiracy and the Protocols of the Elders of Zion* by Norman Cohn. Though the *Protocols* was definitively proven a forgery by the *London Times* in 1921, it continued to be utilized by anti-Semites and believed by millions of people. In the United States, Henry Ford had tens of millions of copies printed under the title *The International Jew* and distributed through his newspaper, the *Dearborn Independent*. While Ford eventually apologized to the Jewish community, his anti-Semitic publications were used by Adolf Hitler throughout the Nazi era. In the 1960s, the *Protocols* were republished by President Gamal Abdel Nasser of Egypt. It was distributed by King Faisal of Saudi Arabia in the 1970s.

The hostility toward Judaism has continued through the generations.

Are names important?

Names signify certain aspects of an individual or a nation's destiny. When God changed Abram's name to Abraham, and Sarai's to Sarah, the change proclaimed a new world outlook in their lives. And so the names "Jew" and "Israelite" by which we are known were not given to us or assumed by us indiscriminately. They represent certain philosophies of our lives, as individuals and as a people.

We have another name, "Yisrael," because that was the name given by the angel of God to Jacob. You recall the story, as told in the Bible, of how Jacob wrestled with the angel and could not be defeated, and how the angel said to him, "Thy name shall be called no more Jacob, but Israel, for you have striven with God and with man and you have prevailed" (Genesis 32:29).

The word Yisrael (Israel) is formed by the union of two words, *yisra*, "he will strive" or "he will fight," and *El*, meaning "God." Note that the verb in its retained form is in the future. Therefore it does not refer to Jacob's struggle alone, but to the struggle, the battle that is to be waged by his descendants. Now we understand why the name "Israel" was given unto us; our whole attitude in life must change.

Why Hebrew names?

Names are very important to Jews. Names are the roots of our families, and each name has a meaning and a history. Jewish tradition holds that God inscribes in each person's record his name and destiny. It is believed that adding a name can change the luck of a person, giving him a new personality or new life. If a person is critically ill and it is felt that there is no hope for him, we sometimes add an extra name. For males, we add the name Ḥayim ("life") Alter ("becoming old"); for females, we add the name Ḥayah Alteh. It will be difficult for the angel of death to find someone and carry out his deadly task if the person's name has been changed. Naming includes a special prayer for the health and welfare of the mother and the newborn child.

Until the Napoleonic era in the early nineteenth century, Jews had no surname. A Jewish male was given his name at the time of the *Berit Milah* (circumcision), and a Jewish girl was named in the synagogue during the Torah reading. The Ashkenazim (Eastern Europeans) named their children either after a deceased relative in the family or after a pious or righteous person, while the custom among the Sephardim (Jews of Spanish background) was to name their children after an esteemed living member of the family.

The idea of utilizing a family name spread over Europe and Asia. Jews adopted different names for various reasons. They called themselves after the group to which they belonged, after the profession they practiced, or after the town or province from which they came. A *kohen* could be called Katz, Kaplan, Cohen, or Cohn; a *levi* could be called Levitt, Levitsky, Levy, Siegel, or Sigal; the name Bielick came from the town of Bielia, Lidski from the town of Lida, Wilner from the city of Wilno.

Names from nature were also chosen and became common: Greenberg—a green mountain; Perlstein—a precious stone; Goldberg—a gold mountain.

Since the establishment of the State of Israel, there has been a trend among Jews to name their children with modern Hebrew names, such as Galit, Lebe, Deor, and Ame. Some Jews still give their children biblical names like Abraham and Benjamin, while others use only the first letter of a biblical name, such as Bruce for Benjamin, Alexander for Abraham. Although 2,800 names may be found in the pages of the Bible, fewer than 10 percent of them are used today.

Names given and selected by parents usually fall into at least one of the following categories:

In memory of a famous person in the Bible or in honor of a religious person in our history

In memory of grandparents, relatives, or close friends

In memory of a hero or heroine in the arts, science, or sports

In honor of beauty, such as a jewel, flower, or animal

In honor or memory of a famous person

My beloved teacher once said: "No father should give his son the name of a wicked man." I should like to repeat, as originally stated in Ecclesiastes 7:1, that a good name is better than precious oil.

"Happy is he that grew up with a good name and departs this world with one" (Talmud, *Berakhot* 17a).

What is holiness?

Holiness (*kedushah*) deals with purity of life, purity of action, and purity of thought. The sanctification of life means infusing all of life, including the necessary physical acts and the sensual joys, with much respect for life and for human values so that it ensures the presence of God.

"Neither shalt thou stand against the blood of your neighbor; I am the Lord" (Leviticus 19:16). Do not stand idly by, without hastening to his rescue.

Saving a life is valued more highly than many good deeds and even more than a pious man's prayer. The sages taught us, "Anyone who destroys a life is regarded as if he had destroyed the entire world, and anyone who saves a life is regarded as if he had brought life to the entire world" (*Sanhedrin* 37a).

The human soul is man's direct link to God. There is no greater sin, therefore, than to destroy this heavenly gift.

How can we become holy of thought? By imitating God, we can strive to be merciful, loving, and patient; by clothing the naked, healing the sick, feeding the hungry, freeing captives, burying the dead, even helping those whom we dislike and by seeking God through prayer.

"Ye shall be holy" (Leviticus 19:2) includes reverence for parents, consideration for the needy, prompt payment of wages to employees, honorable dealing, bearing no malice, loving one's neighbor, being cordial to the stranger, and seeing that justice is done to all alike. It means abhorring everything evil, loathsome, or harmful. In a word, said the prophets, it includes doing justly, loving mercy, and walking humbly with one's God.

To be in a state of holiness implies an awareness of the mysterious and the godly. We must constantly aim for moral perfection in our thinking and in our actions, for this is the purpose and value of our whole life.

A well-known statement by Hillel, a famous sage who lived in the first century, is, "Whatever is hateful to you, do not do unto your fellow man."

The Torah emphasizes, "Be holy, for I the Lord am holy." It is applied not only to matters of human relations but also to the whole panorama of life.

Dr. Pinchas Churgin, my esteemed teacher, taught me that if you are to amount to something in the world, you must strive not merely for material things in life, but also for the spiritual values that are included in the world—holiness.

What is loving-kindness?

Leviticus 19:18 states: "You shall love your fellow man as yourself." This is the teaching of the Bible that every man, no matter what his color, race, or creed may be, is made in the image of God. Loving one's fellow man means Jew and non-Jew alike. Acts of loving-kindness apply to the living and the dead. They are carried out as a personal act of doing good not only to humans, but to the animal world as well.

What is a rabbi?

The title rabbi, or *rav*, came into use during the first century C.E. A rabbi is a teacher without any vested ecclesiastical authority, yet is respected for his knowledge, piety, and scholarship. The title is given when the rabbi is ordained. The ordination ceremony is called *semikhah*. The rabbi, whose function was to teach the members of the community, invariably had his private occupation. He was not salaried until approximately the eighteenth century, when congregations began to expect their salaried rabbis to be more than devotees of talmudic studies. The necessity of preaching and counseling brought about seminaries, which sprang up in rapid succession to ordain rabbis to teach Judaism.

In modern times the duties of the rabbi have been diversified in various fields: counseling, teaching, preaching, visiting the sick, burying the dead, circumcisions, Bar and Bat Mitzvahs, attending public functions, ecumenical functions, and of course, conducting services.

It has been observed that those who accept a rabbinic position when serving as judges must fulfill the biblical command: "You shall not be afraid in judgment: Hear out low and high alike. Fear no man, for judgment is God's" (Deuteronomy 1:17).

What does "shalom" mean?

The phrase *Shalom aleikhem*, "Peace be with you," occurs in Genesis 43:23.

Whenever Jews meet or depart, they greet each other with the word *shalom*. It means "peace." Peace signifies security, contentment, sound health, prosperity, friendship, peace of mind and heart, as well as completeness.

This is the usual saying that Jews exchange in greeting each other. According to a talmudic statement (*Berakhot* 5b), "He who does not return a greeting is called a robber." We are told to "meet every person with a friendly greeting" (*Avot* 4:20).

What is kosher?

Kasher literally means "fit, proper, ritually correct." The word kosher or *kashrut* is usually used to refer to food that is permitted to be eaten, but it also refers to the system of proper slaughtering of approved animal species, as well as regulating the use of dishes and utensils. The prohibition against eating blood is one of the fundamental regulations in the Jewish dietary code (Leviticus 17:11–16).

The basic idea of *kashrut* is that it is a biblical injunction designed as an exercise in maintaining holiness before God. Leviticus 11:1–43 informs us as to which animals, fowl, and fish may be regarded as kosher, or proper. Leviticus 20:25–26 goes on: "So you shall set apart the clean beast from the unclean. . . . You shall be holy to Me, for I the Lord am holy" (clean and unclean refer to spiritual, rather than physical, properties). From this perspective, *kashrut* is observed primarily as a *mitzvah*, a commandment from God, intended both for man's ritual purity and for the maintenance of a proper relationship between God and man.

In Deuteronomy 14:21: "You shall *not* eat of anything that dieth of itself." Also forbidden is the eating of an animal which has not been killed according to the method of proper *sheḥitah* (slaughtering).

"Whatsoever has no scales in the waters, that shall be an abomination unto you." (Leviticus 11:12). Fish such as shark, catfish, and all shellfish are prohibited.

"And these are they which you shall have in abomination among the fowls; they shall not be eaten" (Leviticus 11:13). Forbidden birds such as the eagle, the ossifrage, and the osprey seem to share certain characteristics. They have a tendency to prey on living creatures, including a sharp talon on their feet for hunting.

In order to observe *kashrut* we must learn that only certain animals, birds, or fish are permitted to be eaten: animals that chew their cud and have split hoofs, such as cows, sheep, goats, buffalos, and deer (Leviticus 11:3), birds that are not carnivorous, and fish that have scales and fins.

The animals or birds must be slaughtered in accordance with rabbinic law: animals or birds must not feel pain; the knife must not only be sharp, it must not have any grooves; after the slaughtering it should be examined to see that the lungs are not punctured and whether the liver has a healthy color, and the animal must be free of any other organic diseases. The meat must be kashered, which means drained of blood by soaking and salting.

The process of kashering requires the following steps: the meat is soaked in water for about a half-hour; it is then placed on a grate and covered with salt on all sides so that the pores open up and the blood can be drained freely—this takes about an hour; the meat is then washed thoroughly to eliminate the salt.

Liver, which has more blood than the other organs, can only be kashered by being broiled over an open grate. Meat that has not been washed and salted within three days after slaughter can no longer be used because the blood will have congealed to a point where salting cannot remove it.

Broiling, rather than frying, is the most powerful agent for the removal of blood from meat. Therefore, when meat is broiled (like steak, for example), it needs no kashering. Meat should be kashered before it is ground into chopped meat. Meat should not be frozen for subsequent use unless it has been kashered.

Meat must be kept separate from milk or dairy foods and especially not cooked or eaten together. The term *parveh* means neither meat nor dairy (i.e., fish, nuts, eggs, and vegetables). *Parveh* food that is cooked in a dairy or meat pot is regarded as dairy or meat respectively.

Terefah means unfit, improper, or forbidden by the dietary laws and is the opposite of *kasher*, which applies to animal, bird, or beast. The dishes or utensils used for *terefah* foods are considered *terefah*, unfit.

Two sets of dishes are used; one for meat and one for dairy. Separation is also required for pots and pans, as well as tableware. Two cabinets should be maintained; one for dairy (*milchig*) and one for meat (*fleishig*). The observance of *kashrut* teaches self-mastery and control. *Kashrut* serves as a means of Jewish identification.

What are tefillin?

The *tefillin* (phylacteries) are two small leather boxes of equal size. They are square in shape and colored glossy black. Each contains the same four Hebrew biblical passages written on parchment. To the *tefillin* are fastened long narrow leather strips, which are used to fasten one leather box upon the left upper arm over against the heart. The other case is placed on the front part of the head above the center of the forehead.

Which selections from the Bible are written on the parchments in the tefillin?

The four passages in the *tefillin* teach valuable lessons about Judaism and Jewish commitment.

Exodus 13:1–10 teaches us that it is God who delivered the Israelites from Egypt, and, therefore, we should express our gratitude to God by dedicating our lives to His service. Thus it deals with one's consecration to God.

Exodus 13:11–16 teaches us that the very existence of the Jewish people hinges upon commitment to God's laws. This selection expresses the thoughts that God's laws are eternal. They are binding upon each generation of Jews as they were upon our ancestors who traveled with Moses in the wilderness and who entered the Promised Land under the leadership of Joshua.

Deuteronomy 6:4–9 states: "Hear, O Israel, the Lord is Our God, the Lord is One. And thou shall love the Lord thy God, with all thy heart, with all thy soul, and with all thy might. And these words which I command thee this day shall be upon thine heart." This section, which constitutes part of the *Shema* prayer, proclaims the unity of God and teaches that we must understand our relationship to Him. The duty of the Jew is to do more than just recognize God's existence. God has legislated a Divine Code. It is the duty of the Jews to follow God's teachings and live by his commandments.

Deuteronomy 11:13–21 teaches that the external fortunes of the Jewish people and of each individual are granted by God only in the measure of the fulfillment of God's laws. God will reward those who obey his law, but those who violate it will bring His wrath upon themselves.

Where are tefillin mentioned in the Bible?

Tefillin are mentioned in four places—twice in the Book of Exodus and twice in the Book of Deuteronomy.

> And it shall be for a sign unto thee upon thy hand, and for a memorial between thine eyes, so that the teaching of the Lord may be the words of thy mouth for with a strong hand hath the Lord brought thee out of Egypt. (Exodus 13:9)

> And it shall be for a sign upon thy hand, and for frontlets between thine eyes, for by strength of hand, the Lord brought us forth out of Egypt. (Exodus 13:16)

> Hear, O Israel, the Lord is our God, the Lord is one. . . . And these words which I command thee this day shall be on thy heart. . . . And thou shall bind them for a sign upon thy hand, and they shall be for frontlets between thine eyes. (Deuteronomy 6:8)

> Therefore shall you lay up these my words in your heart and in your soul, and you shall bind them for a sign upon your hand, and they shall be for frontlets between your eyes. (Deuteronomy 11:18)

The *tefillin* are placed on the arm opposite the heart, reminding us of our obligation to serve God both physically and emotionally; upon the forehead to impress upon us that our intelligence and thoughts should be attentive to the teachings of God. By wearing the *tefillin* the Jew makes a symbolic commitment of heart, hand, and mind to God's will.

When are tefillin worn? *Tefillin* are worn every morning during prayer at home or in the synagogue, except on Sabbaths and holy days. *Tefillin* are not worn on the Sabbath or on holy days because these occasions in themselves serve as reminders of the special relationship between God and Israel and bear witness to the sacred ideas that are enshrined in the *tefillin*.

At what age is one required to wear tefillin? *Tefillin* are worn by observant Jewish men from the age of their Bar Mitzvah (thirteen). It is the custom today for a boy to start to wear his *tefillin* two or three weeks before his Bar Mitzvah in order that he will be fully acquainted with the procedure when he becomes Bar Mitzvah. Some very observant women, especially in the Conservative movement, also wear *tefillin*.

What is the tallit? The *tallit* is a Hebrew word for the prayer shawl that worshippers wrap around themselves during the morning services throughout the year. The *tallit* is rectangular in shape, made of silk, wool, or cotton, has black, blue, or other colorful stripes, and has fringes (*ẓiẓit*) at each of its four corners. The *ẓiẓit* are the most important part of the *tallit*. The Bible commanded their use. "Speak unto the children of Israel, and bid them that they make them throughout their generations fringes in the corners of their garments, and that they put with the fringe of each corner a thread of blue" (Numbers 15:38). The *tallit* often has an embroidered band that serves as a collar upon which is inscribed the text of the blessing recited when it is put on.

What are zizit?

The word *zizit* means "fringes." The Torah attaches great importance to the wearing of *zizit* as a visible reminder of the obligation to keep the divine commandments. "And it shall be unto you for a fringe, that ye may look upon it, and remember all the commandments of the Lord, and do them" (Numbers 15:39). There also is the *tallit katan*, a small *tallit*, also called *arba kanfot*, which is worn all day under the shirt to remind the person to remember the commandments and to do them.

Why wear a head covering?

Jews wear a head covering to show reverence for the Creator (*Shabbat* 156b). Reverence requires that the head should be covered. The typical headcovering is a skullcap. It is often called a *yarmulke*, a term of Slavic derivation. Nowadays it is also called a *kippah*, which is a Hebrew word. *Yarmulkes* are made of a wide variety of materials in a multitude of colors and designs. Wearing a head covering is a custom but not a biblical injunction.

Are children guilty for their parents' sins?

The Torah does not teach that the sins of guilty parents shall be visited upon their innocent children. "The soul that sinneth, it shall die," proclaims the prophet Ezekiel. In Deuteronomy 24:16, it states: "The parents shall not be put to death for the children; nor shall the children be put to death for the parents. A person shall be put to death only for his own crime." However, human experience all too plainly teaches the moral interdependence of parents and children. The bad example set by a father frequently corrupts those who come after him. Growing up in a home where parents are not honest or truthful, children will probably be influenced thereby to do wrong. In this way, the sins of the parents are visited on the children (but not the punishment for their parents' sins).

What is tzedakah?

Tzedakah is usually translated as "charity" and "generosity." The term is closely allied to the Hebrew word for "justice," indicating that Jewish tradition sees the giving of funds to the needy as an act of justice. "It is not really me who is giving, but God. I am simply the vehicle of transfer."

When receiving *tzedakah*, know that God is offering you an opportunity to live that you might devote your deeds to goodness. Of course, it is better to give than to receive.

The Jewish ideals of *tzedakah* were taught and summarized by Maimonides, our greatest rabbi and leader of 800 years ago. *Tzedakah*, said Maimonides, is like a ladder; it has eight steps, from low to high, from worst to best.

Here are Maimonides' eight degrees of *tzedakah*. One should decide which step of the ladder one stands upon and how to move upward another step.

The lowest step in giving *tzedakah* is to give too little, unwillingly, and as if forced to give.

The next step is, though giving too little, to do so pleasantly and cheerfully, as if happy to give.

The third step is to give as much as is needed, but only after being asked to do so.

The fourth step is to give as much as is needed and to do so *before* being asked.

A fifth and higher step is to give enough, to give before being asked, and to give in such a way that the poor person knows who gives him help, but the helper does not know who the poor person is. (Some of our sages would tie money in the corner of a cloth and toss it over their shoulder as they walked, so that a poor man behind them could pick it up without being seen by the giver.)

Sixth is to give enough and before being asked, but in such a way that the giver knows who gets the charity, while the receiver does not know who has given it to him. (Many sages used to leave money or food on the doorstep of a poor family or send their gift by a messenger.)

The seventh and the next-to-the-highest way to give *tzedakah* is to do so in a manner in whereby neither the giver nor the receiver knows who the other is. Charity can be given in the secret *tzedakah* room in the Temple and in the synagogues, or by giving to a general welfare fund that is managed by trustworthy and efficient trustees.

Finally, at the top of the *tzedakah* ladder, is the step of helping a needy person to support himself so that charity is no longer needed. This can be done by lending someone money to open a business, joining a needy person in a partnership, or helping someone to find a job. Helping someone to help himself.

When one gives charity, it should be carried out in a righteous manner.

What is ḥillul ha-Shem?

Ḥillul ha-Shem is the destruction of God's name.

In Leviticus 22:32 it states, "And ye shall not profane My Holy Name," a solemn warning against the profanation of the divine name.

The rabbis warn against actions such as any misdeeds toward a stranger

The offense of a single Jew or Jewess can bring shame on the whole House of Israel.

How does a Jew repent?

If a Jew violates the commandments, he has done wrong. The Law enables him to return to God and repent. The process of returning to God, or *teshuvah*, consists of four steps to turn from misdeeds to good deeds:

> The sinner must recognize his sin and acknowledge that he did wrong, admission of guilt (*Viddui*).
> He must feel sincere remorse at having sinned.
> He must resolve to return to fulfilling the law.
> If a person wronged another person, he must ask forgiveness from the person he wronged.

Repentance means an inward change of heart that leads to turning from evil, and to reconciliation with God. It involves an awareness of one's errors and misdeeds: confession, not to others, but to oneself and to God; evading wrongdoings and misdeeds; and finally, following a new way of life.

"Repentance lies at the very root of man's life as a moral blessing" (Talmud, *Pesaḥim* 54a; *Pesikta Rabbati* 169a). Judaism also emphasizes that one may return and be reconciled with God at any time, at any hour of any day.

The prophets emphasized repentance:

> Hosea: "Return, O Israel, unto the Lord your God." (Hosea 14:2)

> Jeremiah: "Return your backsliding, Israel, says the Lord." Jeremiah 3:12 I will not look in anger upon you.

> Ezekiel: "Return you, and turn yourselves from all your transgressions." Ezekiel 18:30 Turn yourself and make others turn as well.

"The Gates of Repentance are always open" (*Devarim Rabbah* 2:12). Offenses against man, however, require rectification and reparation before there can be forgiveness and reconciliation.

The door of repentance is never closed even when one lies on his deathbed.

How do you desecrate one's name?

Great stress is laid on honest and just dealings with a Jew and with a non-Jew, for here the good name of honesty and integrity and the reputation is involved. Every dealing or transaction must be performed in honesty, goodness, and accuracy. Every act of dishonesty tarnishes the good name of the Jewish people and their religion.

What if a Jewish family adopts a non-Jewish child?

An adopted child does not automatically become Jewish. The child would have to undergo formal conversion to Judaism in order to be considered Jewish. He who raises an orphan or adopted child is considered by the Torah to have given birth to the child (*Megillah* 13a; *Sanhedrin* 19b).

What is circumcision?

One of the cardinal precepts of the Jewish faith is circumcision, a sacred rite that, according to the Torah, was transmitted to Abraham by God. Abraham was commanded by God that Isaac was to be circumcised on the eighth day after his birth (Genesis 17:10–12, 21:4). Since then circumcision has been the sign of a Jew and has become a fundamental act of religious existence. The *Berit Milah*, the rite of circumcision, is one of the most deeply rooted institutions in Judaism. The newborn enters the Jewish fold through the rite. The rabbis of the Talmud state that circumcision outweighs all other commandments. It is a positive commandment of the Torah for a father to circumcise his son on the eighth day after the child is born.

It is not merely a surgical operation that may or may not be performed by a surgeon, but a ritual that demands certain procedures, circumstances, and personnel. He who performs the circumcision, in addition to being adept at the operation, must be an observant Jew, one who practices the precepts of his faith.

When Antiochus Ephiphanes prohibited circumcision more than two thousand years ago, the Jews were ready to die rather than abandon this ritual. When the Romans tried to interfere with this rite, the Jews of Palestine rose up in bitter rebellion, leading to one of the bloodiest wars in Jewish history.

The ceremony may be performed on the Sabbath and even on Yom Kippur, whenever the eighth day occurs. If, however, for medical reasons the *berit* cannot be carried out on the eighth day, the circumcision may be postponed. If there is any suspicion of illness, circumcision should not be performed. Danger to life takes precedence over all else, and "You shall live by the commandments" (Leviticus 18:5), meaning "And you shall not die through them" (*Yoma* 85b). The performance of the *mitzvot* should bring life and joy and not cause death. Once delayed, the circumcision cannot take place on a Sabbath or a major festival.

Who are involved?

The participants in a circumcision are:

> The *mohel* (circumciser) (who performs the circumcision)
> The father (who is obliged to have the child circumcised)
> The *sandek* (who holds the child during the operation)
> The *kvater* (the person, usually the godfather, who hands the infant to the *mohel*, usually a relative or close friend)

Two chairs are provided—one for the *sandek* holding the baby, and one for a special "guest," the prophet Elijah, who, according to popular tradition, attends every *Berit Milah* service and protects the infant from lurking danger. In addition to the prayers and blessings performed by the *mohel*, a special prayer is recited by the father of the newborn after the circumcision. The prayer is as follows:

Father: Praised are You, O Lord our God, King of the Universe, who sanctified us with Your commandments, and commanded us to bring our son into the covenant of Abraham our Father.

All present: As he has entered the covenant, so may he attain the blessings of Torah, marriage, and a life of good deeds.

Afterwards a festive meal is usually served.

What is Bar Mitzvah?

Bar means "son," and *mitzvah* means "commandment." A Jewish boy who has reached the age of thirteen marks his formal entrance into the Jewish religious community, as quoted in Ethics of the Fathers 5:23.

Until the age of thirteen, according to Jewish tradition, parents are answerable for their son's conduct. When he becomes a Bar Mitzvah, he reaches his religious maturity and is thereafter held personally responsible as an adult human being. In other words, he remains a Bar Mitzvah, a man of duty, for the rest of his life. This entrance into religious manhood is expressed by extending to the boy the adult privilege of being called up to the Torah as a *maftir*, one who concludes the reading of the Torah and chants the prophetic portion that follows the Torah reading. The purpose of the boy's public reading of the Torah and the Haftarah is to make him a full-fledged adult who is obliged to obey what is written in the Torah.

It is customary for the father of the Bar Mitzvah to pronounce the following blessing: "Blessed be He who has released me of the responsibility of this boy." In this manner parents express joy that their son has attained the age at which he can independently distinguish between right and wrong. One of the many *mitzvot* that the boy assumes is the wearing of the *tallit* and the *tefillin*

(Deuteronomy 6:8). Another privilege is that of being included in a *minyan*, a quorum of adults for religious service.

The day of the Bar Mitzvah offers both challenge and opportunity, for this is an event that carries with it a profound meaning. In America, this rite has become one of the most outstanding events in the religious life of a young Jew.

What is Bat Mitzvah?

Bat in Hebrew means "daughter," and *mitzvah* means "commandment." A Jewish girl who has reached the age of twelve is religiously a Bat Mitzvah.

The Bat Mitzvah has become a significant milestone in the life of a young girl where she takes on the adult responsibilities of Jewish womanhood. It is the time she pledges her determination to link the physical as well as the spiritual to the performance of *mitzvot*, good deeds.

What is the meaning of the six-pointed star?

The Star of David has developed into a specifically Jewish symbol. It is supposed to represent the shape of King David's shield (or perhaps the emblem on it). Some attribute deep theological significance to the symbol. Some say the six-pointed star represents that God is everywhere: north, south, east, west, up and down. Some say that the intertwining makes the triangles inseparable, as are the Jewish people. Some say the three sides represent the three types of Jews: *kohanim*, *levi'im* (Levites), and (*yisra'elim*) Israelites. The *Magen David* (Star of David) gained popularity as a symbol of Judaism when it was adopted as the emblem of the Zionist movement in 1897. In 1933, Hitler decided that Jews in Germany had to wear a brand, and in particular, a "Jew Star" (an insulting name for the Star of David). On May 14, 1948, the State of Israel established the blue Star of David on a white background as the symbol of a proud nation.

What is marriage?

Marriage is a holy institution in Judaism, a wholesome fulfillment, a sacred bond, and a divine command. Its very name in Hebrew, *Kiddushin,* means "sanctification."

The purpose of marriage is twofold, to provide companionship (Genesis 1:28) and to rear a family, so that posterity may receive the blessings from the past and perpetuate its heritage for the Scripture says, "He shall cling to his wife and they shall be as one flesh (Genesis 2:24). "For what value are my earthly belongings," cried Abraham, "if I go childless?" (Genesis 15:2). The first statute in the Bible is "Be fruitful and multiply."

Weddings have always been joyous occasions among the people of Israel. They were often community festivals marked by singing, dancing, and feasting.

What is the ḥuppah?

The *ḥuppah* has undergone a great transformation. Originally, the bride was led to the bridal chamber. This signified her passing from her father's house to her new husband. In the Middle Ages, the opposite took place. The groom went to live with her family.

Although the term is usually used to mean the wedding canopy, the term *ḥuppah* can also be applied to the actual ceremony. The bride and groom stand together during the wedding ceremony under a canopy, the symbol of God's presence over the couple. This is reminiscent of the tent ceremony in biblical times when it was customary to bring the veiled, jewelry-bedecked bride into the groom's tent (Genesis 24:67). The beautifully embroidered *ḥuppah* is usually ornamented in silk, satin, or velvet and supported by four poles held by four unmarried young people. It may also symbolize the future home of the wedded couple. The use of the portable canopy is attributed to the fact that it was customary for the wedding to take place in front of the synagogue or the house under the canopy of heaven.

What is the ketubbah?

The *ketubbah* is a marriage contract specifying the mutual obligations between husband and wife. The marriage contract, formerly an important legal protection for the wife, now stresses the moral responsibility of the married couple. The *ketubbah* is read and then handed to the groom, who gives it to the bride to keep.

The *ketubbah* is a Jewish legal document written in Aramaic detailing all the obligations of husband and wife toward each other. This marriage contract is signed by the bride and groom and witnessed by two people unrelated to the couple just before the actual ceremony. The rabbi reads the *ketubbah* aloud under the *chupah*. It reads (loosely translated) as follows:

The said bridegroom made the following declaration to his bride:

"Be thou my wife according to the Law of Moses and Israel. I faithfully promise that I will be a true husband unto thee; I will honor and cherish thee; I will protect and support thee and will provide all that is necessary for thy sustenance, even as it beseemeth a Jewish husband to do. I also take upon myself all such further obligations for thy maintenance as are prescribed by our religious statutes."

And the said bride has plighted her troth unto him in affection and in sincerity and has thus taken upon herself the fulfillment of all the duties incumbent upon a Jewish wife.

This covenant of marriage was duly executed and witnessed this day according to the usage of Israel.

Do the groom and bride fast on the day of their wedding?

This centuries-old custom evolved from the belief that the young couple, upon entering the matrimonial state, should fast as we do on Yom Kippur to purify themselves of any past transgressions and enter their new life together free of any sins. The fast concludes when the ceremony or betrothal is completed.

What is bedecken?

A number of customs have developed around the marriage ceremony to enhance its joy, solemnity, and meaningfulness emphasizing its sanctity.

Bedecken di kaleh is a ceremonial covering of the face of the bride. Prior to the marriage ceremony, the groom is led to the bridal dressing room to verify his bride's identity, and he lowers her veil over her face while the rabbi gives a blessing. "May you be a beautiful mother in Israel. May you be fruitful and prosper." This custom relates to Genesis 29:25, when Laban covered the face of Leah instead of the chosen one, Rachel. Its origin is also ascribed to the biblical story about Rebecca when she saw Isaac for the first time, took the veil, and covered herself (Genesis 24:65).

What is an aufruf?

The word *aufruf* means to be called up for an *aliyah* (the honor of being called up to the Torah) prior to the wedding day. Today it is customary for the rabbi to bless the bride and groom. The blessing generally stresses that the marriage will be privileged to fashion a Jewish home harboring love and harmony, peace and companionship; that those who are soon to be joined in marriage will be ever faithful to the finest within themselves; and that they will be blessed with children, reared in health and well-being.

Why circling the groom?

The idea of encirclement is found in the Scriptures, where the prophet speaks about bliss and says, "The woman will go around her husband seven times" (Jeremiah 31:21). In this, their most joyous moment, the bride circles around her groom to demonstrate that he is to be the center of her life. Another explanation is that the husband's life has become complete and fulfilled where prophets say that a woman encompasses and protects a man.

Seven are the days of joy upon getting married. Seven blessings are invoked upon the couple by the rabbi during the marriage ceremony, as well as the grace after the meal for the bride and groom.

Some circle around only three times. Three times the word "I betroth you" occurs in Hosea 2:21–22, where God addresses His people: "I betroth you to Myself forever; I betroth you to Myself in righteousness and in justice, in love and in mercy; I betroth you to Myself in faithfulness."

Is there music at weddings? Music is definitely a part of the marriage celebration. There is also special music (*mezinka*) that is played when the youngest child is married and the other children are already married. A popular Yiddish tune congratulates the parents on having married off their children and thus being relieve of parental obligations.

Does the rabbi speak?
It is customary for the rabbi to say a few personal words to the bride and groom.

What are the Sheva Berakhot?
To express our gratitude to God for the miracles of life in general, and the sanctity of married life in particular. The *Sheva Berakhot*, or seven blessings, quoted in the Talmud (*Ketubbah* 8a) are the last part of the wedding ceremony and are recited over wine during and after the ceremony. *Sheva Berakhot* is an ancient tradition dating back to biblical times and celebrates the marriage for seven days following the wedding.

It has been a customary *mitzvah* throughout the centuries to recite the *Sheva Berakhot* during the ceremony, after the feast, and during the seven days. The rabbi (or cantor) raises the cup of wine and gives thanks to God:

For creating the fruit of the vine;

For creating the universe;

For creating human beings;

For creating man and woman in His image, in such fashion that they, in turn, can create life for His grace, as He will make Zion joyful again through (the return of) her children;

For making the groom and bride joyful; may He bring gladness to them as He brought it to His creatures in the Garden of Eden;

For Him, who as the Source of all joy is implored to restore speedily to the cities of Judah and the streets of Jerusalem;

For the voice of mirth and the voice of joy;

For the voice of groom and the voice of bride . . .

Blessed are You, Lord; You are He who makes the groom rejoice with the bride.

The cup is passed to the couple in the same manner as before. They drink from it. From now on, they will share the cup of life together. May it be a "cup of salvation."

What is breaking of the glass?

The custom of breaking the glass under the *ḥuppah* is symbolic recognition of the fact that even in our moment of supreme happiness, we are not forgetful of the sorrows that have overtaken the House of Israel in the course of centuries.

The groom breaks the glass and all shout, "*mazal tov!*" He kisses the bride and then the young couple is escorted to *yiḥud* for a few minutes of precious privacy where the bride and groom break their fast and spend a few minutes of togetherness. There are two people posted at the door to ensure their privacy. After *yiḥud*, the families and friends participate in *se'udat miẓvah*, the festive meal. Taking pictures, dancing, and singing are in order. The dinner closes with grace after meals and includes the repetition of the *Sheva Berakhot*—the Seven Benedictions.

What is mazal tov?

The word *mazal* (luck) occurs only once throughout the sacred Scriptures, and in its plural form in 2 Kings 23:5, where it refers to the constellations or signs of the zodiac. The exclamation *mazal tov* ("good luck" or "congratulations") is derived from it.

What is hospitality?

In an ancient custom, but a modern lesson, we are taught that the tent of Abraham and Sarah had an opening on each side so that wayfarers, from whichever direction they came, would feel welcome to partake of their hospitality. As we read in Genesis 18:1–8, it was not just guests but actually angels in disguise who announced the future birth of Isaac.

Hakhnasat oreḥim (welcoming guests) is a time-honored tradition among Jews. The invitation to "all who are hungry" in the Passover *Haggadah* is well known. Less familiar is the ceremony known as *Ushpizin* in which we extend to our ancestors an invitation to join us in our *sukkot*.

May a non-Jew attend your services?

In Isaiah 56:7, it states: "For my house shall be called a house of prayer for all peoples." Everyone is welcome at Jewish services in the synagogue.

What is a mezuzah?

A *mezuzah* is an outward sign of God's presence and a sanctification of a dwelling place. Inside the case or receptacle is a tiny parchment attached to the doorpost of Jewish homes. The *mezuzah* contains a rectangular piece of parchment inscribed with passages from Deuteronomy 6:4–9 and 11:13–21. This was told to the Jews by Moses to commemorate that God passed over their doorposts when they were in Egypt.

The obligation of the *mezuzah* is derived from the words: "And thou shalt write them on the doorposts of thy house and within thy gates" (Deuteronomy 6:9).

The word *Shaddai*, meaning "Almighty," written on the back of the parchment is made visible through a small opening near the top of the case. *Shaddai* has been explained to represent the initials of the letters:

S̲homer—guarding
D̲altot—gates or doors
Y̲isra'el—Israel

Upon entering the house or leaving it, it is customary to touch the *mezuzah* with one's fingers and then kiss them.

What is a mikveh?

"And he shall bathe his flesh in running water and be clean" (Leviticus 15:13). From this verse, we deduce the commandment of immersion for purposes of ritual purity. A river or sea may be used for ritual immersion.

The rules pertaining to the *mikveh*, or ritual bath, are quite specific. It must be large enough for an adult to immerse completely, and be at least 47 inches deep. It must be filled from free-flowing water or rainwater, not tap water. The most common use of the *mikveh* is by married women who, each month after their menstrual flow, immerse themselves in order to resume sexual relations with their husbands.

This practice is based upon the verse: "You shall not come near a woman who is impure" (Leviticus 18:19).

The primary purpose of the *mikveh* is "spiritual in character, involving a cleansing of the mind, heart and emotions enabling a wife to bring herself once again completely and without reservation to her husband and for her husband to receive her in a like spirit."[12]

---

[12] Rabbi Hayim Halevy Donin, *To Be a Jew*, p. 126.

Is there anything wrong with drinking alcohol?

Drinking liquor is not forbidden, but drunkenness is sharply condemned. In Genesis 9:21 it states: "He drank the wine and became drunk, and he uncovered himself." Jewish law permits drinking for pleasure, and wine is used for rituals to celebrate the Sabbath, festivals, circumcisions, and weddings. A person who is drunk is fully responsible for any violation of the law committed while drunk. Jewish law generally obligates the ill to seek help for alcoholism or any other addiction.

Death and Mourning

Why honor the elderly?

"You shall rise up before the aged and show deference to the old; you shall fear your God; I am the Lord" (Leviticus 19:32).

We must honor and revere our parents in the same manner as it is our obligation to honor and revere God. "It is not the place that honors the man, but the man that honors the place" (*Sanhedrin* 113b).

Honoring our parents means showing respect, obedience, and love. This obligation extends beyond the grave. "Honor your father and your mother" is the fifth commandment (Deuteronomy 5:16).

The dignity of man, which is the basis of Jewish ethics, morality, and spirituality, is expressed not only in how we relate to those who are living, but also in our treatment of the dead. Death is our universal destiny. Therefore, the dead are to be treated with dignity and reverence.

Life has a beginning as well as an end. According to tradition, the human being is made up of both body and soul. The invisible soul is the life-giving force of our earthly existence. The body is merely the vehicle for the soul during its earthly existence.

Over the centuries, Judaism has developed specific rituals and observances that respect the dead and express compassionate concern for the living. The Jewish laws for the dead and the mourners are built into a communal structure that is designed to provide guidance and insight at the time of loss.

Judaism understands the despair, the anger, and sometimes guilt when a loved one is taken from our midst. Our rituals and customs have been shaped to help the survivors face the realities of life. Grief can be very painful and draining. The mourner needs support and understanding.

When I think of death it reminds me of the words from Ecclesiastes 3:1: "For everything there is a season and a time for every matter under heaven—a time to be born and a time to die." These words express the realities of life. To live is to be born. To live is to die. Life is like a jigsaw puzzle, but you do not have the picture on the front of the box to know what it is supposed to look like. Sometimes you are not even sure if you have all the pieces. To live is to know the uncertainty of time. We rarely know what tomorrow will bring, and yet to live is to know pleasure and pain.

When death comes to a loved one, we feel that our own life has been shattered. We are exhausted from the strain. We do not think we will be able to go on, but we do go on.

Death is a reality for which we are never quite ready or prepared. Each day life is present it lulls us into thinking that it will continue indefinitely. Even when death comes, we still are not quite ready to accept its finality and reality. No matter when death comes, we are not ready for the grief, the pain, and the sense of loss it brings.

What is death?

No one lives forever. Those who are born are destined to die. Life is the creation of a benevolent God. The infusion of the divine breath makes man higher than the animals but "a little lower than the angels." Death is a return of the soul and body to the Creator at a time determined by the Creator.

The unknown

Among the things hidden from man is the day of death (*Pesaḥim* 54b). However, says King Solomon, "The living know that they shall die." No one lives forever. Death is a part of life.

It states in Ecclesiastes 3:11, "He has made everything beautiful in its time, also He has set eternity in the heart." Everything heroic in man is significant and perishable, and one's wisdom and virtue stand the crucial test to live on and on.

Death cannot be seen as punishment, or life as reward. There are times when life is a curse and death a blessing. Our faith teaches us that death leads us into life eternal. Life is holy, so is the body. Life is precious, so is the soul. "The spirit returns to God who gave it." (Ecclesiastes 12:7).

Is death the end of life?

Death cannot be and is not the end of life. Man transcends death in many ways. He may be immortal biologically through his children, in thought through the survival of memories, in influence, and by virtue of the continuance of the effect and spirit of his personality.

Fearing death

Judaism teaches not to fear death, for it is not the end of man. Most of us are afraid of death. Our fear stems from terror of the unknown—and nothing is more unknown than "the valley of the shadow of death." We do not know what death is, but we are intuitively certain that it will deprive us of the companionship of those we love, and of everything we cherish and enjoy on earth. Our fear of death relates to not only our own demise, but also to the passing of those we love.

From the time of death through interment, the utmost respect and dignity must be shown to the deceased. To accomplish this, at the time of death the body must be totally covered by a sheet and should remain covered until the arrival of the mortuary people

(*Ḥevra Kaddisha*). A sign of ultimate respect for the deceased is that the body never be left alone. A *shomer* (guard) sits with the body at all times at the funeral home until the actual funeral takes place.

Preparation of the body for the funeral
Taharah is the process of purifying the body. It is prepared in a specific rite of purification that includes ritual washing and fitting of a shroud. People who are specially trained and know exactly what to do perform this. A female is trained to perform this on a female, and a male is trained to perform the ritual on a male. It is customary for a male to be buried in his own *tallit* (prayer shawl) and *kippah* (skullcap). If he does not have these, new ones may be purchased for the burial.

If the body is mutilated, *taharah* is not performed, and the deceased (with the bloodstained clothes) is wrapped in a sheet for the casket to be buried.

Autopsy
Generally, Jewish law does not permit autopsy. If it is required by the state in certain circumstances, then it is permitted. The performing of autopsy may be allowed if the knowledge gained is considered essential for the preservation of life.

Organ donations
Organ donations are permitted when they directly save another's life.

Embalming
Embalming is expressly forbidden by Jewish law because it prevents decomposition of the body back to its natural state, as is stated in the Bible, "from dust to dust." (Genesis 3:19)

Cremation

Cremation is expressly forbidden in Jewish law. Cremation harks back to the pagan funeral pyre. It nullifies the atoning process of the body's underground disintegration. The deceased must be interred bodily in the earth. Jewish law requires no mourning for the cremated. *Shivah* is not observed and *Kaddish* is not recited for the cremated. Cremated ashes may not be buried in a Jewish cemetery unless the deceased was incinerated in war, by an accident, or murdered. Obviously, in such tragic cases, the horrifying mode of death secures atonement.

Casket

Jewish tradition prefers a simple wooden casket with no lining erred. Jewish law expressly forbids metal caskets since they do not decompose.

Between death and interment

Those required to mourn are the deceased's children, including adopted children, parents, brothers and sisters, and the spouse of the deceased. All those who mourn may not pray during interment.

Keri'ah

The tearing of a garment, known as *keri'ah,* symbolizes the emotional distress of the mourners. The torn garment must be worn for thirty days. The funeral home usually distributes a black ribbon for tearing. A tear is made on the left side for parents who have died (close to your heart) and on the right side for all others.

Viewing

Viewing of the deceased is strongly discouraged by the Orthodox and Conservative movements in Judaism. We try to remember our departed when their bodies were full of vigor, creative thinking, doing, and loving rather than as they appear in death, frail in life-less repose, often withered by lengthy, debilitating illness.

Funeral and burial
It is highly recommended that the mourners wait in a separate room at the funeral home until immediately prior to the service. In this way, those who wish to comfort the mourners may do so in an atmosphere of respect for the departed. Usually the rabbi delivers the prayers and eulogy. It is proper and permissible for relatives or good friends to deliver a eulogy.

Pallbearers
There are usually six or eight people previously chosen who carry the casket to the final resting place.

Cemetery service
During the service, the casket is lowered into the ground. Some have the custom of putting three shovelfuls of earth into the grave. It is highly laudable for family and friends to actually perform the entire burial. This act is the most painful. It is the finality and reality of the departed.

If there is only a graveside service, the casket must be escorted from the hearse and carried to the grave before the service can begin.

What is Kaddish?
The *Kaddish* is a short prayer written in Aramaic, the language spoken by the Jewish people for about a thousand years after the Babylonian captivity. Its origin is mysterious. Angels are said to have brought it down from heaven and taught it to men.

Mourners recite *Kaddish* to sanctify God's name. The ritual calls for a *minyan* (10 adult Jews) to honor the deceased so that the memory of the deceased depends on the presence of life.

There is no doubt that Jesus spoke this ancient prayer in the synagogue and that it became the basis for the Lord's Prayer.

The *Kaddish* has five different forms: The *Kaddish* does not mention death, it expresses a fervent hope for the future.

Kaddish de-Rabbanan (Scholars' *Kaddish*) is recited after studying.

Kaddish Shalem (Full *Kaddish*) is recited by the reader at the end of major sections of the service.

Ḥaẓi Kaddish (Half *Kaddish*) is recited by the reader between certain sections of the service.

Kaddish Yatom (Mourner's *Kaddish*) is recited by the mourners.

Kaddish le-Itḥadeta (Mourner's *Kaddish* at the grave) is recited after interment, to honor the death.

The *Kaddish* prayer binds the generations one to another as a sacred thread in love, with respect, and to remember those who have gone to their eternal rest.

The *Kaddish* possesses sanctifying power. Truly, if there is any bond strong and indissoluble enough to chain heaven to earth, it is this prayer. It keeps the living together, and forms the bridge to the mysterious realm of the dead. Can a people disappear and be annihilated so long as a child remembers a parent? Memory sustains man in the world of life.

Kaddish declares that even at this moment of grief and loss, in the face of the ugliness and defeat demonstrated by death, we reaffirm the fact that the purpose of life in this world is that God's name be magnified and sanctified.

The *Kaddish* has become a great pillar of Judaism. No matter how far a Jew may have drifted away from Jewish life, the deepest hold on all Jews is the *Kaddish*.

The essential part of the *Kaddish* consists of the congregational response, "May His great name be blessed forever and ever."

Around this response, which is found almost verbatim in Daniel 2:20, the whole *Kaddish* developed.

The *Kaddish* is recited after the burial.

The rabbi asks all in attendance at the cemetery to form two lines so that the mourners can pass through in the middle. In order to console the mourners a prayer is recited: "May God comfort you among all those who mourn in Zion."

The house of mourning

Upon returning to the house of mourning, or *shivah* house, a pitcher of water and paper towels are placed outside so that those returning from the cemetery may wash their hands before entering. The reason is that water symbolizes life after coming from a place of death. Also, water purifies.

Lighting a candle

A special candle is lit immediately after returning from the cemetery to the *shivah* house. It is designed to burn for seven days. No blessing is recited when lighting the candle, but it should be placed where it can be seen.

What is the meaning of the light?

The human spirit is biblically referred to as the "lamp of the Lord" (Proverbs 20:27). When life ends, we are consoled by the knowledge that the essence of man, which is the spirit, lives with God.

Kindling a light is a positive affirmation of our belief in the eternity of the human soul. Lighting a candle at the time of birth is not part of Jewish tradition because the life of a person can best be summed up at the end of his journey on earth. Mysticism considers the burning wick to represent the soul, while the candle that is consumed stands for the body.

The meal

After returning to the *shivah* house, there is usually a meal including hard-boiled eggs, which is an ancient sign of mourning. The egg is symbolic of the roundness of the world and of mourning, which comes to all. It should be a simple meal.

Shivah

Shivah is the Hebrew word for "seven." It also means "to sit." Our tradition indicates that when a relative passes away, a time is to be set aside for the expression of grief.

After the revelation, Moses established the seven days of mourning by special decree, declaring, as a formal doctrine, that which had been practiced only as a custom. He enacted, and the sages asserted, the seven days of mourning, just as he had enacted the biblical seven days of rejoicing of major holidays. The connection between the two opposites is hinted at in the verse from Amos, "And I will turn your feast into mourning" (Amos 8:10). Just as feasts were observed for seven days, so mourning was to last one week. When our patriarch Jacob died, Joseph, his son observed seven days of mourning.

Shivah is ideally observed at the home of the deceased but may be observed in any relative's home. *Shivah* begins immediately after interment and is not observed on the Sabbath or holidays. It is traditional to hold services in the *shivah* house. It is customary for relatives and neighbors to bring prepared meals to the house to be eaten by the mourners during the week of *shivah* since they are not allowed to prepare their own meals during *shivah*.

It is customary in the *shivah* house to drape a cloth or sheet over the mirrors or to apply window wax to them. Mirrors in the *shivah* house should be covered so that the mourners are not concerned with their personal appearance.

How to console

"To comfort is human; to console, divine."

Your visit to the mourner at home calls for consolation. During this brief visit, you could bring comfort to someone in need. The mandate of our humanity and our religion is that we bring sensitivity and empathy to those who mourn.

In Judaism, we believe that your very presence in the mourner's home marks the beginning of consolation. It is advisable to let the mourner begin to talk and set the tone, especially in sensitive situations such as suicide, young death, or guilt-ridden grief. Listen considerately. It is better to be silent than overly talkative. Show concern for the mourner's well-being. Your face should wear a mien of seriousness, not necessarily sadness. Ideally, your conversation should not be distracting but therapeutic. Speak of the departed. It helps the mourner to unburden himself. Conclude your words of consolation with hope that the values of the departed will be incorporated by his relatives and friends, that the sunlight of health and happiness will shine once again on the family members. Some people conclude their visit with a traditional formula of consolation: "May God comfort you among the mourners of Zion and Jerusalem." "Please accept my sincerest condolences." "Please call on me if I can be of help." "I hope that this will be the last such sadness, and that we will share many happy occasions together."

The above represents the American way. Expressions of empathy and support may vary in different countries. As an example, in England, when visitors leave the house of mourning, they traditionally say, "I wish you a long life."

The *shivah* period allows the mourners to unburden themselves emotionally so that their grief tends not to solidify within them and prolong their period of suffering. Grief does not end with the termination of the *shivah* period, but *shivah* is a prologue for the resolution of grief.

Sitting on a low stool or bench emphasizes discomfort and grief for mourners. Pleasurable activities are limited. The *shivah* period enables us to ponder the ultimate issues of life and death.

Many follow the custom of having all the mourners walk together for a short distance after the *shivah* period. This symbolizes the return to society.

Sheloshim

The avoidance of joyous occasions is considered consistent with the spirit of mourning. The completion of *shivah* does not end the chaos that death has wrought. The process of mourning continues in a lesser degree than during the *shivah* period. Death cannot magically or suddenly be forgotten or ignored. Once outside the *shivah* house, some experience difficulties facing normal daily routines. During *sheloshim*, the thirty-day mourning period, there is to be no entertainment, men do not shave, and one does not attend parties. Marriage is discouraged during this period. Loneliness sets in, especially when the number of visitors has lessened. The experience of bereavement is highly individualistic. Some adjust more quickly, but for some it may take months or longer.

Concern for the dead

Sanhedrin 46b–47a states, "Respect and reverence for the dead and concern for the bereaved in the Jewish tradition are prescribed." A gradual return to normal life can be slow. Recovering from grief takes patience and perseverance.

It is customary for the mourners to recite the *Kaddish* for eleven months after the death of parents. *Kaddish* is one of the most beautiful, deeply significant, and spiritually moving prayers in the Hebrew liturgy. The process of mourning represents a systematic conditioning of the mourner to the full resumption of life's normal activities and responsibilities.

We mourn the loss of those we loved because each death diminishes us and reminds us of the frailty and the fragility of our own lives. We mourn the loss of loved ones because it makes us appreciate the preciousness and precariousness of each moment that we have had with them. Therefore, it is instructive, therapeutic, and right to mourn.

Yet, there is a strange amendment to the law. What is it? If a person suffers the loss of a relative on the day before one of the festivals, namely Passover, Shavuot, Sukkot, and the High Holy Days, he is only permitted to mourn until the festival begins. Then, as soon as the holiday begins, he must rise from the mourner's seat and turn to celebrating the holiday. He must try to free his heart from all feelings of sadness and grief and celebrate the holiday.

Is it realistic to require human beings to stop their sorrow when a festival arrives? What is the reasoning behind the law? The law states: "To rejoice on the festival," which is addressed to the entire Jewish community; this positive commandment has priority over the individual. Why? To be a Jew means to be connected to the community, and you cannot separate yourself from the community. The Jew must identify himself or herself. Each Jew relives and experiences the history of his people. The festivals are all history holidays and anniversaries of events in the life of the people. On Passover, each Jew is required to feel as if he has gone out of Egypt, on Pentecost as if he or she stood at Sinai, and on Sukkot as if he or she is going through the wilderness. Those who celebrate the holidays see not as individuals, but as a link in the chain in not only the past, but also present and future. The festival of the community has priority over the sorrow of the individual. Certainly, each death is a tragedy. The Jew as an individual is mortal, but being a part of his people, he or she is eternal, and since the festivals are the expression of the life of this eternal people, they take precedence over our individual mourning and grief. If the deceased passes away during the holiday, the mourners must continue practicing the rituals of the holiday, and when the holiday ends, the mourners begin to sit *shivah*.

How much should one grieve?

There is no simple and easy way to endure the suffering of a loved one, especially when death comes. The death of a loved one is a traumatic experience. Quite often, it throws one into a state of shock or panic. Because death produces anxiety about the present and future, one sometimes is tempted to make radical changes immediately and prematurely. Trying to deny the pain or avoid the memories that can bring on painful periods does not help. We have been taught that a display of emotions is unmanly. It is not so. It is okay to have a good cry. Grief is an emotion that, if not released, may sometimes lead to physical and even mental symptoms necessitating professional intervention.

Many times reading the Book of Psalms can be a great healer. The psalms reveal almost every conceivable mood of the individual, reflecting the heights of ecstasy and the depths of depression. The psalms contain balm for troubled souls. Psalm 23 can be a great healer. "Walking through the valley of the shadow of death, I fear no evil, for You are with me." Psalm 23 has become the cherished gem of so many people and has helped lift them out of the abyss of dejection. The psalm attempts to help us traverse the highway of pain and trauma, agony and suffering, and return unto the roadway of normal life. This consoling psalm is an expression of dependence on God and faith in Him. When the tide of life is at its lowest ebb and we are perplexed, our faith in a divine source will sustain us. "God is our refuge and strength, a very present help in trouble" (Psalm 46:2).

A person should not mourn excessively. Life must go on. Broken hearts must be mended, and open wounds must be closed. The grieving soul must rejoin society.

Where did we get the idea of erecting a monument?

"And Rachel died and was buried on the way to Ephrath, which is Bethlehem. And Jacob erected a tombstone on Rachel's grave" (Genesis 35:19–20).

Erecting a monument is a very ancient tradition. The monument serves four purposes:

To designate the grave properly so relatives and friends may visit it.

To write the proper name of the departed in Hebrew and English, his or her father's and mother's name, and the date born and died. Sometimes the family emblem or certain descriptions, such as righteous, charitable, good husband, father, are written on the stone.

The tombstone serves as a reminder that we do not forget the deceased from our hearts.

The prayer "May his [or her] soul be bound up in the bond of eternal life. May he [or she] rest peacefully" is inscribed on all monuments.

What is unveiling?

Unveiling is a formal dedication of the monument and the removal of the veil, a cloth draped over the stone. It symbolizes the erection of the tombstone. The children or grandchildren or anyone whom the family designates may execute the unveiling of the stone during the service. The service consists of the recitation of several psalms, the eulogy, the removal of the veil, the *Kaddish* and the *El Male Raḥamim*, the prayer for the departed. It is customary to place stones or pebbles on the monument. They serve as a reminder of the family's presence. The custom may hark back to biblical days when the monument was a heap of stones.

When do we remember the dead in the synagogue?

Recalling the dear departed during the services, an act of solemn piety and devotion, and an expression of profound respect, the *Yizkor* memorial service was instituted so that the Jew may pay homage to his forebears. It is based on the firm belief that the living, by acts of piety and goodness, can redeem the dead. It is accomplished by prayer and contributions of charity in the memory of the departed. The *Yizkor* service is recited four times a year. On the Day of Atonement, the holiest day of the year, when Jews seek redemption for their sins, they seek atonement as well for the departed. The living can redeem the dead. *Yizkor* is also recited on the three pilgrim festivals: Passover, Shavuot (Pentecost), and Sukkot.

Visiting the grave

What is the proper time to visit the grave? Various customs have arisen regarding the proper time for visiting graves. Some visit after *sheloshim* (thirty days after the death), on the anniversary of the death, and before the High Holy Days. There is no rule as to the frequency of such visitation, except that people should avoid the extremes of constant visitation to the grave. Frequent visitation to the cemetery might become a pattern of living, thus preventing the bereaved from placing their dead in proper perspective. Since Judaism puts the emphasis on life, one should not indulge in excessive mourning.

Yahrzeit

Yahrzeit (Yiddish for "year time")is the annual commemoration of the anniversary of our dear departed. It begins with the lighting of a 24-hour candle on the night of the anniversary. It is customary to recite the Mourner's *Kaddish*. The *Yahrzeit* prayer is an expression of reverence and homage for the cherished memory of the departed. It is appropriate to contribute some charity to a worthy cause in memory of the dear departed. It is even customary to fast and to be called to the Torah for an *aliyah*. A prayer for the departed (*El Male Raḥamim*) is also recited.

Finally, the greatest respect we can pay the departed is to have their memory serve as a beneficent influence in our lives. To live with greater reverence for the ideals and values of Judaism, and to fill the spiritual void their passing has created are the greatest honors we can bestow upon our dear departed. Thus, as their souls are bound up in the bond of eternal life in heaven, we give them immortality here on earth.

Chapter 2

ROMAN CATHOLICISM

Rev. Aidan N. Donahue, S.T.L.

Preface

I am pleased to have been invited to be a part of this project by Rabbi Philip Lazowski. As pastor of Sacred Heart Parish in Bloomfield, Connecticut, a community of believers in the Roman Catholic tradition, I feel that I speak in many ways for the rich tradition of faith and praxis that has been the Catholic tradition for some twenty centuries.

In these troubled times, in the wake of the senseless terrorist attacks on our nation that took place on September 11, 2001, the combined effort in mutual understanding that is represented in these pages can do nothing but good. As we come to realize more and more that we are a global community, a diverse community, the sphere of religious faith has become more and more central. It is my hope that my contributions to this book, when combined with those of Rabbi Lazowski and others, will help to promote a greater understanding of the richness in the many faith traditions present and alive in our world. By understanding the faith of others, we might grow in appreciation of the mutual bondedness that we share one with another. It is my hope as well that a greater appreciation of the diversity in faith and praxis among major world religious traditions may speed us toward greater tolerance and mutual understanding.

It is my prayer that the God of Abraham, Isaac, and Jacob, the God of Jesus, whom I profess to be the Christ, may bring us all closer together as one in the human family. May that unity be spurred by an ever-greater awareness of our common heritage of faith rather than a misguided emphasis on the differences that exists among us.

Questions on Roman Catholicism

What does the word "catholic" mean?

The word *catholic* comes from the Greek word which means "universal" or "worldwide." In one sense, the whole Christian Church can be considered *catholic* (note the lower-case *c*) because there are Christians in every corner of the world, on every continent, in every country, and in all cultures. For this reason, most Christians, when saying the *creed,* the solemn statement of what Christians believe, state their faith in "one, holy, *catholic*, and apostolic Church." On a more popular level, the word *Catholic* (note the upper-case *c*) usually refers to *Roman* Catholics. Thus, I can say that I am a *Catholic*, and more than that, a *Catholic* priest.

What are the major branches in Christianity?

Christianity, sadly enough, while unified in essential beliefs, sharing essentially the same creed or profession of faith, is also divided along the lines of church polity (organization) and practice. The three major divisions of Christianity are *Roman Catholicism*, *Protestantism*, and *Orthodoxy*. Roughly, for the first thousand years of Christian existence, the Christian Church was one body of believers. The first major break within Christianity came in the eleventh century owing to political and doctrinal tensions between the *Western* Christian Church, based in Rome under the pope, and some of the *Eastern* Christian Churches, which were loyal to the patriarch of Constantinople. Tensions grew to be so sharp that a formal *schism*, or break, occurred in the year 1054, thereby creating the Roman Church and the Orthodox Church.

Protestantism emerged from the various reform movements that sprang up in the fifteenth and sixteenth centuries and beyond. These movements arose as a reaction to abuses prevalent in the Roman Church, especially the sale of indulgences for the building of St. Peter's Basilica in Rome. These reform movements also arose from a sense that the Scriptures were being neglected. The rallying cry for Protestant reformers was *"sola Scriptura,"* the Scriptures alone, which denied any place for tradition, which is best understood as the *interpretation and application* of the Scriptures by the bishops and theologians of the Roman Church. By the beginning of the seventeenth century, the Christian faith in Europe was massively divided, with Protestantism claiming much of northern Europe, including England, and Roman Catholicism remaining dominant in southern Europe as well as portions of eastern Europe, such as Poland.

In modern times, much lamenting has occurred over the multiple divisions evident in the Christian Church. These divisions stood, and still stand, in stark contrast to the will and the wishes of Jesus, who prayed on the night before his death *"ut unum sint,"* that his followers be one (cf. John 17:21). As a result of the awareness of these multiple divisions in the Christian Church, the *ecumenical* movement evolved, which sought to bring the various Christian denominations together as one. Ecumenical discussions, often in the form of long and painstaking *dialogues*, happen even to the present day. These dialogues are meant to encourage and deepen a mutual understanding among the various denominations in the Christian Church. The Roman Catholic Church, for its part, officially endorsed ecumenical efforts at the Second Vatican Council, held in Rome between 1962 and 1965. As a result, the Catholic Church remains heavily involved in ecumenical efforts to this day.

What specifically is Roman Catholicism?

In their totality, the number of Christian believers worldwide today approaches one-half of the world's population, or approximately two billion people. The largest single grouping within Christianity is *Roman Catholicism*, with the number of Catholics exceeding one billion worldwide. Roman Catholicism is a branch of Christianity. This means that Catholics are Christians. Catholics profess faith in Jesus of Nazareth as Lord and Son of God. Catholics live by the words and the teachings of Jesus of Nazareth. They seek to bring Christ to others and to serve others as Jesus served.

With reference to the word *catholic,* the Roman Catholic Church is found on every continent, in every country, and in each culture. The Church lives within countries and cultures, all of which are diverse, while transcending such countries and cultures. While the Church is open to learning from various cultures and peoples, the Church believes that she has an obligation to teach the truth of the Gospel handed down by the apostles to all peoples and every culture. That teaching must happen without compromise or reservation. Very often, on account of this, the Church is subject to ridicule.

With reference to the word *Roman,* Roman Catholics are distinct from other Christians in a number of ways. Most notable of all is the reverence that Catholics attach to the Pope, the Bishop of Rome, the successor of St. Peter. The Roman Catholic Church is very much an organized and orderly Church, governed by a *hierarchy* (a very structured organization) composed of the Pope and bishops, assisted by priests and deacons. The worldwide Catholic Church is a *communion* of many localized churches often called *dioceses,* each of which is overseen by a bishop, with priests and deacons working under his authority and at his direction typically in smaller communities of believers called *parishes.* Normally every parish is under the direction of a priest, called the *pastor,* who is responsible for the celebration of the sacraments as well as pastoral care for the people. Roman Catholics also have a rather elaborate form of worship, with seven sacraments, the principal sacrament being the Eucharist, commonly referred to as the *Mass.* Finally, another distinctive characteristic of the Roman Catholic Church is found in its teaching authority vested in the Pope and the bishops in communion with him. This body of teachers, called the *Magisterium,* provides teaching and guidance on doctrinal and moral matters.

How does one become a Roman Catholic?

It has been rightly said that "Christians are made, not born." This is certainly true of Roman Catholic Christians. One is never *born* as a Catholic. One may be born into a Catholic family or society. That alone, however, does not make one a Catholic. Normally, one must accept and profess the faith of the Church, express a desire to live that faith as a member of the Church, and then undergo *baptism* with water in a solemn ritual. This having taken place, the person thus baptized thenceforth is considered to be a Catholic, a member of the Roman Catholic Church, a member of the wider Christian Church as well. Once baptized, one can say of himself or herself, "I am a Catholic," or "I am a Christian."

Who is the Pope and what is the role of the Pope in the Catholic Church?

The Pope, simply stated, is the Bishop of Rome. He is considered by Catholics to be the *successor of St. Peter.* In the Gospels, Jesus gave a special position of authority to Peter among the apostles. His faith was the rock on which the Church was to be founded (Matthew 16:18). He was to confirm and strengthen his brothers in the faith (Luke 22:32). This special place of authority, which Catholics call *primacy,* was given Peter by Jesus himself. It is the Catholic belief that this authority lives on in the Church by those who succeed in Peter's place. Since Peter, according to tradition, made his way to Rome and likely died there under the emperor Nero in the 60s of the first century, all those who have served subsequently as the head of the Church at Rome, as the *Bishop of Rome*, have been considered to be the ones taking the place of Peter in the Church of their time. Thus, they are, in fact, "successors of

Peter." The early title of the Pope was simply *bishop*, or "overseer," of the Church at Rome. Gradually, the importance and the power of this bishop extended beyond Rome to the whole Church. Later on, the title *Papa*, (Latin for "father") was used by the Bishop of Rome as stressing his duty to be a chief shepherd and guide for the whole Church. Thus, today we call the Bishop of Rome by the title of *Pope*. The duty of the Pope is to safeguard the unity of the Church throughout the world. To this end, among other duties, the Pope teaches with supreme authority under the gospel, rules on issues affecting the whole Church, and renders judgment on matters of dispute.

What do Catholics believe?

We can say that the basic beliefs of the Catholic Church are summed up very well in the *Profession of Faith,* also known as the *Nicene-Constantinopolitan Creed*. The *Nicene Creed*, dates from the fourth century. It is more popularly referred to as the *Creed*. This summary of the basic beliefs of the Church is recited Sunday after Sunday.

The *Profession of Faith*, which is, ironically, proclaimed almost universally in all branches and denominations of Christianity (with minor variations) reads as follows:

We believe in one God,
    the Father, the Almighty,
    the Creator of heaven and earth,
    of all things, seen and unseen.
We believe in one Lord, Jesus Christ,
    the only Son of God, eternally begotten of the Father,
    God from God, Light from Light, True God from True God,
Begotten, not made, one being with the Father.
    Through him all things were made.

For us [men] and our salvation, he came down from heaven.

By the power of the Holy Spirit, he was born of the Virgin Mary,

and became man.

He was crucified under Pontius Pilate.

He suffered, died, and was buried.

On the third day, he rose again.

He ascended into heaven and is seated at the right hand of the Father.

He will come again in glory to judge the living and the dead,

and his kingdom will have no end.

We believe in the Holy Spirit,

the Lord and Giver of Life, who proceeds from the Father and the Son.

With the Father and the Son, he is worshipped and glorified.

He has spoken through the prophets.

We believe in one, holy, catholic, and apostolic Church.

We acknowledge one baptism for the forgiveness of sins.

We look for the resurrection of the dead

and the life of the world to come.

Amen.

This represents the most concise statement that summarizes what Catholics believe. It also represents what most other Christians, in essence, believe as well.

An examination of the creed automatically leads one to note the *Trinitarian structure and emphasis*. As such, it states most succinctly what Catholics believe about God. Catholics believe that God is one, but that God is also three divine Persons, whom we name as the Father, the Son, and the Holy Spirit. This doctrine of

God is referred to as the *Trinity*. As the creed indicates, the Father is the Creator, the Source of all that is, seen and unseen. The Son of God existed before time and was present at creation, for "through him all things were made." In the fullness of time, the Son of God was conceived by the power of the Spirit of God in the womb of the Virgin Mary of Nazareth. He was born as Jesus of Nazareth, whom Catholics acknowledge and believe to be both LORD and Messiah. He lived as we do, enduring all things we do, except sin. He suffered a horrible death on the cross, but on the third day was raised to life. He sits at God's right hand, clothed in divinity and humanity. He will come as judge of all, living and dead, when all things will be placed under his feet, and God will be all in all (cf. 1 Corinthians 15:28). The Spirit is God's life breath, and power. The Spirit is truly God, LORD, and giver of life. The Spirit inspired the prophets to speak on God's behalf. The Spirit still proceeds from the Father and the Son and, as God, does the work of God in Christ in the Church and the world.

Why are the Virgin Birth and the Immaculate Conception important teachings of the Church?

Before we can even begin a discussion of why these doctrines are important, it is critical that we clearly distinguish between the two of them. The Virgin Birth is a doctrine which refers to the truth that Jesus of Nazareth was conceived in the womb of his mother, Mary, by divine action and power. This is affirmed both by the Gospel of Matthew, where the angel of the Lord tells Joseph in a dream that "it is by the Holy Spirit that she [Mary, his espoused wife] has conceived this child" (Matthew 1:20) and by the Gospel of Luke, where Mary is told by the angel Gabriel that "the Holy Spirit will come upon you and the power of the Most High will overshadow you. Thus, the child to be born will be called holy, the Son of God" (Luke 1:35). The doctrine of the Virgin Birth essentially holds that Jesus was not conceived by an act of human sexual intercourse, but by a special action of the Spirit of God. He had no human father. This doctrine is critical, for the whole constant teaching of the Church has been that Jesus is fully human (through his mother Mary) and fully divine (through his conception by the Holy Spirit in the womb of Mary). A denial of the doctrine of the Virgin Birth inevitably leads to a denial of the full divinity of Jesus, and with that, the whole of the Christian faith is undermined.

The doctrine of the *Immaculate Conception* maintains that the Virgin Mary from the first moment of her existence, was preserved from original sin (the sin of Adam and Eve, as told in Genesis 3) and its effects. Christian doctrine has taught that the sin of Adam has been handed on to successive generations. Sin is universal and has been almost from the beginning, as it is so clearly set down in Genesis 1–11. It is a dimension of being human, and it is this sin, this alienation from God, which called for salvation and redemption by God.

Mary was not conceived virginally, but rather, through natural sexual relations between her parents. The Immaculate Conception is a special privilege granted Mary by virtue of her role as the Mother of God. Her Immaculate Conception, in a sense, represents the "first-fruits" of the redemption wrought by her Son's saving death and resurrection. Mary herself, when approached by the angel Gabriel regarding the desire that God had for her to be the mother of his Son, said, "I am the Lord's maidservant. Let it be done to me as you say" (Luke 1:38). This represents a yes to God's will where a no was just as freely possible. In essence, Mary's yes reverses and undoes the no of Adam and Eve, which brought sin, chaos, and alienation into the world.

The doctrine of the Virginal Birth is clearly attested to and sup- ported by Scripture, as has been indicated. The doctrine of the Immaculate Conception is not explicitly taught in Scripture, but it has a basis in Scripture by implication. Genesis 3:15 has God promising that the woman's offspring shall have victory over the serpent. Mary is called "highly favored" or "full of grace" by Elizabeth in Luke 1:28. Elizabeth goes on in the same chapter to praise Mary as "blessed among all women." These citations imply that Mary, as mother of the sinless One, has a special place and a special role, one that demands that she be preserved from all sin, even from the first moments of her very existence. It is held that Mary did not sin, so dedicated was she to God, so graced was she by God. Yet, having said that, Mary is still saved by her Son, but in a different way than we are. She was preserved by the infinite grace of her divine Son from being touched by sin for even one moment. Thus, gradually in the first Christian millennium, belief in this special grace given Mary developed and spread throughout the Church. The dogma (solemn teaching which must be held by all in the Catholic Church) of the Immaculate Conception was proclaimed by Pope Pius IX (d. 1878) in 1854.

What is the liturgy?
The word *liturgy* comes from a Greek word which means "work of the public." In the Catholic Church, the liturgy is the official public prayer of the Church. The liturgy includes the seven sacraments, the official daily prayer of the Church called the *Liturgy of the Hours,* as well as other rituals and blessings used by the Church that have an official form and standing.

What are the sacraments?
The sacraments are the principal liturgical actions or rites of the Church. As liturgy, the sacraments are official public prayers of the Church. They are never to be understood solely as individual celebrations, but properly as celebrations of the whole Church of which individuals are members. A critical function of the sacraments in this vein, therefore, is the establishment, renewal, and strengthening of *communion* in the Church, a unity with God and a unity one with another as members of the Church.

As rites, the sacraments have an official set form of celebration which, with few exceptions, must be followed. The sacraments, as understood by the Catholic Church, are seven in number: *Baptism, Confirmation, Eucharist, Penance, Anointing of the Sick, Marriage,* and *Holy Orders.* The sacraments, moreover, are rooted, either explicitly or implicitly, in the ministry of Jesus. Some of the sacraments are explicitly commanded by Jesus, such as Baptism (cf. Matthew 28:19; Mark 16:16), Eucharist (cf. Luke 22:19–20; 1 Corinthians 11:23–26), and Penance (cf. John 20:22–23). Others are more implicit, such as the Anointing of the Sick which is grounded in Jesus' own ministry of healing as well as his sharing of the healing ministry with his disciples (cf. Luke 10:9; Mark 6:13).

Sacraments are significant moments in the lives of Catholics. They are celebrated at key junctures of life, such as at Baptism, at Confirmation, at Marriage, or at Holy Orders. They are all moments of grace, that is, celebrations in which God is present, God comes to meet us, and we encounter God. As moments of grace, the sacraments are helps to us as Catholics as we seek to deepen, renew, and strengthen our relationship with the Living God and with the Body of Christ, the Church.

Sacraments are symbolic actions as well. The sacraments all make use of tangible signs and symbols. These include, by way of example, the pouring of water or immersion in water (Baptism), bread and wine as food and drink (Eucharist), the laying on of hands and anointing with sacred oils (Holy Orders, Confirmation, Anointing of the Sick), the joining of hands (Marriage), and the extension of the hand and the sign of the cross imparting forgiveness of sins (Penance or Reconciliation). Tangible signs and symbols are important in Catholicism because we believe that all of creation comes from God's hand and, therefore, natural elements can and do bring the presence and saving action of God to us. As humans, our bodies are crucial. It is through them that we have contact with the world around us. In the celebration of the sacraments, therefore, our senses as well as our minds are properly involved. Thus, the elements of seeing, feeling, touching, tasting, smelling are all part of sacramental celebrations.

What is baptism?

Baptism is a principal celebration in the life of every Catholic, and in the life of most every Christian. It has been said that Christians are made, not born. The means by which Christians are made is *Baptism*, which is a water-bath ritual. The origins of baptism are found in Jewish ritual washings, often practiced as a symbolic washing from sin and guilt. John the Baptist practiced this ritual in the Judean desert (cf. Mark 1:4–9; Luke 3:3–6, 21). Jesus himself may also have baptized in this fashion (cf. John 3:22).

From the beginning, the ritual of a water-bath has been at the heart of the liturgical celebration of initiation, the means by which those who come to faith in Christ are welcomed into the Christian community and become members of the Body of Christ, the Church. Originally, baptism was celebrated only with adults, for they were deemed capable of having the faith needed for such a commitment. Gradually, however, baptism was celebrated with children, and even infants, as whole families converted to the Christian faith. Children and infants not of age were baptized on the basis of the faith of their parents and their parents' commitment to raise them as believers. Indeed, for centuries now, the vast majority of baptisms celebrated in the Catholic Church have been infant baptisms. However, in recent years, a renewed emphasis on adult conversion and adult baptism has emerged.

Baptism itself is celebrated rather simply. Plain water is poured on the head three times as the words, "[Name], *I baptize you in the name of the Father, and of the Son, and of the Holy Spirit,*" are said. Sometimes the person being baptized is totally immersed in a pool of water rather than simply having the water poured in small amounts on his or her head. Other ritual elements, such as anointings with sacred oil, the reception of a baptismal garment, and the reception of a lighted candle, surround the baptismal water ritual. It should be noted that the *Creed,* or the *Profession of Faith,* is made just before the actual baptism is done. This alone should signal the connection between Christian faith and baptism. Adults profess the faith for themselves, whereas children and infants are represented by their parents and godparents.

The Church community itself has an important role in the celebration of baptism, and rightly so, for baptism increases the numbers of members in the Body of Christ. Priests and deacons, as well as other parish members, assist with the preparation for and the celebration of baptism. The godparents themselves have as their primary roles the representation of the community of believers as well as the support of the parents "in their duty as Christian mother and father."

Baptism accomplishes three realities. It joins the baptized person to the Risen Christ, for the baptized identify with Christ in his dying and rising. They die to sin and rise to live for God, to live in Christ. Baptism, furthermore, joins the baptized to the Church, which is the Body of Christ. It admits the baptized to celebrate, in due time, and after proper preparation and formation, the other sacraments. Indeed, baptism has, for this reason, been called the "door" to the sacraments. Finally, on the basis of baptism, there is the good ground for hope in eternal life. This is based on the long-standing insistence of the Church on the centrality of baptism for salvation. It is grounded in the words of Jesus to Nicodemus as found in the Gospel of John: "Amen, amen, I say to you, no one can enter the kingdom of God without being born of water and the Spirit" (cf. John 3:5).

The normal minister for baptism is a bishop, priest, or deacon. However, anyone may baptize if there is danger of death and an ordained minister is not readily available. This often happens in hospitals with newborn infants who are in danger of death.

What is Confirmation?

Confirmation, along with Baptism and the Eucharist, is one of the sacraments of initiation. Confirmation liturgically celebrates and commemorates the outpouring of the Spirit of God on the Church on the day of Pentecost as recorded in the Acts of the Apostles:

> When the time for Pentecost was fulfilled, [the disciples] were all in one place together. And suddenly there came from the sky a noise like a strong driving wind, and it filled the entire house in which they were. Then there appeared to them tongues as of fire, which parted and came to rest on them. And they were all filled with the Holy Spirit and began to speak in different tongues as the Spirit enabled them to proclaim" (cf. Acts 2:1–4).

A baptized person shares in the Pentecost event by being confirmed, just as a person identifies with Christ and shares in his death and resurrection by being baptized.

Confirmation is closely connected to baptism and is important in its own right as a sacrament because it immerses the baptized believer more fully into the Church. It does not celebrate the gift of the Spirit in a believer's life for the first time, for Baptism bestows the Spirit as well. Rather, Confirmation celebrates a new outpouring of the Spirit of God on a believer, the Spirit being given for witness, and with the Spirit, gifts and strength are given so that those who are baptized and confirmed may be effective witnesses for Christ in the world.

Normally, when adults are baptized, they are confirmed immediately, and later in the same liturgical celebration, they receive Holy Communion for the first time. Thus, they in one celebration become fully initiated members of the Church. In the Catholic Church, in most places, for those baptized as infants, some time elapses between Baptism and Confirmation, with young people normally being confirmed sometime in their teen years. There are few exceptions to this rule. In recent years, though, there has been much discussion about the proper age for Confirmation.

The Sacrament of Confirmation is celebrated with the laying on of hands over the candidates accompanied by a prayer calling down the Spirit of God. Then the candidates come forward and are anointed on the forehead in the sign of the cross with a sacred oil called *chrism*, this being olive oil mixed with a sweet fragrance. This anointing bestows the Spirit in a new way, and it conforms, remakes if you will, the confirmed person into the likeness of Christ so that he or she will be able in their own way to be Christ to the world, effective witnesses for him.

The normal minister of Confirmation is the bishop. Priests, under certain conditions, may also confirm. The importance of the bishop in the celebration of Confirmation cannot be stressed enough. Since Confirmation often represents the completion of initiation for a young person, it is entirely proper that this be celebrated and conferred by the leader of the local church or *diocese*, the bishop himself, or if he cannot be present, by someone designated by him.

What is the Eucharist?

We need to clarify some terminology in order to answer these questions effectively. *Communion* refers to the act of receiving (eating and drinking) the body and blood of Jesus Christ under the forms of bread and wine, a central act of Catholic worship. Another common term for this is *Holy Communion. Eucharist* is a word taken from the Greek meaning *thanksgiving*, and it refers to the sacramental celebration of the dying and the rising of Christ for the salvation of all. Part and parcel of this celebration is the rendering of praise and thanksgiving (thus the term *Eucharist*) to God for all God has done for humanity in the past and all that God continues to do even to the present moment for us by way of blessing and deliverance. In the Catholic Church, another name for the Eucharist is the *Mass*. We will discuss the Mass more fully below.

Catholics believe that Jesus is truly and really present in the bread and wine that has been blessed, consecrated, and thus changed into his body and blood. This tenet of our faith is often referred to as the *Real Presence*. As Catholics, when we receive the Eucharist, we do not believe that the bread and wine merely symbolize or represent the body and blood of the Lord. We believe that the bread and wine offered us in Holy Communion *is* the body and blood of the Lord.

How do we explain this? The teaching of the Catholic Church on the Real Presence of Christ in the Eucharistic bread and wine is referred to as *transubstantiation* and it is often misunderstood. This teaching arose in the Middle Ages from attempts to explain that the bread and wine of the Eucharist are more than mere *signs*. Using the thinking of the ancient Greek philosopher Aristotle regarding substance and accidents, the medieval theologians "explained" the mystery of the Eucharist by holding that the *substance* of the bread and wine is changed (transformed) into the *substance* of the body and the blood of Christ, even as the *accidents* of the bread and wine remain the same. This change occurs when the priest, recalling the Last Supper and the words and actions of Jesus on that occasion, takes bread and says the words of Jesus over it: "Take this, all of you, and eat it. This is my body, *which* will be given up for you." In the same way, the wine is changed when the priest takes the cup and says the words of Jesus over it: "Take this, all of you, and drink from it. This is the cup of my blood, the blood of the new and ever-lasting covenant. It will be shed for you and for all so that sins may be forgiven. Do this in memory of me" (cf. Matthew 26:26b–28; Mark 14:22–24a; Luke 22:19–20; 1 Corinthians 11:24–28). On account of this ritual action, which sits at the heart of every Mass, when one receives Holy Communion, one receives the *actual* body and blood of Christ, which is now the substance of what was once simple bread and wine. The *accidents* of the bread and wine remain unchanged, those accidents being, for example, the taste, the smell, the texture, and the appearance, among others.

What is the Mass?

The Mass is, in every respect, the central act of Catholic worship. It is the liturgical event *par excellence* for Catholics, so important a part of Catholic life that no practicing Catholic misses Mass on Sundays for anything but a very good reason. The Mass, the Eucharistic sacrifice, has been described by the Second Vatican Council (1962–1965) as "the summit toward which the activity of the Church is directed; it is also the fount from which all her power flows."[1] So vital is the Mass that it is not only celebrated on Sunday in a solemn fashion, it is also celebrated daily so that Catholics might partake of the sacrament more frequently.

The Mass has its origins in the actions of Jesus himself at the Last Supper. Taking bread and wine, he blessed them and gave them to his disciples as his body and blood. He then commanded that this be done often in his memory, even until he comes again. Having said this, the Last Supper was not a Mass as modern Catholics know the Mass. In the first centuries the Mass evolved to the form that it has even to the present day. It must be remembered that the very first Christians were Jews, devout Jews who regularly participated in Jewish worship in the synagogue and at the Temple in Jerusalem. As the first century neared its end, those Jews who followed and accepted Jesus as Lord and Messiah inevitably were drawn into conflict with official Judaism which did not recognize Jesus of Nazareth as such. Eventually, many of the Jewish Christians were forced to abandon their ancestral faith at great cost. Yet, even as they did so, they brought with them many of the riches found in Jewish traditions and customs. One of these was the form of the synagogue service which consisted of readings from the

---

[1] Cf. *The Constitution on the Sacred Liturgy*, n. 10.

Scriptures, a spoken explanation of the readings and meditation on them, followed by common prayers. Very soon, this format was woven into the Christian Eucharistic service, and it remains as part of the Mass even to this day, that part called the *Liturgy of the Word*. The rest of the Christian Eucharistic service consisted of the "breaking of the bread and the prayers" (cf. Acts 2:42) in memory of the Lord Jesus, what we as Catholics now know as the *Liturgy of the Eucharist*.

The Mass as it is now celebrated is as follows:

Introductory Rites
   Entrance Hymn
   Sign of the Cross and Greeting
   Penitential Rite (in which we call to mind our sins and ask God's mercy)
   Gloria (ancient hymn of praise preferably sung)
   Opening Prayer
Liturgy of the Word
   Reading from the Hebrew Scriptures (in the Easter Season, the Acts of the Apostles)
   Psalm sung in response to the reading
   Reading from a New Testament work other than from the gospels.
   Acclamation before the Gospel (usually *Alleluia!*)
   Gospel Reading
   Homily (explanation, application, reflection on the Scriptures of the day)
   General Intercessions (formal prayers for the needs of the Church, the world, the local community, the sick, and the dead)
Liturgy of the Eucharist
   Preparation of the Altar (during this time a collection is taken and a hymn is sung)
   Prayer over the Gifts of Bread and Wine

Eucharistic Prayer (Great Prayer of Thanksgiving to God for what God has done in Christ)

    Great Amen (the people's response and ratification of what has been prayed)

Communion Rite

    The Lord's Prayer

    The Sign of Peace (usually a handshake, an embrace, or even a kiss)

    The Breaking of the Bread

    Communion of the Ministers and the People

    Hymn sung during or after Communion

Concluding Rite

    Prayer after Communion

    [Announcements]

    Blessing and Dismissal

    Recessional hymn or instrumental music.

This is the general format of the Mass as it is celebrated on Sundays in parishes and dioceses throughout the world.

Why do Christians now celebrate the Sabbath on Sunday, and when did this change occur?

The very earliest Christians were all Jews, and as such they went on the Sabbath to the synagogue to pray and worship. They kept the Sabbath, as Jewish law mandated as a day of rest. The Sabbath was (and is to this day) numbered as the seventh day, or what we know now as Saturday.

However, very early in the Church, a connection was made between the first day of the week (Sunday) and the Lord's resurrection, which took place on that day. As that became more and more emphasized, Sunday came to be called by Christians the "Lord's Day." This happened as early as the end of the first century. Even before that, in some places, Christians gathered for prayer and the "breaking of the bread" in memory of the Lord Jesus on

Sunday evening. We must remember that Sunday was a regular work day for people. It does seem likely that, in the first century at least, Christians did not consider Sunday as the Sabbath in place of Saturday. It is probable that many continued to observe Saturday as the day of rest, and perhaps gathered for worship on various days from one community to another.

We find, however, that around the year 150, Justin Martyr (d. c. 165) writes that the Christian community assembled for the prayers and the breaking of the bread every Sunday, which by then had become the preferred day for doing so. He describes with detail what was done: "the apostles or prophets were read," the presiding minister offered some instruction based on what was read, common prayers were offered, and then bread and wine were blessed with thanksgiving and given to the community.[2]

By the third century, Sunday assumed a special nature among Christians, being called not only the Lord's Day, or the first day of the week, but even the eighth day referring to the creation story of Genesis 1. God created the heavens and the earth and all in them in six days, resting on the seventh. The reference to the eighth day harks us back to the first day when God separated the light from the darkness. Jesus, the Light of the world, rose from the tomb on the "eighth" day (the day after the seventh day, when he rested in the tomb), bringing new, better, eternal light to all. Indeed, the Resurrection of the Lord was seen in itself to be a new act of creation, a sign of the new life, God's power undoing the sin of Adam, destroying its penalty of death imposed on all.

As a consequence of this, labor was seen as incompatible with Sunday. Rest was prescribed. Fasting was suspended, and even kneeling was dispensed with on that day. Therefore, the shift from Saturday observance of the Sabbath to a Sunday observance of the Lord's Day was in place by the third century, and thus it remains.

---

[2] Cf. *Justin Martyr, First Apology, 65–67.*

In the 1970s, in many areas of the world, permission was given for Catholics to participate at Mass on Saturday evening, and thereby fulfill the serious obligation of participating in Sunday Mass weekly. This practice is grounded in the Jewish custom of starting the next day the evening before at sundown. It has proven to be quite popular, with Saturday evening Masses generally well-attended. In recent years, Pope John Paul II has reminded Catholics of the centrality of observing Sunday as the Lord's Day through worship and through abstaining from unnecessary work.[3]

What is confession or the Sacrament of Penance? Who has the power to forgive?

In order to understand the question "Who has the power to forgive?" we need to distinguish between what *kinds* of forgiveness we are discussing. On the ordinary everyday level, of course, everyone has the "power" to forgive, even, in the view of Jesus, the *duty* to forgive those who hurt or offend us. Forgiveness is an essential dimension of healthy human relationships and it is part and parcel of the process of reconciliation on the human level.

On a religious, cultic, or sacramental level as regards the Catholic Church, we speak of forgiveness in connection with the Sacrament of Reconciliation, also known as the Sacrament of Penance, or, more popularly, *confession.* In John 20:22–23, the Risen Jesus breathes on his disciples, and he says to them: "Receive the Holy Spirit. Whose sins you forgive are forgiven them and whose sins you retain are retained." The Catholic Church has always held this passage to be the biblical basis for the Sacrament of Reconciliation.

From the beginning of the Church, the ministry of reconciliation has always been assigned to official ministers of the Church. It was first the responsibility of the bishop, as the leader of the local church, to reconcile sinners with the Church and to pronounce for-

---

[3] Cf. John Paul II, *Dies Domini* [The Day of the Lord], Apostolic Letter, 1998.

giveness on behalf of God and the Church. Later, as the Church grew and expanded, this ministry was also shared with priests, who, acting in the name of the bishop and on behalf of the Church, heard confessions, assigned acts of penance (usually prayers, the giving of alms, or some form of fasting), and then pronounced *absolution*, the formal declaration of the forgiveness of sins in the name of the Father, and of the Son, and of the Holy Spirit. It has not been the practice in the Catholic Church since the beginning to share the formal, official ministry of reconciliation, the "power" of forgiveness, with anyone other than bishops and priests. Furthermore, priests exercise this power only with the permission of their bishop, what is known as *jurisdiction*, given in what is known as the *faculty to absolve*. Such jurisdiction, such a faculty for absolving sin in the name of God and of the Church, is normally given at priestly ordination.

Many people, both inside the Catholic Church, and outside it, question the need for confession to a priest. "Why can I not go directly to God and receive forgiveness for my sins?" they ask. Indeed, it is quite true that one can go to God and ask for forgiveness. Within the Catholic tradition, there are numerous prayers of contrition, asking God's mercy and pardon of our sins. In the case of lesser sins (as opposed to *mortal* or what we term *grave* or more serious sins), these "acts of contrition" as the prayers are commonly called, do bring forgiveness from God if they are sincerely prayed and if the person praying resolves to overcome his or her sins and to make restitution for all harm done by them. Even in the case of mortal or serious sin, an act of *perfect* contrition can be the means by which those sins are forgiven. An act of *perfect* contrition is essentially sorrow for sin solely because it is such an offense against God, a good, loving, and gracious God. Such contrition, such sorrow for sin, must not be motivated by fear of hell or self-loathing at what one has done because of shame and disgrace. An act of perfect contrition is made only when recourse to the

Sacrament of Reconciliation is not possible at the moment. One must resolve to make a sacramental confession as soon as possible.

What is the benefit of sacramental confession? Why should Catholics confess their sins to a priest? One answer to this is found in that we as Catholics believe that Jesus intended it to be that way. The Church was established to carry on the work and the will of Christ, and an important dimension of the work of Christ was the ministry of forgiveness of sins. The Catholic Church carries on that mission through the use of the Sacrament of Reconciliation.

Another answer to those questions is found in the psychologically healthy unburdening of soul that this sacrament makes available. While it may not always be comfortable to admit to another that we have not lived the way we should and then to go on and enumerate what we have done or what we have not done, there is a great sense of freedom, liberation, and relief that comes with actually telling another our sins. The priest, being ordained, represents God, who called him to the ministry. Being human, the priest represents the Church, for he, too, is a member of it. The weakness of the concept of confessing only to God is found in the fact that sin is rarely simply an offense against God. Our sins also hurt other people. The priest, sitting in the Sacrament of Reconciliation, affords us as Catholics to be reconciled effectively both with God and the Church, both of which he represents. An additional dimension of this ministry is found in what is referred to as the *seal of confession*. A priest may never, ever, for any reason, divulge to another what he has heard in the Sacrament of Reconciliation, even if his life depends on it. This seal protects the integrity and the confidentiality of the sacrament.

Finally, the Catholic practice of confession offers Catholics a real assurance that their sins are forgiven. Not only have they confessed their sins with painful honesty, they have also had the assurance that another has heard their confession, prayed with them, assigned them some form of penance whereby they can try to make up in some way for their sins, and then absolved them with beautiful and prayerful words announcing the forgiveness of God.

The Sacrament of Penance is normally celebrated individually, with an individual penitent coming to a priest to confess his or her sins, to receive a penance, and to then be absolved of his or her sins. Very often, there are set times when the priest is available for the celebration of this sacrament, usually sometime on a Saturday afternoon. Of course, a person may request a priest to hear his or her confession at any time. On occasion, the Sacrament of Penance may be celebrated in a group context, with a common gathering for song, Scripture readings, reflection and meditation, and the examination of conscience. At the end of this service, there is opportunity for individuals to confess their sins one on one to a priest of their choice. Usually there are several priests present. Finally, in extreme circumstances, *general absolution* may be granted, that is, absolution of sins without actually confessing them to a priest beforehand. This could be warranted in the event of a sudden catastrophe, such as a plane crash or a military attack. It might be warranted if there are not enough priests on a given occasion to hear all the confessions of the people who have gathered. It must be stated that the bishops of the United States do not generally permit the use of general absolution.

The way the sacrament is celebrated is as follows:

Welcome extended to the penitent.
Invitation to prayer and to trust in God's mercy.
A brief reading from Scripture.
Confession of sins.
Giving of advice and then the imposition of a penance (some gesture meant to signal a change of heart and a desire to make reparation for sin).
Prayer of sorrow (commonly called the *Act of Contrition*) recited by the penitent.

Absolution (see below). The priest extends his right hand over the penitent, saying the words of absolution, ending with the sign of the cross in the name of the Father, and of the Son, and of the Holy Spirit.
Proclamation of praise of God for his mercy, and dismissal.

Those words of absolution would well serve as a fine summary of what the power of forgiveness is in the Catholic Church:

God, the Father of mercies,
through the death and resurrection of His Son,
has reconciled the world to Himself,
and has sent the Holy Spirit among us
for the forgiveness of sins.
Through the ministry of the Church,
may God give you pardon and peace, and
I absolve you from your sins, in the name of the Father, and
of the Son, and of the Holy Spirit.

Can the Church forgive a murderer?

Yes. It is the constant teaching of the Catholic Church that *all* sins are capable of being forgiven by God. Indeed, there are some sins that are far more serious and devastating to others than other sins, but all sins, including murder, can be forgiven by God. What is required of the sinner for God's forgiveness is a true sorrow for sins committed and a desire to amend his or her life. Once the sin is confessed and the person who has so sinned is truly sorry and firmly intends to avoid that sin the future, God's pardon and mercy are assured.

This teaching of the Church in no way mitigates the seriousness of sin, and the particular gravity of very serious sins. Quite to the contrary, the ministry of reconciliation for sinners entrusted to the Church by the Lord is a ground for great hope. As terrible as sin can be, God's goodness, mercy, and love promised to the sinner who is repentant are all the greater.

By way of passing reference, the gospels speak of "a sin against the Holy Spirit," a "blasphemy against the Holy Spirit," which cannot be forgiven. Scholars and theologians have debated for centuries over just what constitutes this sin. A prevailing notion on this question holds that this sin is *final impenitence*, an unwillingness to admit one's sins with true sorrow for them and a desire to turn from them. This amounts essentially to a refusal of God's gracious gift of mercy, a gift which, like all gifts, must be *received* in order to be effective. The result of this is the loss of salvation and eternal damnation, an eternity spent in hell, a state of the total absence of God made all the worse by the ever-present knowledge that this state was freely chosen by no one but the lost soul and the ever-present knowledge that it could have been otherwise had that person so chosen.

What is the Catholic view of heaven and hell?
For Catholics, life in this world is meaningful. Our moral choices, our *life* choices have consequences which lead to our salvation (life with God in heaven for eternity) or our damnation (the loss of eternal life with God, or existence in hell). It has become somewhat fashionable in recent times for many to mitigate or diminish the importance of our moral choices in this life.

When our lives in this world come to an end at our death, it is the Catholic belief that all of us are destined for either heaven or hell, and that this destiny will hinge on the question of whether or not we lived our lives seeking communion with God and accepting the grace of God, what I would say amounts to "placing God and the will of God at the center of our lives." If we have striven to do that, then there is great hope that we will attain the gift of eternal life and communion with God in the state that Christians call "heaven." If we have not done that, that is, if we have deliberately and consistently pushed God and the will of God out of our lives, then there is the possibility that we will in the end be "lost," that is, that we will spend all of eternity in isolation from God in a state of existence that Christians call hell.

Pope John Paul II, in catechetical instructions in recent years, has spoken of both heaven and hell. The Holy Father speaks of both not in terms of places, but of states of being. When life in this world ends, eternity begins, and with eternity, space and time no longer have relevance or force. Thus, we cannot properly speak of heaven as a place up there where we spend all our day with God. Likewise, we cannot properly speak of hell as a place down there where there is fire and everlasting torment. Both of these descriptions, well known in the popular mind, are images, word-pictures as it were, which help us with our limited capacities for true understanding to get at what heaven and hell are like in *actuality*.

Heaven is a state of being, a state of existence which involves eternal communion with God, total union with the Source of all that is. In the past, theologians referred to heaven in terms of the *Beatific Vision* (the "blessed" vision), that unmediated, direct apprehension and delight in God as God truly is. In this life, such an experience is unattainable. It can only become a reality for us beyond the grave. Furthermore, in heaven, should we attain it, we will enjoy communion with all the holy ones, the saints, the "holy men and women of every time and place" who live forever as friends of God.

Will we have a body in heaven? In the past, erroneously, some maintained that death means the liberation of the soul, the spiritual life principle, from the "prison" of the body, and as such, there is, as they maintained, no place for the body in heaven. Yet, we know in our faith that the Risen Jesus appeared visible and tangible in his body after death (cf. John 20:17, 27; Luke 24:39–43; Matthew 28:9, 17), a body that was glorified, freed from the limits of time and space (cf. John 20:19; Luke 24:1–35). Thus, we must maintain, on this basis as well as our firm belief in the resurrection of the body, that we will have bodies in heaven. We are, as it were, embodied spirits here and now. So, too, in heaven, our entire spiritual selves, our embodied spirits, shall be present to God.

Hell is best understood as the state of existence after death characterized by the eternal loss of God. Those who are in hell, if there are any, are there because of the choice(s) they have made in their lifetimes, the free, conscious, and deliberate choice to turn away from God, to refuse God's offer to enter into a life-transforming love relationship with God. All sin finds its grounding in this choice to turn away from God and what God wills, to refuse to enter into and deepen one's relationship with God in love.

Does God send people to hell? Is hell to be best understood as a *punishment* from God? This would seem to not be the case. The New Testament makes it quite clear that God loves the world and all who live in it, and that God desires the salvation of all (cf. John 3:16–18). Furthermore, it is also clear from the New Testament that God shows us generous patience (cf. 2 Peter 3:9), allowing us more than ample time to come to our senses, to repent, and to return to God. Given this, how can we maintain that there is a hell in the first place? The most probable answer to this is found in the likelihood that hell is *not God's* choice, but the ultimate, sad choice of the sinner who finally and definitively rejects God's offer of love and grace. God never rejects us. If there is any rejection, that comes from us and it amounts to a rejection of God by us.

Hell is invariably described in Scripture and elsewhere in terms of fire, pain, and torment. None of this must be taken literally. However, what all of that imagery does underscore is essentially true, and that is that hell is a place of suffering and death precisely because it is a state without God, the only One who brings consolation, true peace, and real healing. A helpful insight is given in understanding hell as the diametrical opposite of heaven. If heaven is a state of eternal communion with God, a communion that brings lasting joy and real peace, then hell is a state of eternal self-chosen isolation from God that brings horror, the pain of loss, and endless torment (no peace). The pain of hell is precisely that of an isolation from God that is both eternal and freely chosen. This isolation will never end, and the one so isolated must "live" with the awareness, the added pain that he or she is "there" because he or she willfully chose it.

Is there anyone in that state called hell? The Catholic Church has never taught that there is. Is it possible that there is no hell? That would be possible *only* if we are not the radically free people created as such by God, radically free to choose to accept or reject many things, but most important of all, a life with God at its center or a life without God. The irony of hell is found in the fact that its existence underscores the truth of our radical freedom as human beings, a freedom that can, in fact, go so far as to reject God, the Source of our being in whose image and likeness we have been created. The reality of hell also clearly stresses how seriously God takes our radical freedom.

Those who lean toward the denial of the existence of hell and the reality of sin tend to focus far too heavily on the *mercy* of God without a balanced focus on the *justice* of God. These people tend to hold that our sins do not matter, that God will readily forgive them, and that we need not fear death and judgment at all. While most of us do hope that God will be merciful with us, not dealing with us as our sins deserve, we should never take the foolish and illogical leap toward holding that God does not take sin seriously. The Scriptures, both the Old Testament and the New, strongly teach that God does call us to holiness of life and repentance of our sins. We need only recall the words from the Old Testament, "Be holy, for I, the LORD, your God, am holy," or the admonition of Jesus found in the gospels in which he states that we must be perfect as the heavenly Father is perfect. Sin is not taken lightly by God. God created us as radically free, and God respects that freedom even to the extent that we might choose to utterly reject God and live eternally in isolation from God.

In summary then, we who are Christians are called to live life seriously in a daily relationship with God and Jesus Christ, living lives grounded in the teaching and example of Jesus. If we do so sincerely, even if not perfectly, there is great hope that God, a God of mercy, will forgive our sins and welcome us into eternal communion with God. We can choose to do otherwise, and we do so at our personal, eternal peril.

What is the Anointing of the Sick?

The gospels again and again relate the concern that Jesus had for those who were sick. He is regularly described by the gospel writers as a man who reached out to the lame, the blind, the lepers, the deaf, the mute, all who were afflicted with maladies of any kind. Jesus' concern for the sick was not something that began and ended with him and his ministry. He commanded his disciples during his lifetime to cure the sick and drive out demons (cf. Luke 10:9; also Matthew 10:8). After the death and resurrection of Jesus, the apostles carried on the healing work of the Lord. They cured the sick, raised the dead, and drove out demons (cf. Acts 3:1–10, 5:12–16, 14:8–13).

In the Letter of James, the author makes specific reference to a special ritual of anointing for the sick: "Is anyone among you sick? He should summon the presbyters of the church, and they should pray over him and anoint him with oil in the name of the Lord, and the prayer of faith will save the sick person, and the Lord will raise him up. If he has committed any sins, he will be forgiven" (cf. James 5:14–15). This passage has been consistently pointed to by the Catholic Church as the basis for the Sacrament of the Anointing of the Sick. This sacrament has been celebrated in the Church from the earliest days to the present.

As the centuries progressed, this sacrament became more and more associated with extreme illness, even death itself. It was understood to be less a sacrament for those facing serious illness, the weakness of advancing years, or mental problems, and more as a final preparation for death. As a result, the sacrament was not called for until the last possible moments, for to call for it indicated that all hope was lost, that death was imminent. Even the name for this sacrament, *Extreme Unction* (the "last anointing"), used for many centuries until it was formally changed by the Second Vatican Council, gives us an insight into how it was understood and used.

The Sacrament of the Anointing of the Sick is celebrated either as a communal event within or outside of Mass, or as a simple ritual in hospitals and convalescent homes, or even dramatically shortened in cases of emergency and imminent death. The ritual calls for anointing the forehead and the hands with the *oil of the sick*, using the formulae: "Through this holy anointing, may the Lord in his love and mercy help you with the grace of the Holy Spirit" (said as the forehead is anointed), and "May the Lord who frees you from sin save you and raise you up" (said as the hands are anointed). There is a provision for other parts of the body to be anointed, if necessary, saying nothing additional.

The effect of this sacrament is not always physical healing and wholeness, although sometimes healing does result. More often, the sacrament has spiritual affects. It imparts a deep sense of peace, of being at one with God, accepting God's will whatever it may be. It can and does help people to prepare for and face death.

The normal minister of the Sacrament of the Anointing of the Sick is either a bishop or a priest. Deacons and lay ministers are not permitted to anoint the sick, likely based on the explicit reference in James to *presbyters*, which excludes all save bishops and priests.

What is a Catholic funeral like?
Catholics are normally buried in richly symbolic rites that extend from the wake to the time of actual burial. The central event in a Catholic funeral ritual is the funeral Mass, normally celebrated in the church to which the deceased belonged and where the deceased worshiped. The afternoon or evening before, during the calling

hours at the funeral home or in the church (where that is the custom), if there are such calling hours, a brief *vigil* service is celebrated. This service, based on the Scriptures, offers hope and comfort to the bereaved as they sit and keep vigil with the body of the deceased.

The funeral Mass itself centers on baptismal imagery. The fact that the deceased was baptized is recalled in several highly symbolic ways. The body is welcomed at the door of the church and sprinkled with holy water which reminds all present of the waters of baptism once poured over the deceased person. A white cloth, or *pall*, is placed on the casket as a reminder of the fact that the deceased person at his or her baptism *clothed* himself or herself in Christ. The casket is placed in the church near the lighted Easter Candle, a symbol of the Risen Christ. The readings and homily are grounded in the hope offered all of us who have died with Christ in baptism and hope to live with him. The body is incensed as a sign of reverence to it which was a temple of the Holy Spirit.

The body is buried in the cemetery after a brief prayer service commending the person to God and yielding his or her body to the ground, "earth to earth, ashes to ashes, dust to dust," until that day when the Lord will waken the deceased person to glory. Very often, in the United States, the family of the deceased may place a flower on the casket, or in some instances throw dirt into the grave. It is uncommon in this country for the family to stay to see the body actually lowered into the grave.

Cremation, the burning of the body of the deceased, is now permitted by the Church, as long as there is implied in the option for cremation no denial of the Church's faith in the resurrection of the body. The scattering of ashes is discouraged. It is strongly recommended that the ashes be buried or entombed.

What is Holy Orders?
Early in his ministry, Jesus gathered close associates around him, men who would share intimately in his mission and continue that

mission after his death. These first close associates came to be known as *apostles* (meaning, literally, "those who are sent"). These men were authorized to preach, to heal the sick, to drive out demons, and to proclaim the coming of the reign of God (cf. Matthew 10:1–4; Mark 1:16–20, 2:13–14, 3:13–19; Luke 6:12–16, 9:1–6). Gradually, others were included in the circle of those authorized to share in Jesus' work, such as the seventy-two sent out to prepare Jesus' way in the towns and villages ahead of him (cf. Luke 10:1–12). After the death of Jesus, still others were added to the number of those ministering in his name, such as Saul of Tarsus, who would become St. Paul (cf. Acts 9:1–30; Galatians 1:11–24), and Matthias, who replaced Judas Iscariot, the disciple who betrayed Jesus (cf. Acts 1:15–26).

The apostles themselves began to realize that they could not do everything by themselves and that they had to associate others in the work of building up the Church. In their missionary work, they moved from place to place, preaching the gospel and establishing local communities of believers (called *churches*). When they left the various locales, they designated certain individuals as leaders of the community in their place. Still others were designated to distribute food and to tend to the needs of the poor. By the end of the first century, we see, even in the New Testament, the gradual emergence of a structured form of ministry in the Christian Church, a three-tiered hierarchy of ministers referred to as bishops, presbyters, and deacons. This was not uniform among all the earliest local church communities at first, but it soon became well established throughout the Church.

It must be stressed that all ministry in the Church is understood to be a *sharing in the ministry and the work of Christ*. As a result, it is Christ who calls individuals to the ministry, and that call (referred to as a *vocation*) is discerned and ratified as authentic by the Church. Only then may that person be *ordained*, that is, officially designated as a minister of one rank or another. The way ordination has been celebrated in the Christian Church has remained fairly simple and uniform for much of the history of the Church. It involves the ratification of the call of the candidate by the bishop, the examination of the candidate as to his willingness to assume the office, the laying on of hands, and the prayer of consecration.

There are three ranks, or levels, in the Sacrament of Holy Orders: bishop, presbyter, and deacon. The highest level, which represents the fullness of priesthood, is that of bishop. Bishops are men known for holiness, integrity, knowledge, and orthodoxy. They are known also for their leadership capabilities. Ultimately appointed by the Pope, the Bishop of Rome, bishops serve as the closest associates and colleagues of the Pope and are called to be concerned for the needs of the whole Church, and not simply those of the local churches over which they preside. Bishops share in the ministry of Christ in a particular way by teaching, governing, and sanctifying. They teach authentically and authoritatively in the name of Christ, relying on the Scriptures and the Tradition of the Church. They govern and lead the Church, ensuring proper order and direction. As such, bishops are often called *shepherds* and *successors of the Apostles.* Their ministry of sanctifying is evident in that they can preside at the celebration of all the sacraments. Only they can ordain. Normally they are the proper ministers of Confirmation. They regulate the celebration of prayer and liturgy both in their own dioceses and in the Church as a whole.

Presbyters, now commonly referred to as *priests*, are the principal co-workers with the bishops. Their presence is more visible to the Catholic faithful than that of the bishops, for priests preside over and direct parish life wherein most Catholics come into contact with the Church. Priests share in the ministry of the bishop by celebrating the Mass, preaching, hearing confessions and absolving from sin, anointing the sick, baptizing, confirming under certain circumstances, witnessing and blessing marriages, and teaching. Priests also conduct funeral and burial services. They provide pastoral care to the people entrusted to them. Priests also work in hospitals, prisons, schools, colleges, and various agencies.

Deacons are assistants to the bishop and work under his direction and that of the pastor of the parish to which they are assigned. In the parish, deacons assist at Mass. They preach, baptize, and witness and bless marriages. They teach in religious education programs and provide instructions to converts. They visit the sick and prepare couples for marriage. They may do other things in the parish and on a wider level as their expertise warrants. In the early Church, the office of deacon stood on its own as a valid ministry. Over time, it suffered from reduced importance, being understood as little more than a step on the way to the priesthood. The Second Vatican Council (1962–1965) ordered that the diaconate (as the order is properly called) be restored in its own right. Furthermore, the council mandated that the admission of married men to the diaconate be studied. Pope Paul VI in 1972 restored the order of deacon to its proper place and opened it to married as well as celibate men.

Does your Church require celibacy? And if so, why?

Celibacy, first and foremost, is a way of life characterized by the voluntary renunciation of marriage in response to a call and a grace from God. Without that call and that grace, the celibate life would be quite difficult, if not impossible, to live out. In the Catholic Church, celibacy is obligatory as a way of life for all bishops, almost all priests, and some deacons.

In the Rite of Ordination for Deacons, there is a moment when the promise of celibacy is noted liturgically. Only those being ordained deacons who are not yet married must make this promise. A married man may be ordained to the diaconate, the lowest level of the Sacrament of Holy Orders, but it is understood that, should his wife die, he would not be permitted to marry again. In some cases, deacons for whom this becomes an issue, either for personal reasons or because they have young children who need a maternal influence, may be dispensed from the diaconal ministry.

Normally, all priests in the Western Catholic Church, referred to as the *Latin Rite,* must live celibate lives. The one exception is for Episcopal priests who become Catholics and seek to exercise ministry in the Catholic Church. They are dispensed from the promise of celibacy and are then ordained Catholic priests. All bishops in the Catholic Church must live celibately.

Interestingly, in the Eastern Rites, such as the Byzantine Rite, the Maronite Rite, and the Armenian Rite, churches in communion with Rome but with their own particular traditions in liturgy and theology, priests may be married, but they must be so *prior* to ordination, and they may not remarry after ordination if their spouse dies. No married man is eligible for the office of bishop.

In the gospels, Jesus commends celibacy as a valid way of life for those who are thus called to that way of life (Matthew 19:11–12). In the Gospel of Luke, the Sadducees, who denied that there was resurrection after death, came to Jesus and presented him with a question regarding a woman who was married and widowed to seven men, all brothers, and yet died childless. Their question? "At the resurrection, whose wife will she be?" Jesus answers their question by stating that in heaven we live as the angels. No one is taken in marriage. Thus, marriage, it seems, is purely an earthly reality. The unmarried celibate life, by implication, is a reflection of the kingdom of heaven. St. Paul, in his First Letter to the Corinthians, commends celibacy for those who can live it. However, he clearly acknowledges that not all can live that life. Those who could not live celibately should marry and thus avoid sin and grow in holiness (cf. I Corinthians 7:1–9, 27–28, 36). Adding to the "glamour" of celibacy was belief in the *imminent Parousia,* the return of Christ, which was expected at any moment, soon and very soon. With Christ coming so soon, what was the point of marrying and raising a family?

Beyond the New Testament period, at first, there was no clear uniformity when it came to the question of a celibate clergy. Indeed, it seems that at first, most in the ministry were married. An interesting point by way of illustration is the imposition of excommunication on any bishop who abandoned his wife for the sake of personal piety. Yet, it seems that quite early on, there were moves made toward imposing celibacy on the clergy. At first, it was enjoined on all who lived as monks or hermits, practicing the life of prayer and self-denial, either in a community or in solitude. Gradually, there were moves made to impose the requirement on all clerical ministers in the Church. At first, owing to several pressuring factors, there was an exclusion of marriage after receiving orders. Later, it was also mandated that a cleric whose wife died could not remarry.

It must be admitted with honesty that this requirement of a celibate way of life, while generally and faithfully lived out by most clergy in the Catholic Church, has not always been universally observed. Violations of the promise of celibacy have occurred, and when they occur today, are often occasions of scandal. Moreover, concerns about Church property and holdings, especially in regard to clergy with children and the question of inheritances, led Pope Benedict VIII (d. 1024) to protect Church property from being bequeathed to children of deceased clergy. Later, Pope Gregory VII (d. 1085) imposed the requirement of celibacy on all clergy.

The Reformers had mixed views of celibacy. Luther was in favor of a celibate clergy at first, but over time he came to condemn it. Calvin held a more moderate view, maintaining that while celibacy was certainly an acceptable means of serving God, it was no more valuable than the married state. At the present, celibacy remains *optional* in most Protestant denominations, and optional with limitations in the Orthodox Church.

Within the Catholic Church, celibacy as a way of life for clerics was reaffirmed strongly, in reaction to the views of the Reformers, by the Council of Trent (1545–1563). In its affirmation of celibacy as a way of life, Trent did not mean to demean marriage. Indeed, Trent affirmed both the value of celibacy as well as the value of marriage.

Subsequently, repeated affirmations of celibacy as obligatory for clerics in the Catholic Church were made. This is the case with the Second Vatican Council (1962–1965), Pope Paul VI (d. 1978), the World Synod of Catholic Bishops held in 1971, and more recently, the present pope, John Paul II.

Within the Catholic Church, the growing shortage of priests is raising the question of the validity of *mandatory* or *obligatory* celibacy as a requirement for priestly ordination. Again and again, the discussion of ordaining married men as priests continues to surface. For his part, Pope John Paul II has resisted any petitions to relax this requirement.

What is the Catholic understanding of marriage?

In Genesis 1:24, after the creation of the man and woman, it is written: "that is why a man leaves his father and mother and clings to his wife, and the two of them become one body." This biblical understanding of marriage was affirmed by Jesus himself, who underscored the sanctity of this union when he quoted this passage in the gospels, in response to a question from some Pharisees: "Have you not read that from the beginning the Creator 'made them male and female' and said 'For this reason a man shall leave his father and mother and be joined to his wife, and the two shall become one flesh'? So they are no longer two, but one flesh. Therefore, what God has joined together, no human being must separate" (cf. Matthew 19:4–6 and Mark 10:6–9).

Following upon this teaching of Jesus, the Catholic Church understands marriage to be a most serious and a most sacred union of man and woman as husband and wife. A marriage is more than a mere social convention, as important as that understanding is for the good order and increase of society. It is more than a mere human relationship. Marriage, in the understanding of the Catholic Church, is a covenantal relationship. It is a *sacrament* in that it involves an encounter with God. It is God who creates the partners in marriage, and it is God who brings the man and woman together, sealing their love in a sacred and permanent bond. Marriage is a relationship that endures, as the wedding vows state, "until death we do part"; or in its more modern form, each spouse says to the other, "I will love you and honor you all the days of my life." Based on the teaching of Jesus and thus reflected in the liturgical celebration of marriage, a true marriage, a relationship entered into with full and proper consent by each spouse, endures for life. It is not possible to break that relationship. Even civil divorce does not render a marriage null in the eyes of the Church. This is the basis of the Catholic prohibition on divorce and remarriage.

Normally, marriage between two Catholic parties is celebrated within the Mass. The Rite of Marriage begins following the homily (sermon). Before the parties may enter into marriage, they must first publicly state their freedom and their intention of doing so. Questions are asked of them, questions to which each party must respond individually. The first question: "Have you come here freely today and without reservation to give yourselves to each other in marriage?" indicates that both spouses are freely choosing to marry and are under no coercion. The second question: "Will you love and honor each other as husband and wife for the rest of your lives?" indicates that both spouses understand the seriousness of this relationship, that it ends only when either one of the spouses dies. The third question: "Will you accept children lovingly from God and bring them up according to the law of Christ and his Church?" indicates the prominence that the Catholic Church gives to marriage as a life-giving union, as the means by which God has ordained the increase of the human race. In those cases where childbearing is not possible (such as is the case when the spouses are beyond childbearing age), the third question may be omitted.

Once these questions are asked and answered properly, the spouses are invited to join their right hands and declare their "consent" before God and the Church. With that, each spouse exchanges the vow of marriage with the other. In essence, each spouse gives his or her heart to the other. This exchange is witnessed not only by the minister representing the Church (either a priest or a deacon) as well as the legal witnesses and family and friends gathered for the wedding. It is also witnessed by God himself, who is the One who brings this union into actuality. Once this exchange has occurred, the man and woman are, in fact, husband and wife. Following upon the vows there is the blessing and exchange of rings, seen as signs of love and fidelity between the newly united spouses. The wedding ceremony also includes a special blessing for the couple.

In cases where a Catholic marries someone who is not a Catholic, the ceremony is adapted accordingly. It is normally best to celebrate marriages that involve another religious tradition, whether Christian or non-Christian, outside of Mass.

Catholics may be married outside of Catholic churches, and even have their marriages witnessed by a minister other than a Catholic priest or deacon, provided that they have received permission from their bishop. This permission, called a *dispensation*, is readily given if there is a sufficient and weighty reason for doing so. Normally, the proper *form* of marriage for Catholics is that it must be celebrated before a priest or deacon and two witnesses. Under no circumstances may a Catholic be married validly by a civil official, such as a justice of the peace, a judge, or a magistrate.

It should also be stressed that marriages involving a mixture of religious traditions require special care and attention, especially as regards the liturgical ceremony and the raising of children. In former times, such marriages, when celebrated before a Catholic priest or deacon, were not celebrated in church, but in another place, usually the *rectory*, the priests' residence or parish house. Such is no longer the case. Indeed, in circumstances wherein the celebration of marriage in a church would cause difficulties for the other spouse and his or her family, permission is readily given to celebrate the wedding in a hall or other suitable place. As regards children, in former times, the Catholic party had to swear to raise the children as Catholics before the marriage could be celebrated. This requirement has been softened somewhat. Now the Catholic party must swear to do all in his or her power to see to it that the children are raised as Catholics.

What is an annulment?

Contrary to popular opinion, an annulment is *not* a "Catholic divorce." As stated above, the Catholic Church firmly holds that a marriage validly celebrated and contracted cannot be broken or ended by anything other than death. "What God has joined, let no man separate," are the words of Jesus, which serve as the basis of this. The practice of granting annulments in the Church arose as a pastoral response to the phenomenon of broken and ended marriages. An annulment is essentially a statement that the marriage entered into by the spouses and now ended by civil divorce was never a valid one in the eyes of the Church based on the law of the Church. An annulment does not deny the existence of a relationship or a marriage recognized under civil law. It states, rather, that in the eyes of the Church, a valid canonical marriage between the partners never existed. Some marriages are declared null because they could not have been entered into validly in the first place, such as would be seen in the rather highly unlikely scenario of a marriage between siblings. Other marriages are declared null because the *consent*, the moment which seals the bond, when the spouses give themselves to each other for the rest of their lives, was defective in some way. Defective consent can be grounded in manifest immaturity, psychological disturbances, and the like. In these cases, such grounds must be established as existent *prior* to the wedding. If it cannot be established with certainty that there were grounds for defective consent evident prior to the marriage, it becomes difficult, if not impossible, for a marriage to be declared null.

What is the Catholic teaching on sexual morality?

In modern society, especially since the 1960s, a great laxity has taken hold as regards sexual behavior and sexual norms. A review of the popular press and the media would lead one to see this dimension of our humanity as a game, something to be played with, something to be exploited for simple physical and emotional pleasure without much responsibility attached to the choices made. Such a view of sexuality is harmful, and more than that, dehumanizing. It flies in the face of the clear biblical teaching on the sanctity of human sexuality. The Old Testament contains numerous passages upholding the sanctity of sexual behavior, with just penalties indicated for the violations of those norms. In the New Testament, both the words of Jesus as well as the writings of the apostles continue the same emphasis. For example, Jesus himself broadens the prohibition on adulterous behavior by considering lustful looks as adulterous behavior. Adultery can be committed not only in deed, but in thoughts and in words (cf. Matthew 5:27–30). St. Paul in his letters identifies certain types of sexual immorality as equivalent to idolatry (cf. Romans 1:24–28, 1 Corinthians 5:1–13). In the face of such temptations, St. Paul urges us to remember that the "body is not for immorality, but for the Lord, and the Lord is for the body." He reminds us that our bodies are temples of the Holy Spirit, that we are not our own, that we have been purchased, and at a price (cf. 1 Corinthians 6:13; 19–20).

Grounded in this teaching, the Catholic Church holds that any and every form of sexual behavior outside of marriage, be it in thought, word, or deed, is contrary to the will of God and sinful. The sexual faculties we have received from God are a tremendous source of power, power given to be co-creators with the Lord in generating new life. Such power can be abused, and often enough with tragic consequences. The only proper medium for the use of our sexual faculties is the marital relationship. It can also be said, in truth, that abuses of sexuality can and do happen in marriage.

One spouse is not to look on the other as an object of lustful pleasure. Rather, sexual behavior in marriage is meant to be an expression of love, an expression of how much one truly values and cherishes the other.

How does the Catholic Church now understand Judaism?

The Second Vatican Council, held between 1962 and 1965, was a landmark event in the history of the relationship between Catholics and Jews and in the official Catholic teaching on Judaism. In its *Declaration on the Relationship of the Church to Non-Christian Religions*, known in Latin as *Nostra Aetate*, Vatican II placed a great deal of emphasis on the relationship between Catholicism and Judaism and a new understanding of Judaism on the part of the Catholic Church. This was rooted in the deep concern that Pope John XXIII (d. 1963), who summoned the council, had about the relationship between the Catholic Church and Judaism.

Vatican II notes that in Judaism are to be found the beginning of the Church's faith and our election for salvation as Christians. The Jews are considered even to the present day the Chosen People, most dear to God. God does not go back on His promises or His choices, and as such there is a permanence to the covenant established by God with Moses. The gifts bestowed and the call to be a people "peculiarly His own" remain intact to the end of time (cf. Romans 11:29). We in the Christian Church are indeed the "new People of God," but our election comes to us through Judaism, for our Savior was Jewish. We are, as St. Paul says, the branch grafted on to the vine, which is Israel (cf. Romans 11:16–24).

The council fathers specifically deplored and condemned the idea long held that all Jews bear the responsibility for the death of Jesus and as such must be reviled and rejected as "Christ-killers" or as guilty of "deicide" ("killing God"). It is certainly the case that no Jews today and indeed not all Jews who lived at the time of Christ bear such responsibility. More than that, to say that the Jews have been repudiated and rejected by God, with an attempt to justify such a view based on Scripture, is to be repudiated. The abuse and mistreatment of the Jewish people at the hands of Christians, seen in their being ostracized, forced to convert to Christianity, discriminated against, stereotyped—all of this is to be deplored as behavior unworthy of the One who has called us in Christ. One cannot keep the commandments as Christ taught us, by loving God and our neighbor as ourselves, if one bears hatred and enmity toward others for any reason. Such attitudes and practices are "foreign to the mind of Christ" (cf. *Nostra Aetate*, 4).

Another point of difficulty in the relationship between Christianity and Judaism is the question of the mandate of Jesus to preach the Gospel to the whole world, the mission of evangelization. Does this mean that the Church should strive to convert Jews to Christianity? Some branches of Christianity, notably evangelical, fundamentalist conservative Christians, actively seek to convert Jews. The Catholic Church does not. In an interesting distinction, Cardinal Walter Kasper, president of the Vatican Council for Interreligious Dialogue, notes that *conversion* implies turning from false gods and idols to the one true God. The cardinal states that this does not apply to Jews, since they already believe in the one true God, even if they do not share our faith in Jesus as Lord and Messiah. Thus, there is no official endorsement on the part of the Catholic Church of any active attempts to convert Jews to Christianity.

Pope John Paul II has tried during his long papacy to promote better relations with the Jewish people. He was the first pope to visit the Rome synagogue. He made an historic journey to Israel during the millennial year. He himself has a number of close Jewish friends from his younger years in Poland.

This official understanding of Judaism on the part of the Catholic Church is one of respect, as a younger to an elder in the faith. The Church sees her roots in faith and worship in Judaism.

She, as St. Paul sets forth in his Letter to the Romans, recognizes that her children share by faith in the promise of salvation that first came to the Jewish people in their great ancestor, Abraham.

Often, Christians are unaware of Jesus' origin and followers. Is understanding the first century relevant or not?
Ignorance of Jesus, his lifestyle, his origin, as well as that of his first disciples, has long led and, sadly enough, continues to lead many people to a weakened and impoverished understanding of their own Christian faith. There are Catholics who in all sincerity and innocence truly believe that Jesus was a Catholic, not a Jew. They hold to this despite the clear witness of the New Testament to the Jewish origins of Jesus. We know that Jesus was circumcised on the eighth day as the Mosaic Law prescribed (cf. Luke 2:21), that the other customs of the law were carried out for him (cf. Luke 2:22), that he was raised as a devout Jew (cf. Luke 2:41–42), that he regularly went to synagogue (cf. Luke 4:15,16), and that he kept the Passover (cf. Luke 22:7–8; Matthew 26:18–19; Mark 14:14). Jesus both read and knew the Hebrew Scriptures (cf. Luke 4:17–19). Moreover, the first disciples of Jesus were also devout Jews, regularly going to synagogues and knowledgeable of the Scriptures and Jewish customs.

Keeping this in mind, it is imperative for a proper and balanced understanding of our Catholic faith that we know and understand the Jewish roots of much that we believe. It is also critical to know and understand the Jewish roots of some of our own practices, such as the origin of the Mass, the ritual of baptism, and the prayers we use. More than half of our Bible comes from Judaism, and we cannot even begin to understand and appreciate the New Testament without reference to the Hebrew Scriptures. Knowledge such as this can only help promote harmony through understanding. A lack of knowledge in this regard has led to many abuses across the centuries grounded in sheer ignorance.

What is the role of the "Old Testament" in Catholicism?
Catholics revere the Scriptures of the Jewish people as the Word of God in the fullest sense of the term. For Catholics, there are some forty-six books in what is referred to as the "Old" Testament. This is a larger number than is found either in the *Tanakh*, the Jewish Bible, or in the Old Testament of Protestant Christian denominations. The reason for this is found in that the Roman Catholic *canon* (or official listing of the books of Scripture) of the Old Testament is based on the Septuagint, the Greek Old Testament. St. Jerome, in translating the Scriptures into Latin in the late fourth and early fifth century, used the Septuagint and not the Hebrew text of the Old Testament books. The Reformers, especially Martin Luther, in the sixteenth century, urged a return to the Scriptures translated from their original languages, the Hebrew in the Old Testament, the Greek in the New Testament. Since the *Tanakh* contains but thirty-nine books, the Protestant Old Testament canon also contains that number. The Roman Catholic Old Testament includes the following seven books that are deemed to be *apocryphal* by Protestant Christians: 1 and 2 Maccabees, Judith, Tobit, Sirach, the Wisdom of Solomon, and Baruch. Most Protestants, while not acknowledging these books as Scripture, that is, the Word of God, do deem them to be worthy of reverence and recognition.

The Catholic Church, in the *Dogmatic Constitution on Divine Revelation* (*Dei Verbum*), issued by the Second Vatican Council in 1965, clearly holds that the books of the Old Testament are, in fact, the Word of God. The document maintains that the books of the Old Testament foretell, recount, and explain the plan of God for the salvation of the human race, a plan that has been in place from the beginning of creation. Since the books of the Old Testament communicate that plan and were written under divine inspiration, they have a lasting value. They are worthy of reverence as the Word of God, and when these books are read, it must be understood that God is speaking the word of salvation to us in them and through them.

Yet, what are we to make of the connection between the Old Testament and the New Testament? It is the clear teaching of the Catholic Church that the Old Testament prepares for and declares especially in prophetic ways the coming of the Messiah, whom Catholics believe to be Jesus of Nazareth, Jesus Christ. These books also prepare us for and declare to us the dawn of the kingdom of God, which we believe was inaugurated in the person and the ministry of Jesus of Nazareth. In doing this, the books of the Old Testament reveal to us a just and merciful God. Even though the books of the Old Testament contain matters that are imperfect and provisional in nature, they are nonetheless repositories of authentic divine teaching. The books of the Old Testament are a virtual treasure trove. In them, we are able to grasp a lively awareness of who God is. We find deep truths about God and about our lives and the meaning of human existence in this world. The Old Testament contains a treasury of prayers, most notably the Psalter itself. Finally, in the pages of the Old Testament, we can find the whole plan of salvation set down before us, a plan fulfilled in Jesus Christ.

Additionally, the books of the Old Testament, inspired by God, are meant to complement those of the New Testament. *Dei Verbum* (n. 16) speaks of a mutuality between the Testaments, with the New Testament "hidden" in the Old Testament, and the Old Testament "made manifest" in the New Testament. The Old Testament books "attain and show forth their full meaning in the New Testament." More than that, the Old Testament sheds light on the New Testament and explains it, leading us who believe in Jesus Christ to a deeper awareness of God's plan for salvation brought to completion and fruition in Christ. It has been rightly said in this regard that one cannot truly understand the New Testament in its fullness without an adequate and sufficient knowledge of the Old Testament.

Very often, especially in the past, but even among modern Christian writers and preachers, there has been a tendency to understand the Old Testament in *typological* terms. What is meant by this is that older realities (called *types*) in Scripture are understood as having foreshadowed, in God's plan of salvation, future realities. A very good example of this is seen in the story of Isaac, portrayed in Genesis 22 as the beloved son of his father Abraham, carrying to the mount in the land of Moriah the wood on which he will be laid for sacrifice. This depiction of Isaac has been interpreted typologically as a representation of Christ, the beloved Son of the Father, who carried his cross to the mount of Calvary, whereupon he sacrificed his life for us all. In the New Testament, St. Paul sees Adam as a "type" of Christ, who is the "New Adam" (cf. Romans 5:14). In addition, St. Paul sees the passage of the people of Israel through the Red Sea as a foreshadowing of Christian baptism (cf. 1 Corinthians 10:2). In the Letter to the Hebrews, Melchizedek is understood and presented as a type of Christ (cf. Hebrews 6:20–7:28; also Genesis 14:18–20). This method of interpreting and understanding the Old Testament in relation to the New Testament would obviously not gain support among Jewish exegetes, for it clearly is a Christian interpretation, one very likely not at all in the mind of the original human authors. Nevertheless, from a Christian perspective, this method of interpreting the Old Testament vis-à-vis the New Testament in its own way has led Christian thinkers and preachers to a deeper appreciation of a unity between the Testaments. This method is not without criticism, even within Christian circles, for it seems to do violence to the fact that the Old Testament has a message of its own and that this message can stand on its own, even in Christian preaching.

The very term "Old Testament" has proven to be problematic in recent years. Many Christians now prefer to set aside that traditional designation for the first two-thirds of the Bible out of a deeper sensitivity and respect for the Jewish tradition. The term "Old" Testament can imply that the books and the message of these books have been superseded and relativized. In this view, the Old Testament is no longer in force. It has been supplanted and fulfilled by the New Testament and its message. The only value these books have is that they can serve as a reference book for consultation in delving more and more into the New Testament. Clearly, such a view is not in line with Catholic teaching. As a result, other ways of referring to these books have surfaced, such as "Hebrew Scriptures" or "Common Testament." While there are problems with these designations as well, and while a universal consensus on what we in Christian circles are to call this collection of divinely inspired works may be impossible to reach, the discussion of this issue has, in any event, raised the consciousness of many Christians about the importance of this collection and its place in communicating God's saving word to the world.

Finally, since the Second Vatican Council, the Catholic Church has undertaken a much wider use of the Old Testament in its liturgy. Most of the rituals of the Church mandate the reading of Scripture, and among the selections given, there are always several from the Old Testament. In the Eucharistic Liturgy itself, the Mass, the first reading (of three in all) on most Sundays of the year comes from one of the books of the Old Testament. This trend indicates both a deeper reverence on the part of Catholicism toward its roots in Judaism, and a deeper awareness of the fact that God does continue to reveal Himself and His will in and through the message of the Old Testament.

The early Christians practiced pacifism. Is this still true? If not, then how and why has it changed?

Pacifism can best be defined as the absolute repudiation of warfare and the use of military force on the principle that it can never be morally justified. The earliest Christians, it is true, practiced pacifism on the basis of the teaching of Jesus that we are to offer no resistance to evildoers and that we are to love our enemies and pray for those who persecute us (cf. Matthew 5:39–43). The earliest Christians lived this out by readily suffering martyrdom for their faith in Christ rather than resist persecution and by refusing to join the Roman legions as soldiers. The Christian refusal to join the army and fight for the causes of Rome was grounded primarily in the clear teaching of Jesus urging nonviolence in the face of evil. This refusal was also grounded in the Roman practice that required all new inductees to the Roman legions to profess loyalty and obedience to the emperor, worshiping him as a deity. This amounted to idolatry and in light of the first commandment of the Decalogue, was unacceptable.

Over time, particularly as the Church came out from the underground and gained more and more social acceptance, even official approval, this stress on a pacifistic approach to life diminished. Emperor worship and oaths of obedience to the emperor disappeared. Indeed, often enough, the Church, particularly after the fall of Rome in the West in 476, found herself much like a worldly power, with popes organizing crusades and even leading troops into battle. How was this justified, given the clear teaching of Jesus regarding love for enemies, mandating that when we are struck on one cheek, we should turn and offer our adversary the other? The answer to this question is found in the emergence in the Christian thinking of what is now known as the *just-war doctrine*. This doctrine was not totally new to the Christian Church. It has roots in classical philosophical and political thought as well as a basis in the Hebrew Scriptures. In the Christian Church, the first great advocate of the just-war doctrine was Augustine (d. 430), and other giants of Christian thought followed in his steps, such as Thomas Aquinas (d. 1274).

The basic principle underlying the just-war doctrine is that warfare and the use of military force is at almost all costs to be avoided as it is contrary to the gospel. However, there are circumstances, somewhat defined and set down by this doctrine, in which the use of military force and a resort to warfare are required. It must be emphasized, however, that warfare and military force are to be used only as a *last resort*, when all other peaceable means of ending the conflict have been tried without success.

Within the just-war doctrine, there are two dimensions of teaching, one of which sets down the criteria necessary before a nation can, in a morally justified way, engage in warfare against another nation. The other dimension of the just-war doctrine sets down a code of moral behavior for those engaged in warfare, what they may and may not do.

In general, the criteria that must be met before a nation can, in a morally justified way, engage in warfare against another are the following:

1. There must be a *just cause*. This cause has traditionally been understood to mean the undoing of injustices already inflicted as well as the recovery of things unjustly taken. In modern times, this understanding of a just cause has been broadened to include defense against aggression.
2. The decision to engage in warfare must be made by competent authorities, either national governments or international bodies which have as an aim the protection and maintenance of security, be it national or regional in nature.
3. The intention behind the use of military force must be morally right, which excludes hatred of the enemy and the seeking of revenge on the enemy.
4. The decision to go to war must be one of last resort, a step taken only when all nonviolent means of conflict resolution, such as diplomacy and sanctions, have been exhausted without success.
5. There must be some reasonable hope of a successful outcome from the use of military force that seeks to attain just goals. If there is no such hope, then warfare is not a morally justifiable option.

As for the criteria set down by the just-war doctrine concerning what may or may not be done morally by combatants, the presupposition is that the military action in the first instance is morally justifiable. The criteria above must all apply. Two additional criteria are established for combatants. The first holds that innocent people may not be killed. Civilians and others not actually engaged in combat may not be targets for direct killing. In modern warfare, owing to the weaponry used, civilians and noncombatants are often killed, but they must not be direct targets. The second principle, called *proportionality*, forbids the use of excessive and unnecessarily destructive force on either combatants or noncombatants. The ramifications of the just-war doctrine for modern weapons of mass destruction, including nuclear, biological, and chemical weaponry, are quite significant.

On the one hand, the just-war doctrine in itself is a sad commentary on the human condition and on how far we as Christians have fallen short of what Jesus has called us to do. Warfare is evil, the result of human sin. It can never be easily justified. Yet there are situations where the use of military force is required in order to correct and redress injustices as well as to counter aggression. The just-war doctrine in this light does offer something positive. It sets down a clear limitation on when military force can be used and how military force can be used.

What of pacifism in the modern Church? The Catholic Church actively works for peace among nations and between disputing national groups through the use of diplomacy as well as through the promotion of justice. Pope Paul VI (d. 1978) is often quoted in this regard. He said in a major document on social justice in 1967 that "if you want peace, you must work for justice." True peace can be attained only when justice is broadly established. While the Church on an official level continues to work for peace and real justice, many of her members have been prominent in recent times in their efforts to promote peace. These include Dorothy Day, Thomas

Merton, Daniel and Philip Berrigan, Archbishop Oscar Romero, and Mother Teresa of Calcutta. The work of peace-making is an ongoing reality, a process that will endure until the end of time, when true peace will be established and God is all in all. Ultimately, the work of peace-making is God's work, but all of us have been called to play an active part in the process.

What is the liturgical year or the liturgical calendar?

In the Roman Catholic tradition, the liturgical year consists of six principal seasons: Advent, Christmas, Lent, the Easter Triduum, Easter, and Ordinary Time. The liturgical year is a manifestation of Catholic belief in the sanctity of time and the Lordship of Jesus Christ over all history. Much of the liturgical year revolves around the mystery of the life of Christ: the preparation for his coming as well as the future anticipation of his glorious return at the end of time (Advent), his birth and manifestation (Christmas), his fasting and temptation (Lent), and his passion, death, and resurrection (Easter Triduum and the season of Easter). The season of Ordinary Time is thus designated because the term "ordinary" refers to the fact that the Sundays during this time of the year are designated by ordinal numbers, such as the "Second Sunday in Ordinary Time" or the "Fifteenth Sunday in Ordinary Time." During these Sundays in Ordinary Time, the fullness of the mystery of Jesus Christ as well as his teaching are unfolded for the faithful so that they might ponder and meditate upon them.

What are the important holidays or festivals in Christianity?

The dominant festivals or holidays during the liturgical year are four in number: the Easter Triduum, Christmas, Epiphany, and Pentecost. These festivals, each of them worthy of explanation on their own, celebrate the core events in the life of the Lord as well as the Church, the community of the Lord's disciples.

What is the Easter Triduum?

The Easter Triduum, the word *triduum* coming from the Latin for "three days," marks the high point of the Catholic calendar and the most solemn time of the Church year. This core festival of the Christian year centers on the passion, death, and resurrection of Jesus Christ. The Triduum begins at sundown on Thursday evening, Thursday being designated as *Holy Thursday,* ending at sunset on Easter Sunday. On Holy Thursday evening, the Church ritually commemorates the Last Supper shared by Jesus with his disciples on the night before his death. At this liturgy, there are several points for meditation and commemoration. Most notably, there is the washing of the feet (often referred to as the *mandatum*, a Latin word meaning "command") in which members of the congregation take part. This foot-washing calls to mind in a vivid fashion the clear example of service given by Jesus. His act of service that evening would be amplified the following day by his death on the cross, a supreme act of service in which he gave his life as a ransom for the many, laying down his life for his friends. Our participation in the foot-washing reminds us of the call Jesus gave to us to be servants to one another, even to the point of giving our lives for others. In addition, the Holy Thursday liturgy commemorates the gifts of the Eucharist, that is, the Sacrament of the Body and the Blood of Christ, as well as the gift of the priesthood, recalled in the words of Jesus after breaking the bread of his body and sharing it and pouring out the wine of his blood and sharing it, "Do this in remembrance of me." The Holy Thursday evening liturgy ends with great solemnity. The Eucharist is moved in procession from the tabernacle (the "safe" or box where the sacrament is reserved for prayer as well as for Communion for the sick and homebound) to a special place of reservation either elsewhere in the church proper or even in a room apart from the church. There is no music played. Silent adoration of the Eucharist continues until late in the night. The altar and sanctuary are stripped, leaving a stark reminder that the next day is a day of solemn mourning and commemoration of the death of the Lord. The Mass, the Eucharist, may not be celebrated in the Catholic Church on Good Friday. Instead, Holy Communion, consecrated (blessed) the evening before and set aside, is given during the Good Friday service.

The Good Friday service normally begins around three o'clock in the afternoon, the traditional time of Jesus' death on the cross. The Good Friday service solemnly celebrates the Lord's Passion and Death. The Good Friday service consists of readings from Scripture, most notably the fourth servant song of Isaiah and the entire passion narrative from the Gospel of John. A homily is given, followed by solemn intercessory prayers. The veneration of the Lord's cross is a key moment in the Good Friday celebration. The cross is carried into the church in procession. Three times the words "This is the wood of the cross on which hung the Savior of the world" are sung, to which the people respond in simple song, "Come, let us worship," kneeling briefly each time. Once the cross reaches the front of the church, it is placed so that all may come and venerate it (honor it). This is done through the bending of the knee in genuflection, through kissing the cross, by bowing to it, by simply and reverently touching it. The Good Friday service concludes with the distribution of Communion and a final prayer. All leave the church in silence. No other solemn official liturgical service is held on Good Friday.

The bulk of Holy Saturday is a day of mourning and watching, very much like a "wake" at the Lord's tomb. An ancient Easter homily compared Holy Saturday to the first Sabbath as set down in Genesis. As God rested on that first Sabbath from all the work He had done, so did the Lord Jesus rest, in death, in the tomb, but in anticipation of a new creation, a new springtime, that would emerge with his glorious resurrection on Easter Sunday morning, a cosmic event which meant victory for God over Satan, holding out hope of eternal life for all who believe in Jesus as Lord and Savior.

The high point, the most important liturgical celebration of the Church year, comes with the Vigil of Easter, which is celebrated at nightfall or after dark on Holy Saturday evening. It is a beautiful if lengthy liturgical ceremony that, if properly and reverently celebrated is profoundly meaningful. The Easter Vigil begins with the blessing of the new fire and the lighting of the Easter Candle, the *Paschal Candle*, a vivid symbol of the Risen Lord who is the light of the world and the light of life. This blessing best takes place outside of the church, for obvious reasons. Then the Easter Candle is borne in procession into the church, which is in complete darkness. The people carry lighted tapers, walking in procession behind the candle. As the Easter Candle and the tapers of the people come into the church, the darkness, symbolizing death and the grave, is dispelled. The church fills with light, and with it, with life. Once the procession with the candle reaches the sanctuary, the *Exsultet*, the "Easter Proclamation," is sung and the candle incensed.

Following immediately thereafter is the Liturgy of the Word, which contains nine readings in all, seven from the Old Testament, the totality of which sweeps across the story of salvation history, how God has worked in and through human persons and historical events to bring to fulfillment His plan of salvation, and two from the New Testament, one from Romans 6, the other a story of the empty tomb from one of the gospels. Each reading has a response, usually in the form of a psalm which is sung. A homily, explaining the significance of the readings and the meaning of this holy night to all assembled, is given after the gospel is read. The Old Testament readings are read in a subdued, watchful manner. The exuberance of the Easter celebration comes with the intoning of the Gloria, an ancient Church hymn used on most Sundays and major feast days, following the last Old Testament passage. The Alleluia is sung for the first time since before Lent began with fanfare before the gospel of Easter is read.

If there are baptisms or receptions into the Church, these are celebrated after the homily. At this point in the liturgy, the new Easter water is blessed, water which reminds us of life and death, as well as the waters of our own baptism. Adults baptized or received into the Church (if they were already baptized in another Christian denomination) are then confirmed, and these will later receive Communion for the first time, thereby completing their initiation. The Mass continues as usual after this.

Easter Sunday is a day of great joy and celebration. The Christian Church sings again the great hymn of praise to God captured in the Hebrew word *Alleluia*, which means "praise God." Flowers and exultant music mark this day which is the greatest day in the Christian calendar. Indeed, every Sunday of the Church year is said to be a "little Easter," a weekly commemoration of the great event of the Lord's saving death and resurrection.

What is the connection between Passover and Easter?

Based on the gospels, there is clearly a connection between the Jewish festival of Passover and the Christian festival of Easter. All four gospels establish that the passion, death, and resurrection of Jesus took place at the time of the Passover. Just as the Jewish people at Passover commemorate the Exodus and celebrate the liberation of their ancestors from bondage and oppression in Egypt, so do Christians, in commemorating and celebrating the passion, death, and resurrection of Jesus at Easter, recall how Jesus Christ has liberated us from more than bondage and oppression in Egypt. The "Exodus" wrought by Christ has freed us from the bondage of sin and the oppression of death. As St. Paul says in Romans 6, "Christ, once raised from the dead, will never die again. Death has no more power over him. His death was a death to sin, once for all. His life is life for God. In the same way, you must consider yourselves dead to sin, and alive for God in Christ Jesus." Both the Exodus and the passion, death, and resurrection of Jesus are events centered on liberation. Christians believe that the Exodus, celebrated at Passover, was a type of the New Exodus wrought by Christ in his passion, death, and resurrection, celebrated at Easter.

The gospels themselves give ample evidence of a clear connection between Passover and Easter. All four gospels state that the final meal that Jesus shared with his disciples before his death (commonly referred to as the *Last Supper*) was either a Passover meal itself (Matthew, Mark, and Luke), or at least a meal with a Passover connotation (John). The Gospel of John makes the connection more specific in that he relates Jesus to the paschal lamb, with Jesus being crucified at the precise hour when the lambs for Passover were slaughtered in the Temple precincts (cf. John 19:14). This is all the more emphasized if we note that one of the favorite images John uses for Jesus is that of the *Lamb of God* (cf. John 1:29). John notes that after the death of Jesus on the cross, the soldiers came and broke the legs of the criminals crucified with Jesus so as to hasten death. They did not do so to Jesus, who was already dead. Instead, they pierced Jesus' side with a lance. John adds a quotation from Exodus 12:46: "Not a bone of it will be broken." This passage in Exodus refers to the Passover lamb.

It is quite evident, then, that there is a profound connection on a biblical basis between the great Jewish festival of Passover and the Christian festival of Easter. More than that, this connection is further stressed in the fact that in the Catholic Church and many other Christian churches, *unleavened* bread and grape wine form the staple food of the Eucharist, the ritual meal that commemorates the Last Supper and, in so doing, also remembers the connection between that meal and the Passover. Yet again, on the level of the liturgical calendar in most Christian churches, the date of Easter is established as the first Sunday following the first full moon following the vernal equinox, a calculation that is also used, essentially, to establish the date of the yearly Passover festival in Judaism.

What is Christmas?
Christmas is an important festival, both from the perspective of the Church as well as in wider secular society. The *Christmas* festival,

celebrated on December 25, commemorates the birth of Jesus at Bethlehem of Judea. While do not know the actual date of Jesus' birth, we do know that he was born and that he actually existed. The origins of the date of Christmas center on an ancient pagan festival in honor of the birth of Apollo, the god of the sun. Christians took over this date and Christianized it in honor of the birth of the one who is called the "sun of justice." Since Christians worship Jesus as Lord and as Son of God, it is only fitting and proper that we mark an annual celebration of his birth. The Christmas festival is a particularly joyous time of the year, marked with various customs across various cultures, including the Christmas crib, the Christmas tree, the singing of Christmas carols, and various types of parties and family gatherings.

What is the origin of the Christmas tree and the Christmas crèche?

Both the Christmas tree and the Christmas *crèche* (nativity scene) are well-known symbols that appear at the time of the annual Christmas festival in December. The origin of these dominant Christmas symbols is quite interesting.

It seems that the Christmas tree had its origins in Germany, for there are ample references to fir trees being used to decorate homes in that region of Europe from the middle of the sixteenth century onward. Early on, these trees were not decorated with candles (which would lead to electrically lighted Christmas trees in the modern era), but with unconsecrated communion wafers, paper roses, apples, and a variety of other things, all of these precursors to the modern Christmas ornaments. The custom of having a Christmas tree spread slowly and unevenly. Not all Christians immediately approved of it, but it gradually became popular just about everywhere and remains so today.

The origin and significance of the Christmas tree is somewhat shrouded in mystery. Evergreens long have been a symbol of rebirth, often used as a symbol of life in the midst of the coldness and death of winter. Yet there is no solid evidence that this is the root origin of the fir tree used as a Christmas tree. The Christmas tree seems to have its roots in what is known as the Paradise Tree, which was the centerpiece of a medieval *mystery play* (a religious drama popular during the Middle Ages in Europe) that presented the story of Adam and Eve and the fall of the human race. The only thing on stage was the Paradise Tree adorned with apples. Eve takes the fruit, eats it, and gives it to Adam, who does the same, resulting in their banishment from paradise, as Genesis 3 tells us. This "Paradise Play" would end with the promise of the coming Savior and his incarnation (grounded in Genesis 3:15).

By the fifteenth century, so many abuses had crept into the performances of these mystery plays that they were forbidden by the Church. Nonetheless, the Paradise Tree had become part of the cultural landscape, and people began putting them up, apples and all, in their homes on or around December 24, the traditional feast, in some parts of the Church, of Adam and Eve. This tree symbolized a tree of sin and a tree of life. Apples (the fruit of sin) were dangled from the tree, and eventually wafers (much like communion hosts) and sweets of various kinds (representing the fruit of life) were also added. The addition of lights was derived from the custom of lighting a large candle, the Christmas light, symbolizing Christ the Light coming into the world to scatter darkness and sin. In parts of Germany in the late Middle Ages, wooden pyramids were constructed and candles set upon them. Glass ornaments were also set on them, with a star placed on top of the pyramid.

The Christmas tree should also remind Christians of the tree of life, the cross, on which our Lord and Savior died to undo the ravages of sin brought into the world by our first ancestors. Because of the death of Jesus, the Light of the World, sin and darkness have been banished, death has been destroyed, and paradise has been restored to us. Thus, in an important sense, the Christmas tree should focus our attention not only on the birth of Jesus, but also on the whole mystery of Jesus, his life, death, and resurrection. The Christmas tree poignantly reminds us that Christmas leads us to Easter, and indeed, draws its meaning and significance from the great Easter event.

The *crèche* or nativity scene (also known as the Christmas crib) is a very ancient tradition in the Christian Church, having roots as far back as the fourth century. Scenes connected with the stories of the birth of Jesus were artistically rendered from the very earliest times. During the medieval period, mystery plays were performed acting out various parts of the Christmas drama.

While it seems clear that the *crèche* predates Francis of Assisi (d. 1226), it was Francis who, perhaps more than anyone, helped to popularize the custom of the Christmas crib. On Christmas Eve in 1223, in the town of Greccio in Italy, having created a manger which he filled with straw, Francis had animals brought and proceeded to sing the Gospel of Christmas and preach very effectively on the mystery of Christmas. From that point on, the custom of having a Christmas *crèche* spread throughout Italy, the rest of Europe, and eventually the world.

What is Epiphany?

Epiphany, celebrated shortly after Christmas, either on January 6 or on the first Sunday in January, is a major liturgical feast. Liturgical scholars note that there was a Christian festival marking the Epiphany quite some time before the feast of Christmas appeared. The basis for this celebration is the commemoration of the visit of the Magi, often referred to popularly as the Three Kings or the Wise Men. On Epiphany, the gospel passage from Matthew is read telling the story of the visit of the Magi (Matthew 2:1–12). Who were the Magi? They may well have been Zoroastrian astrologers from Persia. Matthew calls them "astrologers from the east." Whatever may have happened with regard to the visit of these foreigners, the significance of the Epiphany rests in the manifestation of Jesus to the world, Jews and Gentiles alike, as Lord and Savior. Whoever these Magi were, they were not Jews. The fact that Matthew has them come from a distance bearing symbolic gifts of gold, frankincense, and myrrh stresses the mystery of the Epiphany as one of Christ revealed as Savior of the whole world. The gift of gold traditionally singles out the royalty of Jesus as King of kings, son of David, and Messiah. Frankincense accentuates his divinity, for incense is usually offered only to God. The bitterness of myrrh foreshadows the nature of Jesus as *suffering Messiah*, for he will reveal his true Messianic salvific significance only in his suffering and terrible death on the cross.

What is Pentecost?

Finally, the fourth major annual Christian festival is *Pentecost*, celebrated fifty days after Easter. This feast commemorates the pouring out of the Spirit of God on the apostles, giving birth to the infant Church. The pouring out of the Spirit, which happened in the Upper Room in Jerusalem where only days before Jesus had shared his final meal with his disciples, transformed the first Christians from fearful, cowering individuals to bold, fearless preachers of the gospel, the gospel message being that this Jesus who had lived and walked among them, who had been crucified, had been raised to life by God and made Lord and Savior of the world. The Pentecost festival closes the fifty-day long celebration of Easter, and it is intricately tied into Easter, even bringing to completion the Easter mystery in that it fulfills the promise of Jesus that he would send the Spirit of truth who would lead us into all truth, enabling us to understand everything that has been taught us (cf. John 16:13).

For what is Christianity indebted to Judaism?

Christianity owes much to Judaism. The roots of Christianity are sunk deep in Judaism, and because of this fact, a deeper knowledge of and reverence for Judaism can only enhance the knowledge and reverence that Christians have for their own faith tradition. Much of what Christianity believes and practices is grounded in Jewish tradition, even though Christian faith has colored and altered some of these contributions from our Jewish heritage.

I would summarize the debt that Christianity owes to Judaism in four categories. First and foremost, we owe our heartfelt faith in *the oneness of God* to the Jewish people, who have stood out for much of their history for their singular belief in monotheism, the belief that there is one God and no others. When other cultures and civilizations held to belief in many deities, the Jewish people firmly adhered to the oneness of God. Isaiah the prophet sums up this monotheistic faith well where he writes: "I am the Lord, and there is no other" (cf. Isaiah 45:18). To be sure, Christian belief in God is also unique, grounded as it is in God as Trinity, one God in three divine Persons, who have been revealed to us by Jesus himself as the Father, the Son, and the Holy Spirit. While it is difficult to explain how God can be one and three at one and the same time, it is the essence of Christian faith that *God is one*. This oneness of God is affirmed even as we call upon God as Father, Son, and Holy Spirit.

Second, Christianity is indebted to Judaism for more than half of the sacred writings that we revere as Scripture, the Word of God. What the Jewish people revere as the *Tanakh*, inclusive of the Torah, the Prophets, and the Writings, we as Christians continue to revere as Scripture, words which we believe come from God and speak to us as strongly as they spoke to the Jewish people of long ago and continue to speak to the Jewish people of the present day. The first Christians were Jews, and, as Jews, they continued to read and revere the Jewish Scriptures as their own. This reverence was so deep that when the *canon* (or official listing of the books considered to be inspired Scripture) was decided, the Hebrew Scriptures were included. While these writings have been known by various names in the Christian tradition, ranging from *Old Testament* to *Hebrew Bible* or *Hebrew Scriptures,* we Christians continue to read them, to cherish them, and to pray with them, seeking the guidance of God in them for our time. Even in the Catholic liturgy, when a passage is proclaimed from the Hebrew Scriptures, these words are identified as "the Word of the Lord."

Third, Christianity is indebted to Judaism for a significant body of moral teaching, moral law, and guidance found not only in the Decalogue, but also in the call of the prophets to "cease to do evil, learn to do good; seek justice, correct oppression; defend the orphan, plead for the widow" (cf. Isaiah 1:16–17), as well as in the moral guidance and instruction given by the sages in the body of sacred literature known as the Writings (what many Christians call the *wisdom literature*). Jesus himself quoted from the Decalogue and the prophets, in essence affirming the teaching contained in them, even as he expanded on them and deepened their demands (cf. Mark 10:19–21, with parallels in Matthew 19:18–21 and Luke 18:20–22).

Fourth, Christianity is indebted to Judaism for a great deal of the richness found in its traditions of prayer. The Psalter is used widely in Christian prayer, and many of the psalms have been put to music in the Christian tradition and, as a result, have become beloved and known widely by Christians. Many Christians, as do their Jewish brothers and sisters, pray a number of times each day. In the Catholic Church, there is a venerable form of daily prayer known as the *Divine Office* or the *Liturgy of the Hours*. This official prayer of the Church calls for Christians to pray five or six times each day, at morning, mid-morning, mid-day, mid-afternoon, evening, and at night. Catholic clergy (bishops, priests, and deacons) as well as men and women who are members of religious communities are obligated to pray in this way. The Liturgy of the Hours makes extensive use of the Psalter as well as canticles (hymns) drawn from the Hebrew Scriptures.

Finally, Christianity is indebted to Judaism for a great deal of its liturgical traditions. Much of what now comprises the Catholic Mass, the central act of Catholic worship, comes from the Jewish traditions of synagogue worship as well as the Passover festival meal. The *berakhah* prayers that are part of the Jewish tradition have been incorporated into the Mass in the prayers said over the bread and wine as they are first placed on the altar. The Jewish festivals of Passover and Pentecost have been absorbed into Christian worship, albeit in modified forms which celebrate Christian faith, with Passover being transformed into the Christian celebration of the Resurrection of Jesus (Easter), and Pentecost in the Christian context commemorating and celebrating the bestowal of the Spirit on the nascent Church some fifty days after Easter. However, even in this, with all the Christian interpretation overlaying these feasts, there is due deference given to the Jewish roots of these festivals.

Christianity, in summary, owes *much* to Judaism. It behooves Christians, therefore, to become better acquainted with Judaism. This is true not only for better mutual understanding between two great religious traditions, but also for a better understanding on the part of Christians of their own faith tradition.

For further reading

Boys, Mary C. *Has God Only One Blessing? Judaism as a Source of Christian Self-Understanding*. New York: Paulist Press, 2000.

Catechism of the Catholic Church. Rome: Libreria Editrice Vaticana, 1994.

Fisher, Eugene J., ed. *Twenty Years of Jewish-Catholic Relations.* New York: Paulist Press, 1986.

Flannery, Austin, ed. *Vatican Council II.* Vol. 1: *The Conciliar and Post Conciliar Documents*, new rev. ed. Northport, N.Y.: Costello Publishing Co., 1996.

McBrien, Richard P., ed. *The HarperCollins Encyclopedia of Catholicism*. San Francisco: HarperSanFrancisco, 1995.

Chapter 3

Orthodox Christianity

Dr. Andrew Walsh

The major historical legacy of the Byzantine Empire (324–1453), Orthodox Christianity prizes its unbroken continuity with the church established in Jerusalem on Pentecost. It understands itself to be the universal, unbroken, and normative expression of Christianity. Composed of a network of mutually recognizing local or national churches, mostly concentrated in the Mediterranean, the Balkans, and Eastern Europe, the Orthodox consider themselves members of a single, undivided church bound by common doctrinal, ecclesiastical, and liturgical tradition.

Although the face it shows to the world—in the final forms of its worship, the shape of its theology, the design and symbolism of its churches, the vestments and style of its clergy—reflects the Byzantine period most of all, the Orthodox faith was shaped during the first four centuries of the common era, by both its roots in the religion of Israel and its struggle to express its faith in the context of Greco-Roman culture.

Recognized as the official religion of the Roman Empire in the fourth century, Orthodox Christianity came to be inextricably linked with the Byzantine Empire, in which it flourished and from which it spread, most notably into Eastern Europe, reaching Ukraine and Russia by the tenth century. Major missionary movements and mass migrations since the eighteenth century have turned Orthodoxy into a global faith.

Although contact with the church in Western Europe dwindled after the sixth century, much of the shared dogmatic heritage of

Trinitarian Christianity was articulated by Eastern theologians. Thus, the estranged Roman Catholic and Orthodox churches share a great deal, but are also divided by theological differences, notably about the nature of papal authority and the role of the Holy Spirit in the Holy Trinity. During the centuries that followed the collapse of the Roman Empire in the West, the two regions of the church drifted out of regular communication and into increasing crisis.

The rise of Islam and centuries of conflict with the Roman West eroded the position of the Byzantine Church, especially after the twelfth century. The bitter estrangement between the Catholic West and the Orthodox East is symbolized by the Great Schism of 1054, the sack of Constantinople in 1204 during the Fourth Crusade, and long centuries of tension and rivalry along the long European border, running from Lithuania to Serbia, that divides the two realms of Christian culture and civilization.

The massive dispersion of immigrants from Orthodox homelands that began in the nineteenth century has, however, shattered the neat division between Christian East and West. Orthodox churches are now widespread in Western Europe, the Americas, Australia, parts of Africa, and other areas of the world.

The Orthodox today

Estimates of the total number of Orthodox believers range from 150 million to more than 250 million. More than half of the total number of Orthodox lives in Russia and the Ukraine. The church is organized as a communion of autocephalous (i.e., fully self-governing) churches that recognize one another. The Patriarchate of Constantinople, in continuity with its Byzantine and post-Byzantine role, is recognized as the first among equals, but its leadership does not extend to direct authority over any other autocephalous church. (Autocephalous Orthodox churches are usually, but not always, led by bishops who hold the rank of patriarch, and therefore are often described as patriarchates.)

The oldest local Orthodox churches are the Patriarchates of Antioch, Alexandria, Constantinople, and Jerusalem. The Church of Russia became autocephalous in the fifteenth century; the Churches of Greece, Serbia, Romania, and Bulgaria became autocephalous in the nineteenth century, as the Ottoman Empire broke apart. The Church of Cyprus has also been self-governing for centuries. And independent Orthodox churches were established in Albania, Poland, Czechoslovakia, and Finland during the twentieth century (in all of these countries, unlike the previously listed churches, the Orthodox make up only a small part of the Christian population). The Church of Georgia, in the Caucasus, also reestablished its autocephaly early in the twentieth century.

The Orthodox churches are strongly represented in North America, Australia, and Western Europe, where Orthodox immigrants have arrived from many homelands and many converts have joined the church. In these countries there are many overlapping ethnic jurisdictions, a complex and irregular situation that will eventually be resolved by the formation of new local, autocephalous churches. During the last century, the Orthodox Church also spread significantly in Africa, where the Patriarchate of Alexandria has established many new dioceses in East, South, and West Africa.

What the Orthodox believe

Orthodox Christianity, many of its teachers have said, is best understood as a way of life, by its life as the Body of Christ. Rooted in the Bible, its faith and teachings are shaped by divine revelation, anchored in Sacred Tradition, enriched by the lives of the saints, both past and present, and actively guided by the Holy Spirit. The church exists in living continuity with the teachings that Christ passed on to his apostles and as a living community that affirms both these teachings and the goal of union with God made possible by Christ's loving sacrifice on behalf of creation, his incarnation, death, and resurrection.

The core of the Christian faith, the Orthodox teach and believe, involves several truths: that God is revealed as Trinity, as the creator of the cosmos and everything in it, and as the source of love who wills humanity to be united with him through Christ. The instrument of salvation is Jesus Christ, the Word of God who took on human flesh and lived as a human being in first-century Palestine. The most distinctive aspect of Orthodox theology is that salvation is conceived as union with God, as *theosis*, to use the Greek technical term. God became human, to use the immensely influential language of the fourth-century Egyptian theologian St. Athanasios, so that humans could become God. This loving, ever-expanding relationship with God comes, the Orthodox teach, only through Christ, only through membership in the Church, which is the Body of Christ.

The Christian faith is built on several critical teachings, discussed below.

The Creation and Fall

The Orthodox believe there is a radical distinction between the Trinitarian God and the created order, including humanity, which God made in his own image and likeness, a distinction that can never be overcome by human initiative. The purpose of creation, the Church teaches, was to expand the exchange of love that characterizes the nature and relationship of the persons of the Holy Trinity. Genuine love requires free consent, and so individual freedom of conscience is a fundamental quality of the created order. As the theological account in the Book of Genesis suggests, humanity fell into a disordered, sinful, and separated state by choosing to disobey God's will. Characteristically, Eastern Christian ideas about the nature and consequences of the fall of humanity are less drastic than Western Christian ones, with many Eastern fathers arguing that the Fall was caused by immaturity rather than fully conscious disobedience, and that the "image and likeness" shared by God and humanity was distorted and badly damaged, rather than destroyed, by the Fall. Nevertheless, the human dilemma remained an estrangement from its creator that it could not resolve by itself.

The doctrine of the Incarnation

The Orthodox tradition understands the subsequent history of the relationship between humanity and God as a series of loving initiatives by God to restore the original purpose of creation. Principal steps along the way include the divine covenants with Abraham and Moses, the covenant with Israel. The pivotal point in this process is the Incarnation, the process through which God healed the alienation of the creation by choosing to take on human form, and to obliterate the permanent consequences of the Fall by dying a sacrificial death and creating through the resurrection a path of inclusion that other humans can follow. Orthodox Christians understand that the cycle of Christ's incarnation, life, death, and resurrection marks the pivot point in the history of the universe, the point at which humanity and the whole created order can once again participate in the restoration of creation.

The dogmas of the Trinity and the Two Natures of Christ

Christ's immediate followers in the first century had a strong sense of who he was and what his life, death, and resurrection meant for humanity. But it took almost 400 years for the Church to establish stable definitions of the nature of God and of the relationship between the human and divine in Christ. These critical definitions emerged from the scriptural record, from the authoritative teaching of the church's leaders, internal debate, and the lengthy encounters of church leaders and thinkers with the intellectual structures and traditions of the Greco-Roman world, These two foundational definitions were forged, in the context of vigorous debate at what the church terms ecumenical councils—gatherings of bishops guided actively by Holy Spirit that took place in the fourth and fifth centuries, just after Christianity was established as the state religion of the Roman Empire.

The first three ecumenical councils articulated a stable doctrine of the Trinity, and the fourth described the relationship between Christ's humanity and divinity. These definitions, in a way that would become characteristic of Orthodoxy theology, were not offered as proof-texts that claimed to exhaust the totality of the nature of God, but rather as consciously paradoxical definitions that convey reliable information about divine mysteries, realities that are admittedly beyond the scope of human capacity to grasp fully.

The first dogmatic definition is that God is Trinity: one divine essence in three persons, the Father, Son, and Spirit. The three names of the God are all derived from the New Testament and especially from Christ's words. The final definition was agreed upon at the Council of Nicea in 325 and refined at the Council of Constantinople in 381. The council affirmed that God is one essence, one God, with three persons: Father, Son, and Spirit. The key concern articulated was that the Son—Jesus Christ, the Savior—was actually not simply sent by God but also is God, and therefore has the capacity to save the fallen cosmos.

The second key definition, framed at the Council of Chalcedon in 451, affirms that Jesus Christ had two natures "unconfused, unchangeable, indivisible, inseparable" united in one person. The key concern here was to affirm that Christ was both fully human and fully divine.

Both definitions serve the purpose of illustrating how God could save and restore a fallen humanity. A contemporary Greek Orthodox theologian and bishop, Metropolitan Maximos Aghiorgousisis of Pittsburgh, explains it this way:

> Christ saved humankind through what he is, and through what he did for us. By assuming our human nature, the Incarnate Logos, a divine person, brought this humanity to the

heights of God. Everything that Christ did throughout his life was based on the presupposition that humanity was already saved and deified, from the very moment of his conception in the womb of Mary, through the operation of the Holy Spirit.

The doctrine of the Church

The Orthodox believe that the Church is not merely an institution, but also a vehicle that cuts across the limitations of created time and space to bring humanity into the Kingdom of God. It is a body, the Body of Christ, commissioned by Christ and empowered by the Holy Spirit to act as a vehicle of transformation by preaching the Gospel and through the power of the sacraments, especially baptism and the Holy Eucharist. It is through the sacraments and through the sacramental transformation of human beings and the created world that God is made manifest and creation reordered. That is why worship lies at the heart of both Orthodox teaching and life, because the Body of Christ is an eschatological reality, uniting the fallen world with the Kingdom of God and leading the body of believers on lifelong journeys of transformation that bring them into union with God.

Sources of authority

The Orthodox understand that divine revelation has been made in many ways, but believe that these all form a single, coherent tradition expressed and taught in living continuity by the Church. The Church, established by Christ and guided by the Holy Spirit, is itself the source of reliable authority on the nature of God and the divine economy of salvation. The components of the tradition include:

Sacred Scripture

The texts of the Old and the New Testament form the central deposit of revelation. The Orthodox recognize the Septuagint, a

Hellenistic, pre-Christian Greek-language translation of the Hebrew Scriptures made by Jews in Egypt, as the normative text of the Old Testament. The books of the New Testament, which are considered to contain the witness of the apostles, were assembled and recognized as valid by the church. The Bible is therefore understood as a product of the Church and is best interpreted within the tradition.

Worship and the Divine Liturgy

The Church's Eucharistic worship is a principal source of Christian teaching and the instrument through which the Body of Christ is realized and the process of *theosis* realized. The Divine Liturgy, which means the sacred common work, is the principal event of the Church's life; it is an eschatological reality that leads Christians into union with one another in the Kingdom of God. As celebrated on Sunday and feast days, the Orthodox liturgy expresses the whole history of worship. The first major section of the liturgy carries on the Jewish tradition of synagogue worship and is focused around the reading of Scripture and preaching that explains the significance of the Gospel. The second section of the service, which includes the consecration and distribution of the supernatural Body and Blood of Christ, is a divine mystery that is the central, constituting sacrament of the Christian community. Believers undergo a transformation in this sacrament that is both personal and communal. For the Orthodox, Eucharistic worship is the chief purpose of the Church and its chief connection with the living God.

There are a number of Orthodox liturgies, all of which have roots in the earliest worship practices of the Christian communities in various parts of the ancient world. The two liturgies most commonly used today by the Orthodox churches are products of the local worship traditions of Christians in Syria and include Scripture and prayers that date to the first days of the Christian community. The liturgies, named for two of the most important fourth-century fathers of the Church, St. Basil of Caesarea and St. John Chrysostom, were both refined in Antioch and then adopted in Constantinople during the late fourth and early fifth centuries. From the capital of the Byzantine Empire their use spread throughout the empire and beyond its borders. The texts of these liturgies have changed little since the ninth century. The Liturgy of St. Basil is used about ten times a year, chiefly during the Lenten period before Easter. The Liturgy of St. John Chrysostom, which is somewhat briefer than the Liturgy of St. Basil, is celebrated on most Sundays and feast days.

Orthodox worship takes place within a scheme of sacred time that serves to organize and focus Christian life and belief. At the heart of the church calendar is a structure of feasts and fasts that organize the church year. The feast of feasts, the central rite of the Orthodox faith, is Pascha, or Easter, the Feast of the Resurrection of Christ. Pascha (the Greek transliteration of the Hebrew *Pesach*, or Passover) is celebrated with each liturgy, but it is also the focal point and climax of an annual cycle of worship.

The Orthodox sense of time and worship builds on a nesting set of cycles. Worship, which was developed and refined in the monastic context, has daily, weekly, monthly, and annual cycles. There are also prescribed days and seasons of fasting that function to draw believers into the well-ordered life of the Body of Christ. The most important rituals in the cycle are the celebrations of the liturgy on Sundays, but the celebration of feast day liturgies is also a marked feature of Orthodox piety. There are eight major feasts connected with the life, death, and resurrection of Christ: the Nativity of Our Lord (December 25), Epiphany (January 6), the Presentation of the Lord at the Temple in Jerusalem (February 2), the Entry of Our Lord into Jerusalem (Palm Sunday), Easter, the Feast of the Ascension, the Feast of Pentecost, the Feast of the Transfiguration (August 6), and the Feast of the Exaltation of the Holy Cross (September 14).

Four major feasts also commemorate important events in the life of Mary, the *Theotokos*, or Mother of God: the Nativity of the Theotokos (September 8), the Entrance of the Theotokos in the Temple (November 21), the Annunciation to the Theotokos (March 25), and the Dormition of the Theotokos (August 15).

In addition, the final events in the life of Christ are commemorated with a major complex of services during the week preceding Easter, at the culmination of the penitential season of Lent. These are rites of enormous solemnity, emotional impact, and splendor.

The definitions of the major councils

The Orthodox recognize seven ecumenical or universal councils held between 325 and 787 at which major dogmatic issues were debated and resolved. These meetings, ideally conceived as meetings of all of the bishops of the world, produced statements and canons (legal rulings) that were subsequently recognized as binding, permanent expressions of the teachings of the Church and as revelations of God through the Holy Spirit. The Councils of Nicea in 325 and Constantinople in 381 produced the fundamental Trinitarian definitions that are expressed in the Nicene Creed, a formal statement of belief repeated by Orthodox Christians at baptism and at many of the services and sacraments of the church, including the divine liturgy.

The Councils of Ephesus in 431, Chalcedon in 451, and Constantinople in 681 addressed questions about the Christ's theanthropic standing as both a person of the Trinity and a human being. The Councils of Constantinople in 553 and 680–681 addressed a further set of Christological debates. The Council of Nicea in 787 is best known for its defense of the use of icons in prayer and worship. A number of councils were intended to be ecumenical by those who organized them, but were not subsequently recognized as such. The Orthodox, therefore, believe that the teachings of a synod of bishops must be "received" as Orthodox by the clergy and people before they can be counted as binding (e.g., the teachings of medieval councils at Lyon and Florence, at which reunion with the Roman church were rejected by the clergy and people, even though many bishops had signed the documents of the council).

Many other, smaller-scale or regional, meetings of bishops are also taught to have produced authoritative teachings. Many of these produced responses to overtures or questions from non-Orthodox Christians, or to ratify "confessions of faith" in response to Protestant or Catholic influences. These include the Councils of Jassy (in Romania) in 1662 and Jerusalem in 1672.

The teachings of the fathers of the church

The Orthodox recognize that much authoritative teaching has come in the works of theologians, often from thinkers mobilized to defend the teachings of the church against various heresies. Most of the best-known and most influential fathers were active between the second and eighth centuries. Explication of Scripture was a chief concern of many of the fathers of this period, but many of them are best remembered for their effort to make the Christian Gospel, with its roots in Jewish religion, both intelligible and persuasive to the larger culture of the Greco-Roman world, most particularly by launching an intense dialogue with the schools of Greek philosophy. Other Christians, especially Protestants, have often criticized the patristic synthesis they produced collectively, but the Orthodox embrace it. The canon of the fathers is not closed, and especially gifted theologians are still often linked to the golden age of the fathers.

The canons

The life and understanding of the Orthodox Church is also shaped by the very large and diverse collection of legal rulings by synods and other theological definitions developed over the course of the centuries. The canons regulate the structure and life of the institutional church and express many of the core dogmatic teachings of the Orthodox faith.

Iconography and architecture

The Orthodox tradition is also expressed and taught by the iconography (sacred art) and architecture that inform the church's spiritual life and its worship. In the sacramental context, the Orthodox faith teaches that icons (painted images produced according to a strict set of norms) can serve as a window connecting believers with Christ and the saints. The Orthodox revere or venerate icons, bowing to and kissing them—a practice that Protestants, Muslims, and Jews often find astonishing and unacceptable. But, as the great eighth-century defender of icons, St. John of Damascus, argued, the Orthodox do not worship idols, because they do not believe that icons are gods or supernatural forces in themselves. Instead, icons serve to connect the worshiper with the prototype of the image, with God or with the saint or sacred event depicted on the icon (usually an event in the life of Christ). Orthodox worship relies on the visual, the sensory, and the physical to create the sense that the Body of Christ is elevated into the Kingdom of God during worship. And icons, both as small images and as vast fresco or mosaic schemes covering the entire interior of churches, are powerful instruments both of piety and of instruction. Both icons and the architecture of churches often have distinctive region personalities, although their features all follow a standard scheme. It is easy to recognize Greek or Russian or Romanian or Serb styles of church construction or periods of iconography.

The Orthodox and the Non-Orthodox

The Orthodox tradition makes large claims. In the words of Maximos, the current Greek Orthodox metropolitan (bishop) of Pittsburgh, for example, "Knowing God is not just another kind of knowledge: It is a matter of life and death: For there is no third choice between the Holy Trinity and Hell." The Orthodox do not conclude from this that all non-Orthodox are condemned to hell (which the Orthodox understand largely as a persistent refusal to accept God's invitation to unite with Him). But the Orthodox frankly claim a unique role for the Church in human history, while confessing that God, and not other human beings, stands in the role of judge.

By the standards of the contemporary world, this is not a tolerant or inclusive approach. However, the Orthodox—the meaning of which is "those who worship God correctly"—feel obliged to defend their understanding of the truth. In addition, the Orthodox emphasize that God created humanity for freedom. Respect for freedom of conscience is, therefore, a foundational human right, and religious violence or coercion of others can never be justified

The history of Orthodox interaction with those of other faiths is complex, and the Orthodox have never agreed that there are other legitimate, equally valid paths to God. Nevertheless, many Orthodox churches and individuals support mutually respectful dialogue among groups and individuals. Most of the Orthodox churches have been participants in the ecumenical and interfaith movements of the twentieth and twenty-first centuries, although ecumenism remains controversial within Orthodoxy.

Orthodoxy and Judaism

The topic of relations between the Orthodox and the Jews is a particularly complex, and often painful, topic. In many parts of the world, especially in the United States, relations between Jews and Orthodox have been very cordial, perhaps especially because, more than any Christian group, the Orthodox have lived and struggled as members of persecuted minorities. The Orthodox also know at first hand how it feels to be proselytized by others. Especially in the wake of the Holocaust, Orthodox leaders have spoken and organized against anti-Semitism.

Nevertheless, there is a complex burden of history and many probably irresolvable issues of religious contention. At the heart of this is the fact that both groups believe themselves to be the inheritor of God's covenant with the people of Israel, and both groups understand that covenant to be exclusive

In its prayers and in its theology, Orthodoxy described the Church as the New Israel, as the People of Israel. There are irreducible elements of what some call supercessionism in Orthodox theology, and no discernable way in which Orthodox believers of good will could make those central and authentic elements of their faith less prominent. It must also be confessed that the marks of terrible tension between Jews and Christians can still be seen in scriptural texts and in the liturgical texts of the Orthodox tradition (perhaps especially in the Gospels of Matthew and John and in the services of Great Thursday and Friday during Holy Week).

Legal and religious discrimination against Jews was also a significant feature of social life in the Byzantine Empire and other states that have claimed Orthodox identity, perhaps most especially the Russian tsarist state. Explicit anti-Semitism has also been a recurring feature of Orthodox monastic life, as it is today among extremists on Mount Athos in Greece and in Russia, where many anti-Semitic elements have clustered around the Orthodox Church since the fall of communism.

But, on the other hand, efforts at sincere interfaith dialogue have been a marked and welcome feature of the past fifty years. There have been more condemnations of anti-Semitism by Orthodox bishops in the past several decades than in the previous history of the church. And it is fair to say that the apostle Paul's arguments (in, say, the Letter to the Hebrews) that God's covenant with the people of Israel continues unaffected by Christ's incarnation and by the new covenant that accompanied it is emphasized. While the Orthodox are loath to admit that anything is unaffected by Christ's incarnation, it may well be that more attention will be directed to considering whether the very high authority of Pauline teaching has been acknowledged in subsequent Orthodox theological argument about the validity of God's covenant with the Jews. That is what has happened in the Roman Catholic Church since the Second Vatican Council, and it may portend an eventual shift in theological opinion in Orthodoxy.

The Orthodox churches and the State of Israel:

Most of the autocephalous Orthodox churches do not have a record of taking public policy positions on the validity of the State of Israel or the current Middle East crisis. For most of the period 1948 to 1990, most of the autocephalous Orthodox churches operated in states under communist control and often made foreign policy statements that followed the instructions of their governments. This often meant criticism of Israeli actions, but these statements rarely reflected deeply held, specifically religious opinions. Instead they should be understood as pragmatic expressions that grew from the fact that communist governments used church involvement in the ecumenical movement to advance Cold War interests. Most official policy statements from all Orthodox churches call for good-faith efforts to reach negotiated, nonviolent solutions to problems of civil order and international rivalries, including the Middle East.

The major exceptions to this rule are the Patriarchates of Antioch and Jerusalem, for which the Middle East crisis is a domestic circumstance. The Patriarchate of Antioch operates in Syria and Lebanon. Its people and leadership are entirely Arab, and its policies toward Israel fall closely in line with those of the sitting national governments.

The situation in the Patriarchate of Jerusalem, which functions in Israel and Jordan, is even more complex. The leadership of the Patriarchate of Jerusalem, the largest group of Christians in Israel and the lands of the Palestinian Authority, is mostly Greek in ethnicity, but the church lay membership is overwhelmingly Arab. The

Patriarchate is one of the largest landowners in Israel and in the West Bank, and its relationship with both Israeli and Palestinian authorities has fluctuated. On the whole, and especially before the Second Intifada, the Patriarchate and the Israeli government had a reasonably warm relationship—often too warm for the tastes of many of the Palestinian laity. Since 2001, the situation has been much more difficult, with security restrictions hindering the movement of many clergy and people on the West Bank, the siege/hostage taking at the Church of the Nativity in Bethlehem, and the Israeli government's refusal to recognize the election of Patriarch Irenaios in 2002, largely because they considered him pro-Palestinian.

Chapter 4

PROTESTANTISM

Dr. Frank G. Kirkpatrick

Protestantism was originally defined as an attempt to reform practices and beliefs in the Roman Catholic church, beginning with Martin Luther and John Calvin in the sixteenth century, followed by a number of groups constituting what is now called the Anabaptist or radical reformation.

Over the centuries since then, Protestants have divided into many different denominations, usually along doctrinal lines. Protestantism covers a very broad spectrum from hierarchical churches (e.g., the Anglican or Episcopalian) in which bishops, priests, and deacons have special ordained status, to lay-centered churches in which the lay congregations have the power to hire and fire ministers. There is also a wide range of forms of expressing the faith from highly structured liturgies to free-form evangelical, more emotional ways of prayer and song.

Some generalizations apply to all Protestants:

They reject the authority of the Bishop of Rome (i.e., the papacy).

They stress the centrality of the preached Word of God as found in Scripture. The Bible reveals God's intention for humankind (some believe it is an inerrant, infallible revelation: others hold that it expresses revelation in finite, less-than-perfect human form). They tend to place the traditions of the church in a secondary position as far as authority for contemporary belief and practice are concerned.

They believe that God's grace alone is sufficient for salvation. (Protestantism began with Martin Luther, who believed, erroneously as it turned out, that Roman Catholicism was committed to the view that good works could merit salvation. Luther, in protest, argued that justification [salvation] is by faith in God's grace alone.) They tend to stress the sinfulness (some say depravity) of human nature.

They stress the importance of individual conscience and a personal spiritual experience of divine grace.

Most (but not all) Protestants regard the local congregation as the seat of authority for church governance.

Most Protestants are suspicious of too close an alliance between church and state.

In answering the following questions, I have tried to indicate the dominant positions in contemporary Protestantism.

What is the ultimate authority for belief and practice in your denomination?

Most Protestants would say, of course, that God is, but they disagree among themselves as to how God's authority is revealed or known by human beings.

How do you understand the authority of the Bible?

Some Protestants (sometimes known as fundamentalists or evangelicals) believe that the Bible is literally consistent and true in every word and teaching (it is "verbally inerrant") because it was written by God (using human instruments). Other Protestants believe that it is a somewhat fallible historical document written by people who were faithfully trying to respond to what they understood to be God's intervention in their lives but who wrote in the concepts and language of their own time and place. As such, parts of the Bible are mistaken (e.g., when it declares that the sun stood still), and some of its moral injunctions are outmoded (e.g., stoning to death an adulteress). Most Protestants believe that the Bible conveys the essence of God's intention for humankind. Many believe that the meaning of Scripture has to be provided to the reader through the inspiration of the Holy Spirit.

What is the authority of tradition from the early Church to the present?

Most Protestants put tradition below the authority of the Bible (and in this they tend to disagree with Roman Catholics, who place greater emphasis on tradition). Nevertheless, it cannot be entirely neglected since they believe God has been at work in the history of the Church.

What is the authority of personal experience?

Protestants generally believe that one must have a personal experience of being saved by God through the indwelling of the Holy Spirit. Some make this "conversion" experience central, and locate it at a particular time and place. Others see it as more gradual and cumulative. But personal experience can never contradict the meaning of God's intention as revealed in Scripture.

What is the authority of the historic creeds?

Protestants generally accept the creeds (especially the Apostolic and Nicean) as true reflections of the Christian faith. Nevertheless, many Protestant denominations (mostly in the sixteenth century) have developed their own creedal statements (the Westminster Confession, the Heidelberg Confession, the Augsburg Confession, the Thirty-Nine Articles, etc.).

Do you believe in the divinity of Jesus?

Most Protestants do, while at the same time affirming the complete humanity of Jesus as well. There are some Protestants who tend to downplay the notion of Jesus' divinity and see him, instead, as a perfect moral embodiment (Incarnation) of what God intends for all human persons (though no other human persons have ever lived as perfectly in tune with God as Jesus did).

Do you believe in the resurrection of the dead?
All Protestants accept this claim.

What does it mean to accept Jesus as one's Lord and Savior?
Generally this means that Jesus becomes a guide, a model, a moral example, a personal friend, and the source of one's salvation (by his willingness to die for the sins of others, thus enabling God to forgive them). Generally it means for most Protestants that what Jesus did to procure the salvation of all people makes him their Lord.

How does one attain salvation?
Historically, Protestants believed that their answer to this question distinguished them from Roman Catholics. Believing (erroneously) that Catholics think they can "merit or "earn" heaven by good deeds, Protestants insist that salvation is attainable solely by the free act of God in granting individuals (though not all) salvation by grace. Good deeds *follow out of gratitude for* one's salvation, but unless God has already decided to grant one salvation it cannot be attained by living a good life.

What does salvation mean?
Generally, Protestants understand salvation to mean living forever, joyfully, and fulfillingly, after biological death in the presence of God.

What is the status of the Hebrew Bible or Old Testament as an authority for belief and practice?

All Protestants accept the Old Testament as part of God's revelation to the world of what God is up to and what He intends for humankind. However, they believe that in and through Jesus God extended his actions to include non-Jews (Gentiles) in his plan for the full establishment of the Kingdom of God. Non-fundamentalist Protestants tend to reject parts of the purity codes found, for example, in Leviticus, while believing that God's will is faithfully reflected in such other books as the Prophets. They also accept the general outlines of the scriptural narratives of God's interventions in history on behalf of his chosen people.

Where does authority reside in the church?

It is on this question that most disagreement occurs among Protestants. Many are "congregational," believing that church authority is local, determined by the congregation (assuming it remains faithful to the Bible and creedal affirmations). Congregationally based churches elect their own pastors. Others accept a certain hierarchy in church authority, from bishops down to deacons. The power of the bishop over local congregations and their pastors (priests, or ministers) differs from one denomination to another. Some have the power to appoint clergy to congregations, others simply have the power to license or refuse to license clergy who are elected by congregations. Some Protestant denominations see themselves as global, others more as national bodies, and some as strictly local, often revolving around the authority of a charismatic leader.

How does one become a member of your church?

Protestants believe that one must make a conscious decision to become a member of the church. Membership normally requires baptism and confirmation (or, if already baptized and confirmed in another denomination, reception). Some churches require a profession of conversion; others accept the baptismal assertions as sufficient for membership. Some baptize only adults; most will baptize children provided that they are sponsored by their parents and godparents.

What is your understanding of sacraments, especially Baptism and the Lord's Supper?

All Protestants use at least two sacramental rituals: Baptism and the Lord's Supper (also known as Holy Communion and as the Eucharist). They disagree on what is conveyed by the latter. Some come close to the Roman Catholic position that the substance of Jesus is in the bread and wine. Others believe that the ritual is a remembrance of Jesus' last supper before his death and resurrection. Without agreeing on the details, they all believe that in some way God is present in the sacraments and that they are important for building up the community of the faithful.

Outline the structure of your liturgy or worship service.

This will, of course, differ from denomination to denomination. Some have what are called set liturgies (e.g., the Episcopal Church) in which the services are virtually the same in structure throughout the world. Others are more free-form, developed by the congregation and pastor without relying on a preset text. Present in all Protestant churches, however, are the sermon by the pastor, praise of God, intercessory prayers, and often (but not always) communion.

How do you distinguish your denomination from other Protestant denominations and from Roman Catholicism?

The differences with other Protestant denominations often center around congregational structure, authority in the church (e.g., whether there is a hierarchical structure or not), and the strictness or looseness of biblical interpretation. The difference with Roman Catholicism centers almost entirely around the rejection of the authority of the Papacy, the Magisterium, and the tradition as interpreted by the former (Protestants reject all of these as having no authority over Scripture).

What distinguishes clergy from laypersons?

In most Protestant denominations, clergy need to be ordained by an official body (usually other clergy or a bishop). They are generally trained in accredited seminaries and are expected to have a greater degree of academic knowledge of Scripture, tradition, and theology.

Do clergy need special education/training in order to be ordained (e.g., through an accredited seminary)?

Most Protestant denominations require seminary training, but not all do. In those that don't, election as pastor depends on the individual's facility in interpreting and expounding Scripture, as well as strong pastoral skills as these are discerned and approved by the electing congregation of laypersons.

What is your denomination's view of Judaism?

This is one area in which a great deal of controversy is to be found. Most Protestants are fairly ignorant of the teachings of Judaism, believing that they are to be found only in the Hebrew Bible, with little or no knowledge of the rabbinic teachings and traditions.

Can a Jew be "saved" without first having to become a Christian? Has the Christian Church "superseded" or replaced Judaism in the eyes of God?

This is probably the single most contentious issue today between Protestants and Jews, and even, increasingly, among Christians themselves. A traditional school of thought holds that one must first accept Jesus as one's Lord and Savior in order to be saved. This school holds that the Christian Church has replaced or superceded Judaism (and God's covenant with the Jews) as the precondition for salvation. This means that unless a Jew converts to Christianity he cannot be saved. But increasingly there are Christians (Catholic and Protestant alike) who are revisiting this ancient position, especially in the wake of the long history of anti-Semitism and the Holocaust, which were, at the very least, aided and abetted by Christians and Christian teaching. Some of the new thinking among Christians suggests that God has never broken his covenant with the Jews (and, therefore, they do not need a new covenant or New Testament and thus do not need to convert to Christianity). Christianity, they maintain, is like a graft onto the stem that has grown from the soil of Judaism. This Christian graft has allowed non-Jews to also enter into covenant with God, but the new covenant does not abrogate the earlier one.

Can other non-Christians be saved without first becoming Christian?

Traditionally, the answer has been no. But increasingly, as in the case of the reconsideration of the status of Jews in God's covenant, many are suggesting that God's love and power are so vast and unconditioned that it is up to God whether someone will be saved regardless of whether he/she has become a Christian. As a result they are not inclined to judge whether non-Christians must first become Christians in order to be saved.

Do Christians and the Christian churches bear some responsibility for the Holocaust? If so, what is their moral obligation toward Jews today?

Most Protestants would accept some complicity in the long history of anti-Semitism and, therefore, in the background for the Holocaust. And most would accept a moral responsibility for working for reconciliation between Jews and Christians, as well as for removing theological obstacles between the two branches of God's covenant.

Does your denomination support going to war in a just cause in defense of innocent people? Can Christians be strict pacifists?
Some Protestants are strict pacifists, especially those coming from the Anabaptist tradition (e.g., Amish, Mennonite). But most Protestants accept a version of the just-war theory which morally justifies a nation using military force under restricted conditions: it must be a defensive reaction to attack, it must not cause more harm than failing to fight, it must use the least amount of lethal force to bring the war to an end, it must be winnable, it must protect non-combatants, it must be a last resort.

What is the Protestant position concerning the State of Israel as the eternal home of the Jewish people and the Second Coming of Christ?
There is no official Protestant position on the question of the status of the State of Israel. On the conservative or evangelical side, there are some who believe that Jesus cannot come again until the Jewish people are safely ensconced in their ancient homeland, Israel. Then, when that happens, Jesus will come again and they will all convert to Christianity. (This is the position taken by Jerry Falwell and Pat Robertson, and that is why evangelical Protestants are such strong supporters of the State of Israel.)

On the other hand, most non-evangelical Protestants look at Israel in political terms. It is a nation whose rights to national sovereignty must be absolutely and unequivocally respected. These Protestants are also, for the most part, highly sensitive to the suffering of the Jews historically and most recently in the Holocaust, and that because of this suffering they deserve a homeland. But they would tend to judge the domestic and foreign policies of the

State of Israel by the same standards as any other nation: are they fair, just, and do they provide for equitable treatment of all people under the control of the State of Israel? These Protestants, therefore, are sensitive to the suffering of the Palestinian people under Israeli control, without ignoring the fact that the Palestinian leadership has consistently rejected opportunities for peace with Israel, and that many of them have continued to call for Israel's destruction, thus bearing much of the responsibility for establishing the conditions for peace with Israel. Many (perhaps 20 percent) of Palestinians are Christians, and Protestants want to feel religious solidarity with them, but of course they deplore violent means to resolve the conflict. These non-evangelical Protestants are not particularly attuned to beliefs about the second coming of Christ or to the historical location in which it is supposed to occur. Therefore, their allegiance to the State of Israel is not based primarily on a literal reading of Scripture but on more basic principles of national rights and the protection of peoples and states from internal and external threat.

Chapter 5

African Methodist Episcopal

Dr. Alvan N. Johnson, Jr.

Three of a kind

It is to the distinct advantage of all human beings to explore and understand the world and its people through in-depth examination of what is held in common and celebrated, as opposed to exaggerating our differences and dividing. The Abrahamic religions, namely Judaism, Islam, and Christianity, have powerful and striking similarities and commonalities. When they are thoroughly investigated, universal harmony and peace must inevitably follow.

The Abrahamic religions share the spiritually empowering phenomenon of monotheism. The belief in one God who is Creator and Sustainer secures and bolsters the human psyche through all situations, particularly in seasons of adversity. Not only do we share, not only do we mutually embrace the profundity of reliance on the Unseen, Omnipotent, Peaceful Deity, we also share in a formal ritual that celebrates our commitment to said embrace. For Judaism this celebration is the entry rite of circumcision. In Islam it is the *Shahada,* or "witnessing," to the faith before the faithful. In Christianity the entry rite is the water ceremony known as baptism.

An interfaith mission to the actual geography of the Holy Land reveals another striking commonality that may escape us if we rely too heavily on book learning. The sacredness of holy places, the holiness of places where divinity has kissed the terrain, the interactions among divinity and humanity and locality hold extreme promise for the principles of peace. For a Christian to witness the expression on a Jewish traveling companion's face as he stands on

237

Mount Hermon or as she encounters the Wailing Wall, or for a Jew to journey with a Christian through the pain and treachery in the Garden of Gethsemane and the agony of Golgotha to the indescribable joy at the Tomb of the Resurrection, or for both of them to visit the Dome of the Rock and the Aksa Mosque must be life-changing experiences. When we understand these things in the intimate way we can know things only with friends, we will operate from a position of love and respect, which are the foundation stones of a just peace.

Finally, and perhaps most important, the Creator of Abraham, who was the father of all of our faiths, is the Creator who said, "I brought you out of the land of Egypt and out of the house of bondage." Our God, our Allah, creates us free and intends for us to be liberated from all oppression, if we will only turn our hearts and minds to receive our Creator's love and bend our spirits to our Creator's will. Moses and Jesus and Muhammad all came to liberate us. We celebrate Passover and Easter and Ramadan, all marking liberating events in our entwined and overlapping histories. We all call for compassion for the least among us and for justice for all and for peace on earth. We stand upon these principles because we all believe that a liberated people is a compassionate people, a just people, and a peaceful people. It is impossible for us to liberate ourselves at the expense of our brothers and sisters. Our only hope, as individuals and as members of particular faiths, is to work for the liberation for all people with justice seekers from all faiths.

As pastor of Bethel African Methodist Episcopal Church, it was my distinct pleasure and privilege to travel to the Holy Land as one of the leaders of an interfaith delegation guided by Rabbi Philip Lazowski, rabbi of Temple Beth Hillel. The pastoral family and members of Bethel Church are eternally grateful to Rabbi Lazowski and the good people of Beth Hillel, as well as to our traveling companions from the Church of the Sacred Heart, for a trip well traveled, for bonding in the sacred places we visited, and for bonding over breakfasts and dinners and chance moments of quiet in a heavy touring schedule. There is a closeness and fellowship that comes among travelers that cannot be matched by any number of potluck suppers and joint worship services. We must work tirelessly to keep the spirit of fellowship alive in our midst.

As a diverse yet connected group, we had the awe-inspiring experience of witnessing the Holy Land together from the Golan Heights to Egypt, stopping along the way at Jericho, Mary's house in Bethlehem, the Arab market in Jerusalem, the tomb of Maimonides, the Dome of the Rock where Abraham established monotheism, the Garden of Gethsemane on the Mount of Olives, and Elat, just to name a few. We came away, as I believe everyone must, with a deep-seated appreciation for the entwining of humanity and divinity. We came away, as I believe everyone must, with a sense of hope that springs from observing the creativity of God. We came away, as I believe everyone must, with a new understanding of the holiness of our different traditions and a new respect for our different pathways to the One True and Universal God. When we achieve this, we will be equipped, prepared, and qualified to work for true, universal, and lasting peace.

While monotheism and poker have nothing in common, so to speak, there is a phenomenon in poker that gives us insight into the promise of unified diversity. In poker, one card never wins. Two cards together are very easily beaten. However, three of a kind present a formidable alliance that requires extremely canny fortune to defeat. The enemy of religion is in no wise other practitioners of faith. The real enemy of Islam is not Judaism and the enemy of Judaism is not Christianity. Such a notion is sheer idiocy. The truth of the matter is that the enemies of the faithful are (1) cosmic evil and (2) sinful godless oppression. Those are the enemies against which we are called into Jihad and into a "Crusade." In short, the Creator is calling for us to do battle against the Devil and not one another. By itself, Christianity is able only to conquer some oppression. By itself, Islam can only eradicate a portion of the evil of this world. By itself, Judaism will only defeat a modicum of the results of sin. However, Christianity plus Judaism plus Islam equals three of a kind and, as such, presents a formidable opponent to cosmic evil. Can you imagine how many families can be healed? Can you imagine how many children can be educated? How many homeless people housed? And how many wrongs could be righted, if the diversified unity of three of a kind were to coalesce in one hand—the Hand of God—against evil? Can you imagine if these three forces were to join together? War would be ended because evil would certainly be crushed.

Having crossed the Sea of Galilee and having spent a day on the kibbutz, having taught at the Mount of the Beatitudes and preached at the site of the Resurrection of the Lord Jesus, having prayed with my Muslim brothers outside the Aksa Mosque and having gathered water from the Jordan, having inserted prayers into the Wailing Wall and gathered the soil of Egypt, it is abundantly clear to me that Islam, Christianity, and Judaism are three of a kind, which is the winning hand when that hand is the Hand of God. A Salaam Alaikum. Shalom. My peace I leave with you.

* * *

The mission of the African Methodist Episcopal Church is to minister to the spiritual, intellectual, physical, emotional, and environmental needs of all people by spreading Christ's liberating Gospel through word and deed. The African Methodist Episcopal Church, or A.M.E. Church, is a mainline, mainstream Protestant denomination that is dedicated to seeking out and saving the lost and serving the needy. We adhere to the Twenty-Five Articles of Religion that govern Methodism and will be explained in detail below. Unlike Catholicism, the preaching of the Gospel is central. Further, we are charged to continue programs that feed the hungry, clothe the naked, house the homeless, cheer the fallen, and provide jobs for the jobless. We are dedicated to administering to the needs of those in prisons, hospitals, nursing homes, asylums, and mental institutions. The A.M.E. Church is also dedicated to encouraging thrift and economic advancement. The African Methodist Episcopal Church only has two ceremonies that are designated as sacraments. One is the sacrament of Holy Baptism. Holy Baptism is the entry rite into the Christian Church. We subscribe to the belief in infant baptism. While some Protestant denominations differ on the sacrament of Baptism, we believe in the "Baptism of Believers." However, we also believe in the confession of parents and thus baptize infants and children as well. The second sacrament is the sacrament of Eucharist, or The Lord's Supper, also known as Holy Communion. Communicants receive both elements of the communion. Unlike Catholicism, African Methodism believes that the celebrants add Spirit to substance, thus turning ordinary wine/grape juice and ordinary bread into the symbol of the sacrificial body and blood of Christ. We do not believe that the elements of Holy Communion actually become flesh and blood, but rather the symbols of maximum sacrifice.

The earliest Christian communities were decidedly Jewish Christians who reverenced the Sabbath. However, as belief in the physical resurrection of Jesus became more widespread, worship then moved to what is commonly called Sunday, as opposed to the Sabbath, because each gathering was a celebration of the Resurrection. Thus, Christians worship on the first day of the week.

Just as Judaism has three major branches, Orthodox, Conservative, and Reform, and within these branches smaller subdivisions, including Hasidim and Jews for Jesus, so then does Protestantism. There are at least 450 Protestant denominations. Each one may have something different to say about the relationship between Christianity and Judaism. If that does not speak to diversity on the issue, then add to that the reality that depending on the seminary in which a pastor was trained, each local church may have a different approach to its relationship to Judaism. We at Bethel A.M.E. Church in Bloomfield tenaciously espouse the inherent dignity and worth of all human beings. We teach without exception that God is the Creator of all life, in fact, all that is. We strictly forbid the denigration and/or irreverence of any other human being's ethnicity, physical characteristics, or religious beliefs. We believe and teach that Judaism is the parent faith of Christianity, and that they are, therefore, inextricably conjoined. A careful reading of the New Testament and intense biblical study reveals that Jesus of Nazareth had no desire to institute a movement with Himself as the center. Rather, He was prescribing a particular method of reestablishing relationship with God, the Creator. He constantly refers people to God and, more often than not, averts attention from Himself to the God of Abraham, Isaac, and Jacob. Anti-Semitism has absolutely no role in Christianity whatsoever. In fact, it is contrary to the essence of the faith. Further, we believe emphatically that all occupants of Palestine are Semites, and, thus, all are directly related to essential Christianity.

We believe beyond a shadow of a doubt that the Holocaust is historical reality. It was the second-most-horrible attempt at genocide, superseded only by the Middle Passage. We deeply regret the role of European-based Christianity, which one must argue is considerably away from the Palestinian experience of the faith. European Christianity was at the heart of the cause of slavery and at the heart of the cause of the Holocaust. We, as African American Protestants, distance ourselves from either enterprise. In fact, we have suffered mightily from the same phenomenon. The silence of the Christian Church in these God-awful tragedies is both theologically indefensible and socially reprehensible.

The Christian Church is critically divided on the issue of abortion. Our denomination is somewhat divided on the issue as well. Our position can best be stated as the "choose life" position. We

African Methodist Episcopal / 243

must use every strategy at our disposal to convince people not to abort fetuses. However, at the conclusion of our protestation, should the person choose to proceed, that procedure must be private, clean, and safe. Likewise, war is very often essential to preserve human life from those who do not share its value. On the other hand, capital punishment has never proven to be a deterrent. The state of Texas has the highest number of capital punishments, but also maintains the highest per capita murder rate. Clearly, capital punishment "ain't working." More importantly, it is in no wise distributed justly or evenly between the rich and the poor and between whites and minorities. It is to cease until a rationale evolves that sustains it.

Bethel African Methodist Episcopal Church seriously regrets the historical misstatement of the Catholic Church. Further, the recent restatement of the present Pope was most unfortunate. A clear understanding of the activity of God vividly assures the enlightened believer that God reveals God's presence universally. There is no one pathway to God. And it is abundantly clear (a) from biblical truths and (b) from recent discoveries that Isaiah 53:6 is abundantly clear when it states, "All we, like sheep, have gone astray."

God alone is Sovereign. No human being can ever fully know the mind of God. No one can ever know whom God forgives and whom God does not. We teach that God's mercy and forgiveness are infinite. However, they must not be taken for granted. The much more difficult issue is whether or not we can forgive even the minor infractions that we so tenaciously cling to. We need to learn how to forgive one another in our households and in our daily relationships. Then, murderers and rapists and other dangerous criminals have a prayer of a chance of being forgiven. Forgiveness is an art form that righteous-thinking people of all faiths need to perfect.

We believe profoundly and wholeheartedly in the Resurrection of the Lord Jesus Christ. We believe that Jesus of Nazareth was crucified and was buried in the tomb of Joseph of Arimathea. However, before the morning of the third day, His body underwent a metaphysical transformation. His body and His spirit were reunited. He emerged from the tomb and is still "alive," and even though invisible to the naked eye, will be alive until we all undergo the exact same process.

All Christians believe that the person of the Lord and Savior Jesus Christ fulfills the requirements of the Messianic Liberator called for in the prophecies in the Hebrew Bible to a large extent. Some believe that Jesus fulfills every requirement, but many do not. Those Christians who struggle with the fulfillment issue struggle with the existence of war and the other prophetic assurances that were to accompany Messiah. Some would postulate that it is the rejection of Messiah that perpetuates war. Here at Bethel it is clearly believed that Jesus is the Messiah and that, if He had been universally accepted by Romans, Jews, and pagans, the Messianic conditions predicted would have obtained. However, it is much more important for us at Bethel to point out that Christians are anticipating the *return* of the Messiah, while the Jews are anticipating the initial advent of Messiah. We are convinced that when the Jewish Messiah arrives and the Christian returns that they could very well be the same being. This is our hope.

We have a profound belief in the concepts of heaven and hell. However, it is extremely difficult to communicate that they are not spatial realities. These two realities are both physical and metaphysical. Hell is the condition of a torment of the spirit. However, constant and perpetual bombardment of racism and sexism, anti-Semitism and dehumanization render earthly existence hellish. Heaven, which is the synonymous term with the Kingdom of God, is both present reality and future condition. The Kingdom of God is already, but not yet.

We are absolutely and unequivocally opposed to any presence of coercion as it relates to conversion. People are not to be forced into the Kingdom. Belief is a purely voluntary act, the importance of which is taught, not indoctrinated. Human beings are endowed with free will, and the Scripture is clear, God is most pleased when we voluntarily affiliate with His presence. Very much akin to this thought is the concept of pacifism. The Bible is replete with allowances for just war. The process of proof-texting or isolating Scriptures can clearly lead to a justification of pacifism. Further, scant few Christians have either read or remember that Martin Luther considered pacifism to be sedition because pacifism too far extended would destroy the police power of the state. We, however, interpret the words of the Lord Jesus, "Render unto Caesar that which is Caesar's," to mean that it is justified to defend the state from external threat, as any good citizen would.

As it relates to the person and work of Jesus the Christ, we are convinced that He is the Son of God. What if the word "Son" is interpreted to mean "brainchild" or the idea of God? What if the term "Son" of God means the decision of God to take that which is invisible and make it visible? We believe that all human beings are the children of God. However, we believe that Jesus of Nazareth was the *only* child of God that is not made visible through the processes by which all other human beings are made visible. This, in fact, falls into the realm of miracle, which leads us to a discussion of the Virgin Birth. If we were to assemble every single scientist on this planet and make available to them every single chemical known to humanity, they would be utterly unable to produce even one apple seed. Therefore, it could be said that an apple seed is a miracle—a happenstance unable to be duplicated by humanity. The Virgin Birth falls into the realm of belief in God's ability. The Creator Life Force (a) can never be fully understood by finite humanity and (b) must be believed to be able to effect *any* phenomenon. Thus, God is certainly capable of effecting a virgin birth or a sunrise or an apple seed.

The concept of the Trinity, or three entities being one God, is decidedly the most difficult to explain to the rational mind, especially one predisposed to disbelief. However, there are three concepts that aid us in comprehending that which is incomprehensible. The first help is the concept of revelation. The concept of revelation, succinctly stated, is that Adonai reveals God's self at Creation and, thus, reveals creative power. Second, in the person, the physical manifestation (the idea of God to reveal God's intent for our lives), namely, Jesus the Christ, God reveals love. God intends for us to love one another so profoundly that we are prepared to sacrifice all for one another. He demonstrates this on the Cross at Golgotha. Finally, Ruach revealed God's companionship, namely, the Spirit of God, as an ever-present reality. Thus, we see three distinct aspects of the same reality separately revealed. The second help, as it were, is the concept of function. If a woman is married, has children, and her parents are still alive, she is one being that is at once daughter, wife, and mother. It is disconcerting that people so readily grasp how three can be one in that instance, yet are so slow to grasp the exact same concept in the supernatural arena. God is at once supreme parent, divine example, and constant companion, simultaneously. The third concept or help is the concept of substance. That is to say, that the Creator God, the physical manifestation of the person, Jesus, and the continuing presence of the Holy Spirit are all three of the same substance. Water, ice, and steam are the same substance in different forms. Therefore, God eternal parent, God liberating redeemer, and God spirit companion are of the same substance.

We at Bethel A.M.E. Church depend heavily on the biblical concept of atonement. There is a four-step process revealed in Scripture that precipitates atonement. The first is confession. One must admit that behavior is sin. Second, there must be a cessation of the offensive behavior. Third, there must be a reversal in the behavior of the offender. And fourth, there must be a restoration of the victim. The concept of atonement for others is much, much more difficult to understand. The Hebrew Bible affords us the ritual of placing the sins of others on a proverbial scapegoat. Further, the Bible assures us that the prayers of the righteous availeth much. Atonement for others is possible through the process of mediation and can be accomplished by a neutral intermediary. We believe that Jesus is the classic example of the process.

In the matter of the relationship between faith and works, we believe that a person must have both, that true faith will lead necessarily to works. The New Testament clearly states that faith without works is dead. We wholeheartedly believe that once the status of faith is established, it will necessarily lead to good works. The question arises: Can a person who does good works and does not have faith inherit salvation? It appears to be a moot point. Anyone who has no faith is not concerned with salvation. So salvation is not in their grasp simply because it does not concern them. However, one must also raise the question: If they truly have no faith, why are they doing good works? We would suggest that they have faith in something.

We, as African Methodists, support the position of celibacy before marriage and fidelity in marriage. We categorically reject the idea that celibacy is a mandatory prerequisite for the spiritual leadership.

As it regards the relationship between Passover and Easter, the perceived differences are woefully exaggerated—ad nauseam. Conversely, the similarities are ultimately ignored. Passover is the powerful demarcation of freedom from Egypt. The Resurrection is the demarcation of liberation from the fear of death. Christians must never, ever teach anyone that the Jews killed Jesus, when ethnically it was the Romans. Second, Christians must never teach that the Jews killed Jesus when it was the absence of love and the presence of jealousy and the practice of deceit and evidence of the demonic, which are all endemic to humanity, that killed Jesus. That is why in the Black Christian tradition we are loath to espouse any notion that it was a group of people that destroyed the God-Man.

But rather, we raise the question as to whether or not you and I are in possession now of any of the character traits that accompanied the death of Jesus. We raise the question, Were you there when they crucified my Lord? Was the jealousy and suspicion resident in your personality responsible for the death of the Savior? We must celebrate Passover because it engenders the mysterious, miraculous ability of God to liberate those whom God loves from the clutches of evil. Likewise, we must celebrate the Resurrection because it symbolizes God's miraculous and mysterious ability to liberate us from the clutches of evil.

The Book of Revelations is to be understood as prophetic cryptology, as was the Book of Daniel. People of faith have always codified their communications with one another, and Revelations is no exception. There can be no doubt that the book was written to send secret messages to believers throughout the Diaspora. That is to say, it predicts the fall of Rome and the end of oppression, but only in terms that other Christians would understand.

The concept of *Christos Imitatio* will keep pure first-century Christianity relevant for all time. The recording of the actions of first-century Christians simply illuminates the consistency of human nature. The imitation of Christ is the strategy that empowers Christians to respond to the foibles in human personality, to contribute successfully, and to survive triumphantly. Faith will always be relevant. Working for justice, as did first-century Christians, will always be relevant. Reducing pain and interacting with other like-minded human beings will always be relevant. Thank you and God bless.

African Methodism and Its Relationship to Judaism

What is the ultimate authority for belief and practice in your denomination?
The Holy Bible, consisting of the Hebrew Bible and the New Testament, is the ultimate authority for belief and practice in the

African Methodist Episcopal Church. *The Doctrine and Practice of the African Methodist Episcopal Church* provides the regulatory authority for the governance of the denomination.

How do you understand the authority of the Bible?

Is the Bible literally consistent and true in every word and teaching, or is it a somewhat fallible historical document written by people who were faithfully trying to respond to what they understood to be God's intervention in their lives even though they expressed their response in flawed human language and thought-forms?

Our denomination understands the Bible to contain unequivocal truth as revealed by God to God's people. However, we make a distinction between fact and truth. Our denomination does not adhere to a literal understanding of the Bible, but rather understands that through careful interpretation, the truth that is embedded in every periscope and passage will be brought to light.

What is the authority of church tradition from the early church to the present?

The authority of church tradition supersedes that of the Bible in one instance. It is an extremely significant instance, but for all intents and purposes the only one. It is the case of infant baptism. The early church believed that Jesus' return was imminent. They began baptizing infants, thus establishing the tradition that dominates Christendom to the present. African Methodism stands in the mainstream, mainline Methodist tradition that was born in the Great Awakening under the theological leadership of John Wesley and John Knox. These theologians redirected the Christian experience away from the excesses of the hierarchical Roman Catholic structure and theology back toward a theology that encouraged a direct, personal relationship with God, using the Bible as the ultimate authority. The "method" of worship designed by early Methodist theologians is still followed by the A.M.E. Church. With the establishment of African Methodism in 1787, a denomination founded in social protest against racism, a new Afrocentric church tradition, centered around the liberating activity of God in the world took root and was grafted on to the Methodist church tradition.

What is the authority of personal experience?

While we validate personal experience, it has scant authority to determine doctrine. Rather personal experience is a potent tool in the evangelistic thrust of the church. Prayer meetings provide a formal environment where believers can witness to their personal relationships with God.

What is the authority of the historic creeds, especially Nicea in 325?

In order for Jews to understand the Christian experience, they are requesting to understand that which a huge segment of the Christian Church does not understand. The entire problem of authority, especially for those of us in the Protestant Episcopal wing of the Christian Church is answered in what we call the Quadrilateral:

1. Holy Scripture, including the Hebrew Bible and the New Testament, contain all things that are necessary to salvation. Thus, it is the prime authority.
2. The Apostles Creed and the Nicene Creed enjoy authority second only to the Bible in that they are the sufficient statement of the Christian faith.
3. The third authority is that of the two sacraments, Baptism and the Lord's Supper, ministered with the unfailing use of Christ's words.
4. Last, the tradition of the church stands as an authority.

Therefore, the creeds of the church, especially Nicea, have authority as it relates to the clear, faithful articulation of the beliefs of Christianity.

Do you believe in the divinity of Jesus?

The simple and direct answer to the question of belief in the divinity of Jesus is an unapologetic yes. However, let us have a brief discussion. We believe that all human beings are mundane creatures that are possessed with a modicum of divinity, the proverbial spark of the divine. Jesus, though human, was possessed of much more than a spark. Rather, His being was filled with the Spirit of that which is divine.

Do you believe in the resurrection of the dead?

The clearest articulation of the resurrection is found in Paul's Epistle to the Thessalonians. We thoroughly believe in the resurrection of the dead that is predicated on the belief that at conception spirit and body are united and that at death spirit and body are separated. At the resurrection, the same spirit and the same body are reunited and radically transformed into a supernatural, eternal state of being.

What does it mean to accept Jesus as one's Lord and Savior?

At Bethel A.M.E. Church in Bloomfield, we attempt to instill in believers that we are to worship Jesus, and therefore God, as a physical manifestation of a transcendent reality. Lord and Savior, then, means allowing the theology/Christology, the philosophy and the wisdom of Jesus Christ to determine one's actions and inform one's decisions. The term "Lord" must mean the being that controls our lives. Savior, then, engenders a sense of emulation. If we live our lives the way Jesus lived His, then we escape eternal damnation, as well as punishment and ignominy in this life.

How does one attain salvation?

For us, particularly as Black and minority and female Christians, salvation is synonymous with liberation. We are set free from the power of sin and the forces of oppression and gain everlasting life by identifying our spiritual essence with Jesus, and we submit our lifestyles to the Christ.

What does salvation mean?
Historically, the Book of Genesis in the Hebrew Bible has been interpreted to portray the spiritual condition of all humanity. It attempts to explain the fact that all human beings are born with the ability, yes, and worse, the proclivity to sin. All human beings are to be punished for actual sin committed, much of which qualifies us for eternal punishment. Salvation, then, means that we have a relationship with God because we are followers of Jesus Christ that averts eternal damnation and existential punishment and assures us of present safety and future security.

What is the status of the Hebrew Bible as an authority for belief and practice?
The Hebrew Bible, also known as the Old Testament, is clear and distinct authority for belief and practice. In fact, it is quintessential and nonreplaceable. We believe that both the Hebrew Bible and the New Testament contain all that is necessary for salvation. This is important for all faiths because we teach that no one needs Tarot cards, Ouija boards, prayer cloths, psychic hotlines, or crystals for salvation. Rather, the Word of God is contained in the Hebrew Bible and augmented in the New Testament. Christ has come to fulfill Torah, not to dislodge it.

Where does authority reside in the church?
Do you have a hierarchy of authority in the church (e.g., bishops, priests, deacons, laypersons, etc.)? Does the local church have the power to hire and fire its pastor?

The African Methodist Episcopal Church is governed by episcopacy. That is to say, there is a cadre of twenty bishops that govern nineteen episcopal districts and one ecumenical post. There is an intermediary order of presiding elders who assist the bishop in administration. Each local church is presided over by a pastor appointed by the bishop. The local church does not have the authority to hire or fire a pastor, but the lay leadership of the church, known as stewards, does have the ability to petition the bishop for the removal of the pastor

How does one become a member of your church?

There are two methods of becoming a member of the African Methodist Episcopal Church. The first is through the sacrament of Holy Baptism. The second is by volunteering to become one, having already been baptized into the Christian faith, and then being trained in the A.M.E. tradition.

What is your understanding of sacraments, especially Baptism and the Lord's Supper?

The African Methodist Episcopal Church only subscribes to two sacraments or ultimately sacred acts. They are holy Baptism and Holy Communion. Many Christian churches, including our church, teach that Holy Baptism is to Christians what circumcision is for the Jews, and that is the sacred entry rite into the faith. The sacrament of Holy Communion is the rite of remembrance, and that is to remember that the cost of true freedom very often requires the sacrificing of human life.

Outline the structure of your liturgy or worship service

A December service: Fourth Sunday in Advent
The Devotional Period
The Processional
The Doxology (Contemporary)
The Call to Worship
The Hymn of Praise

The Invocation
The Choral Response
The Interlude
The Holy Scripture Lesson
The Choral Selection
The Decalogue (Contemporary)
The Gloria Patri
The Choral Selection
The Offertory
The Exercise of Christian Stewardship
The Choral Response
The Sermon
The Invitation to Christian Discipleship
The Doxology
The Benediction
The Postlude

How do you distinguish your denomination from other Protestant denominations and from Roman Catholicism?

The African Methodist Episcopal Church is, as are other Protestant denominations, distinguished from Roman Catholicism primarily by the doctrines of the infallibility of the Pope, the necessity of intercession by priests, the availability of both elements (until recently), and the belief that the elements of Holy Communion are changed in their essential nature. We are distinguished from Baptist and some Pentecostal denominations in that we are thoroughly convinced of the spiritual efficacy of infant baptism. There are other distinctions of a historical nature, but please be given to know that we here at Bethel A.M.E. Church spend an enormous amount of time focusing, concentrating on the similarities of Protestantism, Catholicism, Judaism, and Muhammadism. We have and we hold much, much more in common than that which divides us.

What distinguishes clergy from laypersons?

Do clergy need special education/training in order to be ordained (e.g., through an accredited seminary)?

We believe that all believers have a ministry. The laity have specialized ministries; namely, music, education, youth, missions, and so on. Likewise, the clergy have ministries as well. The only difference is that the clergy require special training and education and are set apart for sacred duty; namely, to perform marriages and baptisms, to consecrate Holy Communion, and to bury the dead. In our denomination an aspirant must have an undergraduate degree in order to begin the pursuit of ministry and must be a graduate of an accredited seminary in order to be ordained.

What is your denomination's view of Judaism?

Can a Jew be saved by God without first having to become a Christian? Can other non-Christians be saved without first becoming Christian? Has the Christian Church superseded or replaced Judaism in the eyes of God as God's chosen people? Do Christians and the Christian churches bear some responsibility for the Holocaust? Did Christianity and Christians contribute to anti-Semitism? If so, what is their moral obligation toward Jews today? Does your denomination support going to war in a just cause in defense of innocent people?

To be perfectly honest, there very well may be a difference of opinion as it relates to Judaism, depending on one's training and experience. Our denomination, per se, has not made a declarative statement in this matter. However, we here at Bethel African Methodist Episcopal Church, definitively, unequivocally, categorically, and any other "-ly" that there is, hold tenaciously to the notion that God and God alone is the author and determining factor in salvation. Jesus stated quite clearly that not everyone who claims to be a Christian will enter the Kingdom of heaven. He goes on to say that the person who does the *will of the Father* shall enter the eternal Kingdom. There are some people who claim to be Christian who will burn in eternal damnation, and there are agnostics and monotheistic Jews who are doing the will of God. We have nothing else to say on this matter. In terms of being God's chosen people, Jews and Christians alike must understand that we must be God's choosing people. God is now, and always has been, at war with idolatry, not the Abraham faith. No one, but no one, has special standing in relationship to a Common Creator. The issue is whether or not a human being worships the One, True, and Living God or places his or her trust in the lottery, diamonds, their practice, the casino, or any earthly toy.

We believe that Christians bear the same responsibility for the Holocaust that Jews bear for the oppression of minorities today. Whenever any human being ignores the plight and oppression of any other human being, they are, in fact, anti-Semitic, anti-Christian, anti-Black, and anti-Palestinian. Jews and Christians are morally obligated to one another today. The Holocaust accounted for the loss of more than six million Jews fifty years ago. Slavery accounted for the loss of twenty million Africans 200 years ago. The task before us is to address one another's suffering here and now today.

Our denomination encourages every practitioner to be a good citizen, not only to cooperate with the state, but to participate in the state and to help to protect it and preserve its freedom. This may call for military operations to participate in an unjust war, as opposed to suborning anarchy. However, we must at all costs work tirelessly for the state to be just in all its actions. Therefore, war for self-defense and for the defense of innocent people very well may become justified.

What is your denomination's position concerning the State of Israel as the eternal home of the Jewish people, and the Second Coming of Christ?

Again, our denomination has not made a public pronouncement specifically regarding the State of Israel. We accept by acclamation Israel's right to exist. However, we make a resoundingly clear, categorical, emphatic distinction between the State of Israel and Judaism. We thank God for Rabbi Philip Lazowski, who enabled us to see Israel from the Syrian border to Egypt. We thank God for that experience. There we learned that perhaps 50 percent of the population of Israel are non-practicing or ethnic Jews. This is an incredibly important factor. The State of Israel is a political entity that must evaluate her actions by Torah if she is to be the home of the spiritually Jewish people. Lastly, we know for a certainty that absolutely no one, absolutely no one, knows the chronology or the geography of the Second Coming of Christ.

We are more than elated to be involved with this extremely important work. We thank God for the opportunity, and we thank God for Rabbi Philip Lazowski.

Chapter 6

EVANGELICAL PROTESTANTISM

Rev. Terry Wiles

Who are the Protestants?

Protestants are one of two distinct channels of Western Christendom. The other is Romanism, the Latin church, which is commonly known as the Roman Catholic Church.[1] In broad terms a Protestant is a Christian who is not of the Roman or the Eastern Church. In more specific terms a Protestant is a Christian who believes in (1) the authority of Scripture rather than the authority of the papal system, (2) justification by faith in the work of Jesus Christ on the cross, and (3) the priesthood of every believer.

What are you protesting against, and are you still protesting?

While it is common to use the term "protest" in a negative way, it also has a positive meaning. The term "protest" means, according to *Webster's Ninth New Collegiate Dictionary*, "to make a solemn declaration or affirmation of." As such, Protestants are any of several church groups that affirm or bring witness to a set of tenets that set them apart from the Roman or Eastern Church. In that sense a Protestant is "protesting," but I personally prefer the concept of "Pro-Testament.

What are the basic tenets of Protestantism?

The basic principles of Protestantism are:

---

[1] From *Schaff's History of the Church*, Electronic Database, 1999, by Biblesoft.

1. The New Testament teaching that a person is justified not by works of any kind but by faith in the redeeming substitutionary work of Christ on the Cross. We believe that Jesus Christ was the "sacrificial Lamb of God," the sinless sacrifice that was made for the sins of all mankind.

2. The principle of the *priesthood of the believer*, which means that every redeemed person has access to God through prayer and need not go through any other human being to reach God.

3. The primacy of the Bible, both the Old and New Testaments, as the only source of revealed truth, the written word of God to mankind, inspired by God, and preserved for our guidance in Godly living.

What do you as an Evangelical Protestant believe in?

The Bible, composed of the sixty-six books of the Old and New Testaments, is the revealed word of God. Scripture in its entirety originated with God and was given through the instrumentality of chosen men. Scripture thus at one and the same time speaks with the authority of God and reflects the backgrounds, styles, and vocabularies of the human authors. We hold that the Scriptures are infallible and inerrant in the original manuscripts. They are the unique, full, and final authority on all matters of faith and practice, and there are no other writings similarly inspired by God. (2 Timothy 3:15–17; 1 Thessalonians 2:13; 2 Peter 1:21)

We believe that there is one true, holy God, eternally existing in three persons (Father, Son, and Holy Spirit (each of whom possesses equally all the attributes of deity and the characteristics of personality (Deuteronomy 6:4; Isaiah 43:10–11; Matthew 38:19; Luke 3:22).

We believe in the Deity of the Lord Jesus Christ. The Scriptures declare:

His virgin birth (Matthew 1:23; Luke 1:31, 35).
His sinless life (Hebrews 7:26; 1 Peter 2:22).

His miracles (Acts 2:22, 10:38).

His substitutionary work on the cross (1 Corinthians 15:3; 2 Corinthians 5:21).

His bodily resurrection from the dead (Matthew 28:6; Luke 24:39; 1 Corinthians 15:4).

That by voluntary transgression man fell and thereby incurred not only physical death, but also spiritual death, which is separation from God (Genesis 1:26–27, 2:17, 3:6; Romans 5:12–19).

That man's only hope of redemption is through the shed blood of Jesus Christ, the Son of God, and that to appropriate that salvation comes through repentance toward God and faith toward the Lord Jesus Christ (Luke 24:47; John 3:3; Romans 10:13–15; Ephesians 2:8; Titus 2:11, 3:5–7).

The ordinance of baptism by immersion is commanded in the Scriptures, and all who repent and believe in Christ as Savior are to be baptized. Thus they declare to the world that they are followers of Jesus Christ (Matthew 28:19; Mark 16:16; Acts 10:47–48; Romans 6:4).

The ordinance of Holy Communion, the Lord's Supper, consisting of the elements bread and the fruit of the vine is the symbol expressing our sharing the divine nature of our Lord Jesus Christ (2 Peter 1:4), a memorial of His suffering and death (1 Corinthians 11:26), and a prophecy of His second coming (1 Corinthians 11:26), and is to be practiced by all believers until He comes again.

That a life of holiness and obedience should be the target of believers which is attained as they follow the Scriptures and submit to the work of God's Spirit. This process, called sanctification, results in separation from that which is evil and dedication unto God. (Romans 12:1–2; Hebrews 13:12; 1 Peter 1:15–16).

That God will empower us to live for Him if we seek that empowerment which we call Baptism in the Holy Spirit, not to be confused with the Baptism in Water mentioned earlier (Luke 24:49; Acts 1:8).

That there is one true Church universal, comprised of all those who acknowledge Jesus Christ as Savior and Lord (Ephesians 1:22–23, 2:22; Hebrews 12:23).

That believers are people of time and eternity, and we are to live our lives in anticipation of our Lord's return. That return will be sudden and God's own timing: a second coming of Christ in which Christ will reign on the earth. This will bring the salvation of national Israel and the establishment of universal peace (Zechariah 13:5; Matthew 24:27–30; Revelation 1:7; Ezekiel 37:21–22; Zephaniah 3:10, 20; Romans 11:26–27; Isaiah 11:6–9; Psalm 72:3–8; Micah 4:3–4).

That there will be a final judgment with the wicked being consigned to everlasting punishment (Matthew 25:46; Mark 9:43–48, Revelation 19:20, 20:11–15, 21:8).

Explain your denomination. How is it different from Catholicism?

First, we distinguish between Catholicism and Romanism. The term Catholic means "Universal." Romanism is the Latin church headed by the Pope.

Romanism holds to a large number of traditions, such as the papacy, transubstantiation, the sacrifice of the mass, prayers and masses for the dead, purgatory, indulgences, and various other things which we reject as extra-scriptural or anti-scriptural.

Our church is a sovereign church, voluntarily in cooperation with a fellowship of other churches. Our mission is to serve God and man by reaching nonreligious people and turning them into fully devoted followers of Jesus Christ. We believe this is what the Scriptures command us to do.

We are a community of believers who recognize that God wants us to be something together and represent Him with our unified diversity.

We gather to worship God because God is worthy to be praised. This includes public gatherings where we sing, pray, receive instruction from God's word, and bring our offerings of service and financial support.

We believe that all people matter to God and understand that God's message of grace is to be presented to all. This is done through relational evangelism and missionary outreaches both at home and abroad.

We help one another in the development of personal character, the discovery and use of spiritual gifts, and seek to follow Christ in the concepts of servanthood and pursuit of biblical goals.

As a fellowship of churches, we work to promote these ideals.

Do you have sacraments, and what are they?
We have two, Water Baptism and Holy Communion.

What are the teachings of Christ?
The teachings of Christ are those things recorded in the Bible. In a narrow sense they are the four Gospels: Matthew, Mark, Luke, and John. In a broader sense, because we see Christ as a member of the Godhead, the teachings of Christ include the Bible, both the Old and New Testaments, which is the Word of God.

Why do Christians now celebrate the Sabbath on Sunday, and when did this change occur and why?
The general understanding is that Christians worship God on Sunday because they believe that is the day Jesus rose from the grave.

First-century believers referred to Sunday as "The Lord's Day" (Mark 16:9).

Now when He rose early *on the first day of the week*, He appeared first to Mary Magdalene, out of whom He had cast seven demons (Acts 20:7).

Now on the first day of the week, when the disciples came together to break bread, Paul, ready to depart the next day, spoke to them and continued his message until midnight. (1 Now concerning the collection for the saints, as I have given orders to the churches of Galatia, so you must do also: *On the first day of the week* let each one of you lay something aside, storing up as he may prosper, that there be no collections when I come (1 Corinthians 16:1–2).

Other considerations probably pertained to issues that arose between Jews and Believers. The decision in Acts 15 (New Testament) was one that dramatically turned the direction of the church. During the early years the church was mostly Jewish, and it retained a solidly Jewish approach. However, when Gentiles became believers, the Acts 15 council in Jerusalem decided that Gentiles were not to be subjected to the requirements of the Jewish law. Jewish believers gave their blessing to the Gentile church at this council.

How does a Christian view a non-Christian religion?
With respect for the tradition of that religion yet as being short of the biblically revealed relationship that God desires to have with people. Christianity at its heart is a relationship and not a religion. Religion says, "Do." Relationship says, "Done."

True believers have one thing in common, and that is a deep and personal relationship with God that they did not have before becoming a person of faith. Thus, there is a desire in their life to tell others about it so they too can have this relationship.

Why did the Church encourage anti-Semitism until modern times?
Sincere people can be sincerely wrong. We believe that *the Church* you refer to in the question does not reflect biblical Christianity, but rather institutional religion.

The first Christians were Jews. These believers were not against other Jewish people but desiring that Jews would come to the understanding concerning the Messiah whom the Jewish Christians were convinced was Jesus Christ.

In future centuries some of the "Church" (which was now a majority of Gentile believers) began to see Jewish people themselves as the problem. Pride and ungodly desires for power probably motivated the anti-Semitic attitudes and actions that developed.

Whatever the reason, it was wrong and does not represent biblical Christianity.

What was the role of your Church during the Holocaust?

According to *Assemblies of God, HERITAGE*, a magazine collection of articles from *Assemblies of God* archives, vol. 2, many of our missionaries were imprisoned by the Nazis, and many were martyred for their faith.

Our fellowship, at its General Council in 1945, passed the following resolution under the heading of "Anti-Semitism":

WHEREAS, We have witnessed in this generation an almost universal increase in anti-Semitism and this has resulted in the greatest series of persecutions perpetrated in modern times, and

WHEREAS, Even in the United States of America there has been an alarming increase in anti-Semitism;

THEREFORE BE IT RESOLVED, That the General Council hereby declare its opposition to anti-Semitism and that it disapproves of the ministers of the Assemblies of God identifying themselves with those who are engaged in this propaganda.

BE IT FURTHER RESOLVED, That the editor of publications be instructed to prepare an article including Section 1 of this resolution in which our position on anti-Semitism is set forth and that it be published in the *Pentecostal Evangel*.

In response to this resolution, the October 20, 1945 edition of the *Pentecostal Evangel* contained a lengthy article, the summary of which states:

> Our position is that God has redeemed the children of Israel unto Himself to be His people *forever* (2 Samuel 7:23–24).
> God has a great love for Israel. (Deuteronomy 7:7–8; Jeremiah 31:3).
> God continually works to restore Israel to Himself (Ezekiel 37:24–29, 39:25–29; Jeremiah 32:37–41, 33:7–9).
> God has promised Israel land from the river of Egypt unto the river Euphrates, land more vast than Israel has ever received, boundaries that cover a territory which includes the whole of the Arabian Peninsula according to boundaries foretold in Ezekiel (Genesis 15:18; Isaiah 35:1).
> God gives strong warnings to those who hate and persecute Israel (Jeremiah 2:3, 30:16).
> God promises to bless those who bless Israel (Genesis 12:3).
> That we should pray for Israel and its salvation (Romans 10:1; Isaiah 62:6–7).
> We should not be anti-Semitic because our Savior was a Jew.
> We should bring a loving witness to Jewish people because Jesus told His disciples to first think of His own people (Acts 1:8).
> We should pray for the peace of Jerusalem (Psalm 122:6).

If Protestants are pro-life, how do you explain killing in war or capital punishment?

The Bible, Old and New Testaments, contains many references to war. While we abhor war, we recognize it is sometimes necessary in the human effort for peace and stability.

The New Testament predicts that "wars and rumors of wars" will be one of the characteristics of the end of times (Matthew 24:6; Mark 13:7; Luke 21:9, 24).

The apostles trace war to the selfishness and greed of men (James 4:1 ff.).

We believe that modern war is the result of the sinfulness of mankind and/or the age-old struggle against good and evil. When mandated by civil authorities, it is sometimes necessary to take up arms in order to defend oneself.

Capital punishment is recognized in the Scriptures as a means of dealing with certain crimes.

A court could inflict for a crime against the person, a sentence of (1) death in the form of stoning, burning, beheading, or strangling, etc.; (2) exile to one of the cities of refuge in case of manslaughter (Numbers 35); or (3) stripes, not to exceed forty, in practice thirty-nine or less (Deuteronomy 25:3; 2 Corinthians 11:24).

The earliest theory of punishment seems to have been that of retaliation—"blood for blood," and to some extent this principle appears even in the Law of Moses (Leviticus 21:19–20; Matthew 5:38).

The words of Lamech (Genesis 4:24) indicate that death was regarded as the fitting punishment for murder, and the same thought apparently was in the minds of the brethren of Joseph (Genesis 42:21).

Under the Law of Moses, the murderer was to be put to death without mercy. Even if he took refuge at the altar in a sanctuary or in an asylum city, he would not be immune from arrest and execution, and the same principle was applied in the case of an animal (Exodus 21:12, 14, 23, 28, 36 parallel).

Under the Mosaic Law, the offenses that made one liable to the punishment of death were: (1) striking or reviling a parent (Exodus 21:15, 17); (2) blasphemy (Leviticus 24:14, 16, 23; 1 Kings 21:10; Matthew 26:65–66); (3) Sabbath-breaking (Exodus 31:14, 35:2; Numbers 15:32–36); (4) witchcraft and false pretension to prophecy (Exodus 22:18; Leviticus 20:27; Deuteronomy 13:5, 18:20; 1 Samuel 28:9); (5) adultery (Leviticus 20:10; Deuteronomy 22:22);

(6) unchastity: (a) before marriage, but detected afterward (Deuteronomy 22:21), (b) in case of a woman with someone other than her betrothed (Deuteronomy 22:23), (c) in a priest's daughter (Leviticus 21:9); (7) rape (Deuteronomy 22:25); (8) incestuous and unnatural connections (Exodus 22:19; Leviticus 20:11, 14, 16); (9) man-stealing (Exodus 21:16); (10) idolatry, actual or virtual, in any form (Leviticus 20:2; Deuteronomy 13:6, 17:2–7); (11) false witness in capital cases (Deuteronomy 19:16, 19).

Various methods of capital punishment are mentioned in the Bible as appropriate for specific offenses:

> Stoning: Exodus 19:13, Leviticus 20:27, Joshua 7:25, Luke 20:6, Acts 7:58, 14:5.
> Hanging: Numbers 25:4, Deuteronomy 21:22.
> Burning: Genesis 38:24, Leviticus 21:9, 20:14.[2]

Some Christians recognize the civil authorities' authority to make law and carry such laws out. But the individual Christian is called upon to be forgiving.

War and capital punishment are the results of mankind's attempts to right wrongs and/or properly punish someone for a crime.

Today, when the word "abortion" is used, it almost immediately brings to mind the legal practice of destroying unborn children. Even though abortion on demand has been legalized, it is still immoral and sinful.

The Bible recognizes that a woman is "with child" even in the first stages of pregnancy (Luke 1:31, 36, 41, 44).

The Bible recognizes that the taking of the life of an unborn child is a monstrous crime (Exodus 21:22–23).

---

[2] Much of the information in the preceding discussion is taken from *Encyclopaedia, an electronic database by Biblesoft, 1996*.

The Bible recognizes that God is active in the creative process of forming life, and to abort such is to abort the work God is doing (Genesis 29:31–32, Job 31:15, Isaiah 44:2, 24, Psalm 139:13–16).

Abortion is the taking of innocent life. God's Word is very explicit concerning the taking of innocent human life (Exodus 20:13).

Please explain the present Pope's statement, "The Catholic Church is the only instrument for the salvation of all humanity."

The Roman church sees itself as the dispenser of salvation. Obviously we disagree.

Who has the power to forgive?

God alone. Forgiveness comes as a result of repentance of sins (Mark 1:4). This forgiveness was made possible by the sacrificial atonement of Jesus Christ (Romans 4:25, 5:1).

Do you believe in the resurrection of the dead?

Yes. We believe that death seals the eternal destiny of each person. For all of mankind there will be a resurrection of the body into the spiritual world and a judgment that will determine the fate of each individual. Unbelievers will be separated from God into condemnation. Believers will be received into eternal communion with God and will be rewarded for works done in this life.

We reject the teaching of reincarnation.

What is the Protestant's view of the coming of the Messiah?

We see the coming of the Messiah as a twofold event. First, we believe that Jesus Christ is the Messiah. He came first to die and atone death on the cross for the sins of mankind. Second, He will come as the reigning King at the end of the age (Zechariah 14:5; Matthew 24:27, 30; Revelation 1:7, 19:11–14, 20:1–6) This millennial reign will bring the salvation of national Israel (Ezekiel

37:21–22; Zephaniah 3:19–20, Romans 11:26–27) and the establishment of universal peace (Isaiah 11:6–9; Psalm 72:3–8; Micah 4:3–4).

What is the Protestant meaning of heaven and hell?

Hell is the place where those not found written in the Book of Life, together with the devil and his angels, will be consigned to everlasting punishment in the lake of fire which burns with fire and brimstone. In hell they experience the second death, which is eternal separation from God's relationship (Matthew 25:46; Mark 9:43–48; Revelation 19:20, 20:11–15, 21:8).

Heaven is the place where those found written in the Book of Life will spend eternity, a place of righteousness (2 Peter 3:13; Revelation 21 and 22).

What is the justification for the use of force in regard to conversion?

There is no justification for the use of force in regard to conversions. True conversion only comes as a result of the free will of someone who hears a message and responds freely to that message.

The early church practiced pacifism. Is that still true today?

The early church practiced pacifism in regard to the defending of their faith. That is still true with biblical believers today.

Pacifism in regard to the defending of one's faith and pacifism in regard to defending one's country should not be confused. As a body, our church is not opposed to the bearing of arms for the settlement of civil disputes. In such cases the individual's own conscience sets the standard.

What impact did Martin Luther have on your church? His later writings included anti-Semitic sentiments. How do you justify this to your church?

Martin Luther and others stood against the Roman Church and elevated instead (1) the authority of the Holy Scriptures pertaining to life and salvation versus the decrees of the Romanists which continue even to this present time, (2) the biblical doctrine of *the* Justification by Faith versus justification through the works established by the Romanists, and (3) The biblical teaching of the Priesthood of the Believer versus the vicarious priesthood of the Romanists.

Beyond that Martin Luther has little impact on our church. There are many things in Luther's life that are objectionable. Anti-Semitic sentiment is wrong.

What does it mean to a Christian to say that Jesus is the Son of God?
We believe that Christ existed eternally as a person within the tri-une God prior to anything else, including the created universe, and that this eternal Christ is the same person who came into the world as the human being Jesus of Nazareth.

This transition from the eternal Christ to the human person Jesus is called the Incarnation (which means "to provide with body").

This Christ became human through his birth as a baby and came to die on the cross as the victim of his own creation, thus completing the plan of God for the redemption from sin.

Thus, in His incarnate form, He was uniquely the Son of God and the son of man.

As the son of man He had human attributes. As the Son of God he had the unique attributes of God, such as supernatural manifestations of angels announcing His coming, the visits of wise men who came with royal offerings, prophecies of Simeon and Anna, evil designs of Herod the Great, prophetic introductions by John the Baptist (John 1:29) and by God Himself (Matthew 3:17; 2 Peter 1:17).

As the son of man, He was subject to the Father from the time of his birth until the end of all things. As the Son of God, He was the "finger of God" working at God's behest (Luke 11:20).

As the son of man, His body was laid in the grave. As the Son of God, death could not hold Him. He was resurrected, having completed His atoning work, ascended back to the Father (Acts 1:1–11), is seated at the right hand of God today (Psalm 110:1; Acts 2:33–34; 1 Corinthians 15:25; Ephesians 1:20; Hebrews 1:3, 13), is the mediator between God and humans (Hebrews 7:25), is exalted by God as Lord over all (Philippians 2:9–11), and will return one day as the Messiah to establish an earthly Kingdom (Acts 1:6–11).

Judaism believes that when the Messiah comes, there will be peace, tranquility, and people will not harm others any more. Since Jesus is considered the Messiah, what kind of peace do we have?
We believe the Messiah came first to be the atoning sacrifice and will come again at a future time to establish a Kingdom of peace.

Why is the Virgin Birth of Jesus and the Immaculate Conception an important teaching of the Church?
Protestants believe in the Virgin Birth but not the teaching of the Immaculate Conception.

"Immaculate Conception" is a product of the Roman Church, a teaching that says Mary, the mother of Jesus, was conceived without sin. Protestants honor Mary as the mother of Jesus, but the Roman Church has venerated her. This is not taught in the Bible but in the dogma of the Roman Church.

The Virgin Birth is important because it is the process wherein God became man. Without the Virgin Birth there would have been no sinless sacrifice for the atoning of sin.

How can you believe in one God and still speak of the Trinity?
We believe that the Bible reveals God as a trinity of persons within one being. By the Trinity we mean that there are three eternal distinctions in the one divine essence, known respectively as Father,

Son, and Holy Spirit. Since God is Spirit, there is a unity of essence, purpose, and endeavor.

We believe this plurality is revealed in many places in the Scriptures, including hints in Genesis 1 that use plural forms when speaking of God.

In the New Testament, this revelation is given much fuller treatment.

How does one atone for his sins?

There is nothing one can do to atone for his own sins. The Scripture says that he who sins shall die. Atonement can only come through a sinless sacrifice.

We believe that Scripture teaches that Jesus became the atoning sacrifice as the Incarnate Son of God. Forgiveness from sin comes by bringing oneself under the blood of the Lamb.

Forgiveness of sins, according to Scripture, is given through confession of sin, repentance (turning and following God), and faith toward the work of Jesus Christ on our behalf.

What is the role of confession in your Church?

Confession of sin is the initial step a person must take in order to find peace with God. 1 John 1:9 says, "If we confess our sins, He is faithful and just to forgive us our sins and to cleanse us from all unrighteousness."

Beyond that, confession has many benefits. Regular confession reminds us of our continuing need of God, brings personal cleansing, brings healing of relationships, and much more.

Can the Church forgive a murderer?

Every believer should forgive. However, this forgiveness is not to be interpreted as an escape from accountability.

Sin has its consequences, not the least of which is an impact on relational credibility. Proper accountability may require punishment.

But a believer who harbors hatred in his or her heart is not taking care of his or her own heart.

The Church emphasizes faith versus works. Is this true of your Church?

Our salvation is through faith in the atoning work of the Sinless One. Good works are one evidence of true salvation in that the person who has no good works does not have active faith. But no work from sinful man can atone for sin. So we say, "By Grace are you saved, through faith."

The work of the Son of God was the work of Grace that makes it possible for us to be saved. Our active faith in that expresses itself through good works.

Can a person who does good deeds but does not believe in Jesus achieve salvation? On the other hand, does one who is a big sinner but accepts Jesus achieve salvation?

No sinner can save himself or herself. No amount of good deeds can atone for sin because they are sinful sacrifices. We have all sinned. The Bible indicates that even a lie is a sin that brings us under the curse of sin which is separation from God. All sin can be forgiven by sinless sacrifice. This is seen in the Old Testament by the offering of atoning blood of animals.

We believe that the Good News is that God's plan of salvation included the sacrificial Lamb, Jesus, the sinless Son of God, who died on the cross for our sins. Salvation comes through bringing oneself under the atoning work of God by confessing our sin and trusting in the work of the Savior on the Cross.

Does your church require celibacy?

Before marriage yes, but not after marriage.

How does Judaism fit in with Christian theology?

Israel is God's chosen people. Christianity is the extension of God's plan to redeem fallen man. Christians fully embrace the Old Testament and its teachings. We recognize that those professing Christianity and those professing Judaism can miss the mark that God has set. The Old Testament is full of illustrations of this, as is the New Testament. We believe that God looks on the heart and seeks those people who will worship Him with all their heart.

Gentile Christians have the privilege of being grafted into the family of God through the grace of God that makes provision for the salvation of all men.

Jews and Gentiles alike must live by faith. "The Just shall live by faith" (Habakkuk 2:4; Romans 1:16–17; Galatians 3:11; Hebrews 10:38).

How can one person atone for others?

The price of atonement for sin is death and requires a sinless sacrifice. Thus atonement is only possible if that one is sinless and is willing to pay the price of atonement. The New Testament Book of Hebrews teaches in detail about the atoning work and its requirements.

Jesus Christ could atone for the sins of the world because He was sinless.

What is the significance of the resurrection of Jesus?

The resurrection of Jesus is the evidence of the truth of His teachings. He said He was going to die and be resurrected. Either He was a liar, a lunatic, or Lord. The resurrection gives evidence to His Lordship.

It provides a confirmation of Jesus' teachings and of His claims. The resurrection evidences the new life that can be had in Christ. The resurrection is the first evidence of the hope of a resurrection of us today.

What is the connection between Passover and Easter?
The Passover was the meal where Christ shared with His disciples about His being the Lamb of God who would die for the sins of the world. It was at the Passover meal where Jesus instituted the Christian celebration of remembrance, Holy Communion.

From the Passover meal Jesus was arrested and eventually crucified. Christians celebrate Easter as the day Christ rose from the grave, triumphant over sin and death.

What is the teaching of revelation? What is your reaction to the Book of Revelation?
The full title of the book is "The Revelation of Jesus Christ." It is the revelation that Jesus gave John on the Isle of Patmos to show unto His servants that which must come to pass.

Its teachings deal with the Church age and the things to come following the Church age. These things include a time of tribulation here on earth such as has never been seen. It also includes the regathering of Israel from the nations and the establishment of Temple worship, the rise of an evil world ruler who desecrates the Temple, and an ultimate battle to be fought at Armageddon. This battle will conclude with the return of the Messiah to establish an earthly Kingdom of peace, ruling from the throne of David. The book ends with a final judgment and a separation of good and evil and a new heaven, new earth, new Jerusalem, new Temple, new light, and new paradise.

Christians are often unaware of Jesus' origin and followers. Is understanding of the first century relevant or not?
Understanding of the first century is very relevant.

What is the role of the Old Testament in Christianity?

The Old Testament is a record of the promise God gave to Abraham and through him (ultimately) to all mankind.[3] This promise is fulfilled and is being fulfilled in the history of Israel and through the continual workings of Jesus Christ.

Jesus Christ is the principal in the history of Israel, the promised Messiah through whom God works to complete His promises. The single promise of redemption given through Abraham is fulfilled in the Messiah, Jesus Christ. The promises given to Abraham in the Old Testament were continually fulfilled in the Old Testament. Jesus Christ, as the Messiah, continues the fulfillment by making it possible for mankind to be redeemed from sin by becoming the ultimate Passover Lamb. This was accomplished during His first advent.

The promise and plan of God to Abraham will be ultimately fulfilled at the second advent, when the world will revolve around Israel, with Christ, the Messiah, reigning in a Kingdom of Peace from Jerusalem.

God's promise to Abraham (Gen. 12:1–3) can be seen as the center point for the Old Testament. Genesis chapters 1–11 serve as a prolegomena to the promise contained in 12:1–3. The promise is further developed in subsequent chapters.

The history books carry the story of how the promise formed a people. The prophets became "covenant enforcers" as they called Israel back to the promise. Wisdom literature calls one to live a life in the promise.

The Old Testament in a sense, then, is salvation history. The history of the Old Testament reveals how the people were formed into His people.

One can trace the pattern of the salvation work of God in many ways. One such pattern takes us from Genesis to Revelation.

---

[3] The answers to this and the next question were given as a contribution to this chapter in whole or in part by Dr. Richard Lafferty.

From the one to the many (Adam to Noah's day)
From the many to the one (pre-flood to Noah)
From the one to the many (Noah to Babel)
From the many to the one (Babel to Abraham)
From the one to the many (Abraham to Israel)
From the many to the One (Israel to Jesus Christ)

At this point we have come from the first Adam to the Last Adam, Jesus Christ. Through Jesus Christ, God's plan of salvation is extended to the totality of the human race who will turn from their sins to God. And so the pattern continues:

From the One to the many (Jesus Christ, the ultimate Paschal Lamb, to mankind)
From the many to the One (see Revelations 3:21–22)

How does one distinguish in the Old Testament between the ethical and the ritual?

First, I would say that all ritual is rooted in the ethical. Rituals were given or developed as visible signs of the ethics mandated in the Promise.

Rituals are not empty patterns of behavior, but have rich meaning. Rituals are given (e.g., the procedures in the ordination of priests), developed because of historical events that transpire (e.g., the Festival of Lights), evolve (e.g., liturgy), or even, as we believe, added to (e.g. Passover—Communion). All of the rituals are outward signs of inward ethics.

Values are that which ethics rests upon. Ethics refers to behavior, while values refer to core beliefs. So a ritual is a ceremonial display of core beliefs and thus calls one to a life of ethics. In Judaism and Christianity, rituals serve to *remind* and *proclaim* e (cf. Passover and Holy Communion) the way of life mandated by God.

In order to distinguish between the two, one has to have an understanding of the history and the culture. We believe this is revealed in the Bible. To understand the Scriptures is to understand ritual (the way God desires to be worshipped) and ethics (the way people worshipped God).

Thus, in reading the Old Testament we are seeking for ways God desires to be worshipped and taking lessons from the ways God's people worshipped Him. Obviously there are positive and negative examples.

What is Communion? What is the Eucharist? How do you explain Jesus' presence in the Communion?

In Jesus' day the most important religious festival of the year was the Passover. This observance reminded the people of their deliverance from the bondage in Egypt. It involved the sharing of the Passover meal and required the sacrifice of a lamb whose blood symbolized the salvation of the Israelites from death (Exodus 12:1–14).

Communion was instituted by Jesus the last time He gathered with His disciples prior to His crucifixion. They had gathered for the Passover meal.

As the Passover meal was finished, Jesus chose the Communion meal (the taking of the bread and the cup) to be the way Christians would celebrate their new deliverance from sin and death.

The Passover lamb that had given salvation to Israel from Egypt was a foreshadowing of the real Lamb of God, whose blood could save the whole world from sin (John 1:29). Christians would later say, "Christ, our Passover lamb, has been sacrificed" (1 Corinthians 5:7).

This meal, given to the Church by Jesus, goes by several names. It is called communion or holy communion (1 Corinthians 10:16), the Lord's Supper (11:20), the Lord's table (10:21), the Eucharist (from giving "thanks") (10:16, 11:24), and the breaking of bread (Acts 2:42, 20:7).

Each component has its significance. The gathering, the sharing, the bread, and the wine, the explanations as "This is my body . . . my blood," the invitations to "take and eat . . . drink," and the mention of the new covenant, of the resurrection, and of the Kingdom of God (1 Corinthians 11:17–26).

Partaking of this meal is an outward sign of our inner ownership of the eternal benefits gained for us by the death of Jesus. Faith in His atoning work is the only source of our salvation. His broken body and shed blood atone for our sins, making peace with God.

Communion does not save. But the Communion meal is a love feast for the Christian. It provides them a Christ-ordained opportunity to celebrate their salvation. Each time they gather for communion, Christians proclaim that Christ is as indispensable to their spiritual survival as food and drink are to their physical survival, and they rejoice because Christ and His salvation are as easily accessible to them as bread and wine are available at a rich man's table.

Jesus' presence in Communion is there through the Spirit of God, just as the presence of God is with us every day. The elements do not become the body and blood of Christ.

Supplemental Questions

What is the ultimate authority for belief and practice in your denomination?

The Bible, consisting of sixty-six books of the Old and New Testament, is our ultimate authority for belief and practice.

We hold that the Scriptures are the unique, full, and final authority on all matters of faith and practice, and there are no other writings similarly inspired by God.

How do you understand the authority of the Bible?

We believe the Bible is the Word of God written; it is the revelation of the truths of God conveyed by inspiration through His servants to us. As such, it is infallible and without error.

We believe the original autographs to be inerrant (Jeremiah 36:2). God, the divine Author, prompted the original thought in the mind of the writers (Amos 3:8). He then guided their choice of words to express such thoughts (Exodus 4:12, 15). God then illumines the mind of the reader in a way that the reader potentially may comprehend the same truth as was originally in the mind of the writer (1 Corinthians 2:12; Ephesians 1:17–18).

We understand inspiration to mean that special act of the Holy Spirit by which He guided the writers of the Scriptures.

We define inerrancy as meaning exempt from error, and infallibility as a near synonym meaning incapable of error. Such inerrancy and infallibility apply to all of Scripture. The Scripture is truth (2 Samuel 7:28; Psalm 119:43, 160; John 17:17, 19; Colossians 1:5).

We believe that the Bible is a supernatural book, written by people but inspired by God. It is God's revelation of Himself and is the authoritative guide whereby we know His will for us for all time.

What is the authority of church tradition from the early church to the present?

We recognize no authority of church tradition from the early Church to the present except that which is mentioned in the Holy Scriptures. Our sole source of faith and conduct is the Bible, which is the Word of God.

What is the authority of personal experience?

We recognize no authority of personal experience that cannot be supported by the written Word of God. However, personal experience can verify the authority of the Bible.

From a personal level, as I read and study the Bible I find myself being drawn near to God. I find myself being nourished in my soul. God's Word brings counsel, guidance, direction, and correction for my life that over time proves wise. In other words, it affirms itself through personal experience.

As I "taste and see that the Lord is good" (Psalms 34:8), and as God's Word becomes a "lamp to my feet and light to my path (Psalms 119:105), then my personal experiences become a testimony of its authority.

What is the authority of the historic creeds, especially Nicea in 325?

We believe the authority of the historic creeds is limited to their attempts to define doctrine and faith and their ability to stay true to divine Scripture. Where the creeds are true to Holy Scripture, they are beneficial in bringing clear and precise understanding to the meaning of Scripture.

The Apostles' Creed contains clear and concise meaning to the fundamentals of the Christian faith that are necessary for salvation.

The Nicene Creed contains definite and explicit statements concerning the divinity of Christ and the Holy Spirit. The Nicene Creed provided the needed clarification to combat the heresies of the Nicene age, and is useful to combat those same heresies today, which invariably reoccur in differing forms.

Do you believe in the divinity of Jesus?

We believe that the Lord Jesus Christ, God with us, is divine and eternal in nature. He is the only Begotten of the Father. As to His human nature, He is the proper Son of Man. Scripture acknowledges Him to be both God and man; who because He is God and man is Immanuel, "God with us" (Matthew 1:23; 1 John 4:2, 10, 14; Revelation 1:13, 17)

Christianity teaches that Jesus Christ is the one and only Son of God, that He is fully human and fully God, without sin and the only one worthy or qualified to forgive sin. He proved that He had the ability to forgive sin, and He proved that He was God when He was resurrected.

Do you believe in the resurrection of the dead?

We believe in the resurrection of the dead. Those who die in the Lord will be resurrected to live and reign with Christ for eternity (Job 19:25–27; Romans 8:23; 1 Corinthians 15:51–52).

The wicked dead will be raised and judged according to their works. Whosoever is not found written in the Book of Life, together with the devil and his angels will be consigned to everlasting punishment in the lake which burns with fire and brimstone (Matthew 25:46; Mark 9:43-48; Revelation 19:20, 20:11–15, 21:8).

The choices that we make here and now in this life will determine our eternal destiny. If we choose to ignore God or reject God or to ignore our individual sin problem, then we will spend an eternity separated from God.

But if we choose to solve the sin problem God's way by receiving Jesus Christ into our lives and allowing Him to forgive our sins, then we will spend an eternity with God in heaven.

That is why Christianity is so adamant about warning us to solve the sin problem in our life. The decision that we make now is very important because eternity weighs in the balance.

What does it mean to accept Jesus as one's Lord and Savior?

To accept Jesus as one's Lord and Savior is central to the Gospel message.

First, it means to recognize Jesus as Lord.

The Bible tells us that God has made Jesus both Lord and Christ (Isaiah 45:23; Romans 14:11; Philippians 2:9–11). He was, is, and forever will be the supreme Governor of all things and all persons, Jews and Gentiles, angels and men. He was sent from God to be the sinless sacrifice and as such is the servant Messiah who came to redeem people from their sins (Luke 19:10; John 10:10, 20:31, 12:26–33).

King David looked forward to His coming (Psalms 16:8–11). His coming was evidenced by His miraculous birth, sinless life, sacrificial death, and resurrection.

As Lord, He is Immanuel, which means "God with us."

Second, it means to embrace His saving work as sufficient to cover and forgive our sins. As Lord He is the governor of all. As the Christ He is the redeemer of all who will put their trust in Him.

His work of salvation is not with the blood of goats and calves, but with His own blood He entered the Most Holy Place once for all, having obtained eternal redemption (Hebrews 9:12). As such, Jesus Christ is the Paschal Lamb, the sinless sacrifice, and He is the Mediator of the new covenant, by means of death (Hebrews 9:15). Christ was offered once to bear the sins of many (Hebrews 9:28).

To accept Jesus Christ as one's Lord and Savior is to embrace His Lordship over all and to believe in His atoning grace as being sufficient to make peace with God. Thus, as it says in the introduction to the book of Revelation:

Revelation 5:9–14

And they sang a new song, saying:

"You are worthy to take the scroll, and to open its seals; for You were slain, and have redeemed us to God by Your blood out of every tribe and tongue and people and nation, and have made us kings and priests to our God; and we shall reign on the earth."

Then I looked, and I heard the voice of many angels around the throne, the living creatures, and the elders; and the number of them was ten thousand times ten thousand, and thousands of thousands, saying with a loud voice:

"Worthy is the Lamb who was slain to receive power and riches and wisdom, and strength and honor and glory and blessing!"

And every creature which is in heaven and on the earth and under the earth and such as are in the sea, and all that are in them, I heard saying:

"Blessing and honor and glory and power be to Him who sits on the throne, and to the Lamb, forever and ever!"

Then the four living creatures said, "Amen!" And the twenty-four elders fell down and worshiped Him who lives forever and ever.

How does one attain salvation?

Salvation is attained by repentance of sin and faith in the atoning work of Jesus Christ (Isaiah 64:5–6; John 3:16–18; Acts 3:19, 16:30–31). It is the process through which a guilty, sinful person gets right with God.

The Bible is very, very clear about this issue. The central message of the Bible is how to relate to God. It starts by describing God, who is holy and perfect and righteous above all else. And all of us, every single one of us, have fallen short of His standard. And that falling short is called sin. It separates us from God.

But because God loves us so much, He planned to bring a solution to the separation. He sent His Son, Jesus Christ, to die on a cross and pay the penalty of death which we deserved on our behalf. The shedding of Righteous blood provided the covering so we could be reconciled with God.

To attain salvation we must come to God honestly about who we are, confess our sins, admit our need for a Savior, and receive Jesus Christ as our Savior. When we do that, when we put our faith and trust in Jesus Christ and Him alone for the forgiveness of our sins, the Bible tells us our sins are forgiven and cleansed (1 John 1:9). This brings us into a growing, dynamic, and loving relationship with God.

What is the status of the Hebrew Bible as an authority for belief and practice?

We believe that the Bible, both the Old and New Testament, is the only authority for belief and practice. As such, the entire Bible is a revelation of God's plan for redeeming His creation from sin.

Where does authority reside in the church? Do you have a hierarchy of authority in the church (e.g., bishops, priests, deacons, laypersons, etc.)? Does the local church have the power to hire and fire its pastor?

Authority on a human level resides in those in whom God has given leadership gifts and are called by God into leading, guiding positions. The Bible gives titles to these offices, such as bishops, presbyters, elders, and deacons. Those who hold these positions are to exhibit characteristics of servanthood and service (Mark 9:35; Ephesians 4:11–16; 1 Timothy 3:1–13).

Local leadership comprised of ordained ministers along with the watch-care of elders and other supportive leadership enable laity to work together in love and unity with the intent on the one ultimate purpose of glorifying Christ.

While some denominations appoint the pastors of individual churches, our church is sovereign in government and calls its own pastor. If there is reason to make a change, there are provisions provided within the local church to make that change.

The New Testament gives us some indications that the local church is responsible for its own government. First, each church elected its own officers and delegates (Acts 1:23, 26, 6:1–6, 15:2–3). Second, each church had the power to carry out its own church discipline (Matthew 18:17–18; 1 Corinthians 5:13; 2 Thessalonians 3:6, 14–15). And third, the church together with its officer rendered decisions (Acts 15:22), received delegates (Acts 15:4), and sent out solicitors (2 Corinthians 8:19) and missionaries (Acts 13:2).

We attempt to follow that pattern.

How does one become a member of your church?

Evangelical Christianity comprises many different churches and denominational groups. Each group, and even each individual church, has a standard for membership. Generally membership is open to all who give evidence of their faith in the Lord Jesus Christ, who voluntarily subscribe to the tenets of faith and agree to be governed by the constitution and bylaws of the local church.

What is your understanding of sacraments, especially Baptism and the Lord's Supper?

We believe that the ordinances of Baptism and the Lord's Supper are outward rites appointed by Christ to be administered in the Church as a visible sign of the saving truth of the Christian faith.

The ordinance of baptism is a symbol of the believer's identification with Christ in burial and resurrection (Romans 6:3; Colossians 2:12, 1 Peter 3:21). It is an outward testimony that the individual has confessed his sins and believed in the Lord Jesus Christ for salvation. Water baptism does not effect the salvation: it testifies to it and symbolizes it.

The ordinance of the Lord's Supper was instituted by Christ during the Passover meal (Matthew 26:26–30; Mark 14:22–26; Luke 22:17–20). We are expressly told that the Lord's Supper symbolizes the sacrificial death of Jesus Christ (1 Corinthians 11:26). Thus, it is a memorial meal reminding us of the provision that God made for mankind by sending His own Paschal Lamb to redeem us from sin. And it is a perpetual reminder that is to be practiced regularly until Christ returns.

Outline the structure of your liturgy or worship service.

Our church has no set liturgy, but our worship service generally consists of the singing of songs of worship by the entire congregation, individuals, or choirs, prayers of thanksgiving and petition by individuals and/or the congregation at large, the sermon, and an opportunity to respond to the sermon at an altar of prayer.

It would be common to see people freely expressing their faith, clapping their hands, singing joyfully or tearfully in worship, and praying with one another.

How do you distinguish your denomination from other Protestant denominations and from Roman Catholicism?

The primary difference between Christian denominations is found in nonessential doctrinal differences, the system of governance, and/or the structure of liturgy. Nonessential is defined as being things pertaining to other than eternal salvation.

Then there are conservative and liberal differences. Conservative Protestants attempt to preserve certain social traditions, in opposition to liberal religious groups and others who are trying to bring about social change in society. We believe that the Bible teaches a conservative social tradition on matters such as abortion, homosexuality, and general lifestyle.

Generally, Christian denominations agree on major theological matters, such as Jesus' incarnation, bodily resurrection, the return of Jesus to earth in a second coming, heaven, hell, the Trinity, and the virgin birth of Jesus.

A sample of some differences between Evangelical Christians and Roman Catholicism is as follows:

Conservative Protestants	Roman Catholic Church
Believe in the priesthood of the believer and reject the concept of apostolic success as historically invalid.	Believe in apostolic succession. Ordinations traceable back to St. Peter.
Authority is vested within the believer as the individual believer follows the teachings of God's Word.	Authority vested in the hierarchy of the church.

Conservative Protestants	**Roman Catholic Church**
Sacraments such as commu- nion and baptism are symbols of grace.	Sacraments are the means of grace.
The original writings of the authors of the Bible are inerrant.	Same as conservative Protestants.
Church structure is democratic, elected, and mostly male, sin- gle or married.	Hierarchical male, unmarried.
Communion/Eucharist is a memorial meal looking back to the ultimate redemptive act of God.	Christ's body and blood are physically present in the ele- ments.

Both Evangelicals and Romanists believe in grace, which is the free and unmerited salvation that comes from the sinless sacrifice of the blood of Jesus Christ, God's only Begotten Son. Evangelicals view grace as a direct action by and from God that comes to the individual believer through confession and faith in Jesus Christ. Roman Catholics see grace as flowing through the conduit of the sacraments

What distinguishes clergy from laypersons?
Clergy are divinely called men or women whose purpose is to pre- pare the people of God for their ministries.

While the word "ministry" is often associated with the work of the clergy, in its biblical sense it properly denotes the work of the entire church, the body of Christ in the world. We believe that min- istry belongs to the entire church.

All are called in some way to be ministers. Spiritual gifting for ministry is without regard to race or sex. Quoting the prophet Joel (Joel 2:28–29), Acts 2:17–18 says, "I will pour out my Spirit on all people. Your sons and daughters will prophesy . . . even on my servants, both men and women, I will pour out my Spirit in those days, and they will prophesy." The ministry of the laity is integral to the accomplishment of the mission of the church.

These laity must be trained and led on a massive scale if the work of the church is to be accomplished. Clergy leaders equip laity for ministry and are Christ's gifts to the church for that purpose (Ephesians 4:7–12).

Do clergy need special education/training in order to be ordained (e.g., through an accredited seminary)?

Ordination can be defined as the public ceremony by which the movement acknowledges the divine call, commission, and qualification of a person to ministry. The movement extends its blessings, fellowship, and opportunities; receives a pledge of dedication, faithfulness, and loyalty; and invokes divine enablement for success in life and ministry.

All Christians are equal, but ministers are set apart for special, full-time Christian service and leadership. When necessary, the laity can perform all of the functions of ministry except those for which the state requires an ordained minister.

We require a careful examination, written and oral, of the candidate as to qualification on six essential points:

- The genuineness of their Christian experience.
- The sufficiency of their spiritual, moral, emotional, and social maturity.
- The reality of their divine call.
- The correctness of their doctrine.
- The adequacy of their preparation and practical abilities.

- The acceptability of their allegiance to the movement's policies and programs.

While no certain level of academic pursuit is required, the qualifications for ordination include the qualifications for bishops as set forth in 1 Timothy 3:1–7 and Titus 1:5–9.

A person seeking ordination first seeks counsel from his pastor and a letter of recommendation from that pastor to the sectional presbyter. The candidate must maintain an acceptable ministry at a licensed level for a minimum of two years and be at least twenty-three years of age before being invited to write for ordination. The candidate must complete coursework on and be tested in areas of Bible and theology, examined by a sectional credentials committee, undergo a home interview, and be examined again by a district-level credentials committee and affirmed by peers and overseers.

Upon completion of educational and practical requirements, the candidate may be ordained in a public ceremony. This credential is renewed annually.

What is your denomination's view of Judaism?

Evangelical Christians (who in America number some 60 million adults, or one-third of the Christian community) feel passion for Israel. Evangelicals support Israel for biblical, historical, political, and moral reasons.

The birth and continued existence of Israel signals for us the second coming of the Messiah and the world's redemption.

We believe that it is not possible to love a spiritual Israel and hate the earthly one. For us to turn our back on Israel and the Jewish people is to rebel against God.

While there are real issues that separate Evangelicals and Jews (most notably our missionary zeal and religious fervor to preach the message of our Christian faith), we are genuinely your friend.

Can a Jew be saved by God without first having to become a Christian?

Many Jews were saved before the word "Christian" was ever used (Acts 11:26). Their salvation came through faith in the offering that God Himself provided (Hebrews 10:1–10).

Salvation is the result of having faith in God. Both the Old and New Testament tell us that "the just shall live by faith" (Habakkuk 2:4; Galatians 3:11; Hebrews 10:38).

Salvation, as we understand the Bible's teaching, includes the desire of God, who is not willing that any should perish (2 Peter 3:9), and the provision of God whereby man can be saved (Galatians 4:4–5).

We understand that provision to be complete in the shedding of the blood of the eternal Paschal Lamb, Jesus Christ. Thus Romans 5 tells us:

Romans 5:6–9

> For when we were still without strength, in due time Christ died for the ungodly. For scarcely for a righteous man will one die; yet perhaps for a good man someone would even dare to die. But God demonstrates His own love toward us, in that while we were still sinners, Christ died for us. Much more then, having now been justified by His blood, we shall be saved from wrath through Him.

We believe that Old Testament people of God looked forward to the coming of a Messiah who would save people from their sins. This faith saved them. In the New Testament Book of Hebrews there is a listing of many Old Testament individuals who were saved by faith in the coming Messiah (see Hebrews 11).

Today, we have the privilege of looking back to a cross where that Immanuel died in our place. The Messiah came first as the redeeming Savior. He will come again as the reigning King.

No Jew must give up his Judaism to put his trust in the redemptive work that God provides. In Leviticus 17:11 it is written, "for it is the blood that makes an atonement for the soul." Our belief is that the ultimate atoning provision of God is found in Jesus Christ, His death, burial, and resurrection. That is the gospel message.

Can other non-Christians be saved without first becoming Christian?

The biblical world-view is that there are two types of people: the people of God and the heathen. Another way to describe this is Jew and Gentile. The Gentile, or heathen, world has the privilege of salvation through Jesus Christ.

Alternative religions, whether the widespread forms of animism (belief in the existence of spirits separate from bodies), or more sophisticated religions such as Hinduism, Buddhism, and Islam, each contain their own distinctive world-views. However, all of these alternatives supply pictures of God, of man, of the universe, and of the way of salvation very different from the Judeo/Christian view.

If one is willing to accept the logic that two competing alternatives cannot both at the same time be right, one is obliged to make a choice. Paul, the New Testament Apostle to the Gentiles, spoke at the Areopagus in Athens about the need to choose between Christ and the contemporary competing options available in his day. Paul defended the claims of the Christian message as superior to all others by pointing to the resurrection of Jesus Christ (Acts 17:29–31).

The Bible is very clear that "Salvation is found in no one else, for there is no other name under heaven given to man by which we must be saved" (Acts 4:12). This, without apology, is a claim to the exclusive nature of the Christian message.

Since the Bible is clear in its insistence on belief in the Lord Jesus Christ as the only way for sinners to get right with God and to be ready for heaven, then to tolerate non-Christian alternative views is to deny to masses of people the only way of salvation. We disavow universalism and the acceptance of world-views that do not require entering the kingdom of God through the narrow gate of the God-man, Jesus Christ.

Has the Christian church superseded or replaced Judaism in the eyes of God as God's chosen people?

The simple answer to this is no. We believe that the Jews are God's chosen people. God has not cast away His people (Romans 11:1). God makes a way even for individuals in rebellion to be saved (Romans 11:26–27).

God, in His grace, has extended the opportunity to all mankind (Romans 1:16). As a Gentile believer I have the privilege of being grafted into the family of God through Christ's redemptive work (Galatians 3:8–11).

Do Christians and the Christian churches bear some responsibility for the Holocaust? Did Christianity and Christians contribute to anti-Semitism? If so, what is their moral obligation toward Jews today?

There is no question that some Christians and some Christian churches must bear some responsibility for the Holocaust. Some who profess Christianity contribute to anti-Semitism. They are wrong and should repent of their wrong and ask forgiveness.

All Christians have a moral obligation to love what God loves and hate what God hates. God loves people. God hates sin. A Christian's moral duty is to love God with all their heart, mind, soul, and body and love their neighbor as themselves. We should pray for them, love them, and support them.

Our movement has a great love for Israel and the Jewish people.

Does your denomination support going to war in a just cause in defense of innocent people?

As a movement we affirm our loyalty to the government of the United States in war or peace. We shall continue to insist, as we have historically, on the right of each member to choose for himself whether to declare his position as a combatant, a noncombatant, or a conscientious objector.

The biblical principles which support this position (1) call for civic loyalty (Romans 13:1), and (2) call for the employment of personal conscience in all matters (Romans 14:12).

We understand the sixth commandment, "You shall not murder" (Exodus 20:13), to refer to an act of *willful* and *personal* vengeance. While the outcome may be similar to the killings of war, the motive and driving force are quite different. The preservation of peace and tranquility sometimes makes this response imperative.

We deplore war. We are committed to its avoidance as much as accountability, sensibility, and responsibility allow. But we understand that war is sometimes unavoidable and will continue to be so until the Prince of Peace, Jesus Christ, establishes His reign over a world that is now characterized by violence, wickedness, and war.

What is your denomination's position concerning the State of Israel as the eternal home of the Jewish people, and the Second Coming of Christ?

We believe that the land of Israel is the eternal home of the Jewish people and that Israel includes all of the territory given by God to the twelve tribes as identified in the following passage of Scripture:

Genesis 15:18

On the same day the Lord made a covenant with Abram, saying: "To your descendants I have given this land, from the river of Egypt to the great river, the River Euphrates.

A more detailed and precise description is given in the book of Numbers 34:1–15.

This land and the planet will one day come under the divine rule of God through the Lord Jesus Christ. The second coming of Christ includes the rapture of the saints, which is our blessed hope, followed by the visible return of Christ (Zechariah 14:5; Matthew 24:27, 30; Revelation 1:7, 19:11–14, 20:1–6), who will rule from the throne of David in a future, rebuilt Temple and will establish universal peace (Isaiah 11:6–9; Psalms 72:3–8; Micah 4:3–4). It will include the salvation of national Israel (Ezekiel 37:21–22; Zephaniah 3:19–10; Romans 11:26).

Chapter 7

Baptists

Bishop LeRoy Bailey, Jr.

The Baptist Perspective of Faith in Modern Times

Where did we come from?

The Baptist denomination originated in the early seventeenth century in England and Holland. Its beginning was influenced by the reformed theology of Ulrich Zwingli and John Calvin. These separatists believed in baptism for believers only and later held the belief in baptism by total immersion. This practice became the claim to the name Baptist.[1]

Roger Williams organized the first Baptist church in America in 1639 in Providence, Rhode Island. African Americans make up the major portion of Baptists in the United States. Most Baptists affiliate with one of three national Baptist conventions. A new convention has substantial numbers. It is called the Full Gospel Baptist. This group has challenged the more traditional patterns of worship and doctrine.

The earliest known African Baptist was "Jack," a slave who was baptized into the First Baptist Church of Newport, Rhode Island, in 1652. The first free African American Baptist of record was Peggy Arnold, who joined the Newport Seventh Day Church in 1719.

Most historians recognize the Silver Bluff Church, formed in 1773 in Aiken County, South Carolina, as the earliest organized African American Baptist church. However, Mechel Sobel, in a work entitled *Trabelin On*, contends that William Murphy and

---

[1] H. Leon McBeth, *The Baptist Heritage*, p. 21.

Philip Mulkey preached in the Bluestone community of Mecklenburg County, Virginia, in 1758.

Time does not allow all the distinctives of the Baptist faith to be presented. However, several things should be shared.

What do we believe?

There is, first, the faith in Jesus Christ as Lord. The key to being Baptist is being Christian. There is the notion that this need not be stated, but so many miss its importance. Being Christian is significant, and holding to the notion of being Baptist secondarily will always keep one from being cultic. A cult is anything that is not authentic and distorted.

Many claim to be Baptist but are cultic in the sense that they hold to Baptist tradition over Christian balance. This has produced extremists who are dogmatic and detrimental to the faith of Christ.

There are many distinctives concerning us, but one in particular is that of autonomy. We are all independent, but we choose to be in collegium.

There are twenty or more articles of faith that we adhere to, known as the New Hampshire Confession, which date back to 1830. These may be found in the *Baptist Hiscox Guide for Baptist Churches*.

I will summarize these for our brief encounter. However, I will not cite the many scriptures that validate these articles. Baptists believe:

The Scriptures: All Scripture is inspired by God.

The True God: There is One True God whose name is Jehovah.

The Fall of Man: Man was created in holiness but voluntarily transgressed and fell from his holy position. He is positively inclined to do evil and is therefore condemned.

God's Purpose of Grace: God has provided a resolution for man's fall in the person of Jesus Christ. Whoever believes in

Him receives pardon. Man cannot be saved on his own through works but through faith in the shed blood of Jesus that alone atones for his misdoing.

The Way of Salvation: The way of salvation is only by grace on the part of the Father through His Son, who has made us right with the Father through His death and providing sympathy, the Father finds us suitable.

Regeneration: Regeneration is a disposition of the heart whereby a person believes and submits his will to God through the Son whom we know to be Jesus Christ. Through the process of regeneration, sin in a person's life is broken and the love he has for God is translated into daily living.

Repentance: Repentance is Godly sorrow for sin often repeated.

Faith: Faith involves the assent of the mind and consent of the heart through belief and trust to the will of God.

Justification: Through justification, we have pardon of sin and the promise of life eternal based on the death, burial, and resurrection of Jesus. A person is justified solely by the blood of Jesus the Righteous, who has never been contaminated.

Adoption: Whoever believes in the Lord Jesus is adopted by the Father as His child, and all who believe are members of the family of faith and become joint heirs with Christ concerning the heritage of the saints on earth and in heaven.

Sanctification: Sanctification enables us to become partakers of His holiness. It is a progressive work begun in regeneration.

The Perseverance of Saints: Those who are truly regenerate will not fail but continue in the works of God. They will not perish.

The Law and the Gospels: The law of God is the eternal and unchangeable rule of His moral government. It is holy, just, and good, given to deliver men from their sinful nature.

A Gospel Church: A Gospel Church is a congregation of baptized believers in Christ who observe the ordinance of Christ and exercise the gifts, rights, and privileges given them by the Word. The only scriptural offices are bishops or pastors and deacons whose qualifications are found in the books of Timothy and Titus.

Christian Baptism: A believer in Christ is immersed in water in the name of the Father, Son, and Holy Spirit as an emblem of their faith in Christ.

The Lord's Supper: The Lord's Supper consists of a provision of bread and wine, symbols of Christ's body and blood. This meal commemorates the death, burial, and resurrection of Jesus Christ.

The Christian Sabbath: The first day of the week is to be kept sacred for religious purposes. It is known as the Lord's Day in honor of the resurrection of our Lord.

Civil Government: Civil government is divinely appointed for the interest and good order of society. Civil authorities have no control over religious matters.

Righteous and Wicked: There is a difference between the righteous and the wicked. Those who refuse to receive Christ are unrepentant in their unbelief and are under the curse. This will lead to eternal damnation.

The World to Come: The world as we know it is coming to an end. Christ will return from heaven and raise the dead, and a separation will take place of the righteous and the wicked. The righteous will reign with Him and the wicked will go to everlasting punishment.

What is our desire?

Baptists in the twenty-first century maintain the traditions of their fathers in the faith. The greatest of these traditions is civil and religious freedom.

Freedom has its benefits and consequences. Those who are truly Baptist do not accept many of the negatives of our society.

However, we are tolerant enough to understand that we are not to legislate but we are to ensure the rights of those who choose to be wrong. We understand that our freedoms call us to a faith in Christ to reclaim the dignity and morality that once was innate to our spiritual progenitors.

Baptists are Christocentric and Bibliocentric, as is elaborated by the following excerpts:

> Baptists generally do not believe in a social gospel or that the kingdom of God can be established simply through social reform of an individual or a society as a whole but Baptists do believe in a spiritual gospel that has social implications.

> In order to make the greatest impact on society, Christians should be ready to work with all men of good will for any good cause, always being careful to act in the sprit of love without comprising their loyalty to Christ and His truth.

> Jesus taught that Christians should be both salt and light in the world. The very presence of Christ should be judgment upon all that is corrupt and evil.[2]

Those statements are indicative of the very fabric that makes us appealing and productive to our society and this generation. We adjust to the common godly good that is defined for us in Scripture (i.e., the Sermon on the Mount in Matthew 5), and we are resistant to the common evil (i.e., the works of the devil) that threatens our peaceful co-existence (as is taught in the New Testament by Christ and the Apostles).

We do not claim to be right in ourselves but right in Christ. This is not an innate righteousness. We strive to reach the perfection that

---

[2] Herschel H. Hobbs, *Concerning Social Action in Baptist Faith and Message*, rev. ed. (Nashville: LightWay Press, 2000), pp. 112, 114, 113.

is in our Savior Christ Jesus (Matthew 5:48). Our righteousness comes to the fore as we fight for the right of others to become all that God wants them to be.

The larger Baptist family

The Baptist family is a large one. Their roots are in the nineteenth century or before. I will list a few for you:

General Baptists
Seventh Day Baptists
Freewill Baptists
Primitive Baptists
Regular Baptists

Of course, the aforementioned Baptist denominations, and others not mentioned, are perhaps the offspring of personality conflicts, or, might we say, theological differences.

There are many ethnic Baptist groups, including:

Czechoslovakian Baptists
Hungarian Baptists
Polish Baptists
French Baptists
Scandinavian Baptists
Romanian Baptists
Russian Baptists
Swedish Baptists
German Baptists
Hispanic Baptists
Asian Baptists
Chinese Baptists
Japanese Baptists
Korean Baptists

Indo-Chinese Baptists
Filipino Baptists

There are also many different Baptist associations. Other well-known groups are the Southern Baptists and the American Baptists.

There are liberal, conservative, moderate, and fundamentalists in the Baptist family. Each group has its own spin on the Scripture's interpretation that forms its beliefs and practices. Just last year the Southern Baptists mandated that women should be kept silent in the church. Other Baptists feel that women should speak, but the Southern Baptists will only allow women to teach. I don't know the difference between preaching and teaching!

Some Baptists are like the Taliban who restrict the freedom of women.

We are shaped by our time and fashioned by our vision.

The Baptist Church is a good body that has its problems because the people who make up this Church have their problems. The wonder of this is that the Spirit of Christ is yet at work in us to perfect us but at the same time to work and do according to His good pleasure (Philippians 2:13).

There used to be an old adage when I was a child that went like this: "I was Baptist born, Baptist bred, and when I die there will be a good Baptist dead." Allow me to close by saying, "I was Christian born, Christian bred, and when I die will be a good Christian dead." The Lord Jesus said it so well: "There is none good but the Father" (Matthew 19:16–22).

Thank God for all believers. And thank God for Baptists.

Chapter 8

UNITARIAN UNIVERSALISM

W. Robert Chapman

Unitarian Universalists: Who they are and what they believe in
A joke about Unitarian Universalists is that they believe—at most—in one God. There is a grain of truth in that. But modern Unitarian Universalism—the result of the 1961 merger of two historically liberal Protestant sects, the American Unitarian Association and the Universalist Church of America—cannot be easily pigeonholed. A creedless religious body that emerged in the United States largely from separate strains of New England Puritanism, today's Unitarian Universalist can easily be a theist, a deist, a pagan, a humanist, or even an atheist—bound together by religiously informed moral and ethical principles drawn primarily from the Judaic and Christian traditions.

At one extreme there are congregations whose worship services follow a religious liturgy not unlike those of an Episcopal church; on the other extreme, certain congregations eschew any resemblance to liturgy altogether, offering instead discussions or programs led by the laity that might focus on moral or ethical issues. But most Unitarian Universalist societies are somewhere in between, with services like those of liberal Protestant churches—congregational hymns along with instrumental or vocal music, inspirational readings from sacred and secular sources, prayers and sermons by a professionally trained, ordained pastor. Although each congregation is loosely linked by membership in the Unitarian Universalist Association, each is self-governing within the framework of UUA principles.

Historically a product of the radical left wing of the Protestant Reformation, Unitarianism's chief theological distinction was its biblically based rejection of the doctrine of the Holy Trinity—essentially a revival of the Arian heresy of the fourth century, which unsuccessfully challenged nascent Christianity to reject Trinitarianism and return to the Judaic form of monotheism. Universalists rejected the Calvinistic doctrine of Election—whereby God arbitrarily chooses a few righteous souls for eternal salvation—and taught instead that God's salvation was available to all believers. In time, Unitarians came to be perceived as overly intellectual, although their dwindling congregations were among the most affluent in America. Universalists, by contrast, were poorer, less educated, and more evangelical. By the middle of the twentieth century, however, their similarities outweighed their differences—hence, the merger.

Unlike mainstream Christians, Unitarian Universalists tend to regard Jesus as an important ethical and moral leader rather than the Son of God or Messiah. Perhaps reflecting their strong educational backgrounds, most Unitarian Universalists are uncomfortable with religious dogmatism and have come to this liberal religion after leaving another faith tradition. Like Judaism, Unitarian Universalism is largely a here-and-now religion, greatly concerned with issues of social justice. One of its strongest selling points—especially for parents—is its lack of a creedal test: All are welcome to join in a common quest for religious truth, guided by reason, respectful of other traditions, and inspired by one's own conscience.

What is the ultimate authority for belief and practice in your denomination?

The ultimate authority is vested in the individual conscience, informed historically by reason, history, and religious tradition. Although Unitarian Universalism does not prescribe a creedal test for membership, there are certain principles to which most UUs would happily assent. In our congregation, we covenant to affirm and promote:

The inherent worth and dignity of every person.

Justice, equity, and compassion in human relations.

Acceptance of one another and encouragement to spiritual growth in our congregations.

A free and responsible search for truth and meaning.

The right of conscience and the use of the democratic process within our congregations and in society at large.

The goal of world community with peace, liberty, and justice for all.

Respect for the interdependent web of all existence of which we are a part.

The living traditions we share draw from many sources:

Direct experience of that transcending mystery and wonder, affirmed in all cultures, which moves us to a renewal of the spirit and openness to the forces that create and uphold life.

Words and deeds of prophetic women and men that challenge us to confront powers and structures of evil with justice, compassion, and the transforming power of love.

Wisdom from the world's religions that inspires us in our ethical and spiritual life.

Jewish and Christian teachings that call us to respond to God's love by loving our neighbors as ourselves.

Spiritual teachings of Earth-centered traditions that celebrate the sacred circle of life and instruct us to live in harmony with the rhythms of nature.

Humanist teachings that counsel us to heed the guidance of reason and the results of science, and warn us against idolatries of the mind and spirit.

Grateful for the religious pluralism that enriches and ennobles our faith, we are inspired to deepen our understanding and expand our vision. As free congregations, we enter into this covenant, promising to one another our mutual support and trust.

How do you understand the authority of the Bible?

Unitarian Universalists are not creedally bound to have a single view, thus making each adherent of this faith an arbiter of the Bible's authority. There are many among us who find particular spiritual wisdom in the metaphors and stories of the Bible, but there are few among us who would insist upon its literal and absolute truth.

What is the authority of church tradition from the early church to the present?

The earliest Unitarian thinkers would be the Arians and Socinians, who took issue with the Trinitarian doctrines developed by the early church, finding them not to be scripturally based, and believing that elevating Jesus to the stature of God made Jesus as a person inaccessible and thereby spiritually distant from believers. This strand of thinking, which ultimately became organized as Unitarianism and Universalism in the late eighteenth and early nineteenth centuries, clearly differentiated itself from church hierarchy and tradition, and held that people have an inborn ability to develop their own spiritual impulses without compulsion or restriction from church authority.

What is the authority of personal experience?

Since ultimate authority is vested in the individual, personal experience counts for a great deal. Personal experience does not take place within a spiritual vacuum, however; we call upon the experiences of co-religionists as well as spiritual people from many faith communities.

What is the authority of the historic creeds, especially Nicea in 325?

As a noncreedal faith community, none are binding on Unitarian Universalists as members of a denomination. Individual UUs are free to accept or reject these creeds as their consciences direct them.

Do you believe in the divinity of Jesus?

Unitarian Universalists are free to accept or reject the divinity of Jesus. While most would reject that notion as it is generally understood by Christians, some could accept that divinity was present in Jesus in the same way as it was in Abraham and Moses, the Buddha, the Prophet Muhammad, Mother Theresa, and countless extraordinary persons.

Do you believe in the resurrection of the dead?

While Unitarian Universalists are free to believe or disbelieve in the resurrection of the dead, they are not required to state such a belief as a condition of membership in the denomination.

What does it mean to accept Jesus as one's Lord and Savior?

For most Unitarian Universalists, this concept rarely concerns us.

How does one attain salvation?

See the next question.

What does salvation mean?

According to Alice Blair Wesley,

> The English word *salvation* derives from the Latin *salus*, meaning health. Unitarian Universalists are as concerned with salvation, in the sense of spiritual health or wholeness, as any other religious people. However, in many Western churches, salvation has come to be associated with a specific set of

beliefs or a spiritual transformation of a very limited type. Among Unitarian Universalists, instead of salvation you will hear of our yearning for, and our experience of, personal growth, increased wisdom, strength of character, and gifts of insight, understanding, inner and outer peace, courage, patience, and compassion. The ways in which these things come to, change, and heal us, are many indeed. We seek and celebrate them in our worship.

What is the status of the Hebrew Bible as an authority for belief and practice?

Like the Christian New Testament, the Hebrew Bible is a source of great religious insight and occupies a welcome place in our pulpits and our daily lives. As Alice Blair Wesley explains,

In most of our congregations, our children learn Bible stories as a part of their church school curricula. It is not unusual to find adult study groups in the churches, or in workshops at summer camps and conferences, focusing on the Bible. Allusions to biblical symbols and events are frequent in our sermons. In most of our congregations, the Bible is read as any other sacred text might be—from time to time, but not routinely. We have especially cherished the prophetic books of the Bible. Amos, Hosea, Isaiah, and other prophets dared to speak critical words of love to the powerful, calling for justice for the oppressed. While biblical prophets inspired many Unitarian and Universalist social reformers, we do not hold the Bible—or any other account of human experience—to be either an infallible guide or the exclusive source of truth. Much biblical material is mythical or legendary. Not that it should be discarded for that reason! Rather, it should be treasured for what it is. We believe that we should read the Bible as we read other books—with imagination and a critical eye.

Where does authority reside in the church? Do you have a hierarchy of authority (e.g., bishops, priests, deacons, laypersons)? Does the local church have the power to hire and fire its pastor?
While the Unitarian Universalist Association provides a denominational structure, ultimate authority resides within each local congregation—a democratic system most commonly known as congregational polity. The congregation elects its own lay leaders, who have ultimate authority over setting budgets and congregational policies. The congregation as a whole votes on calling ministers, approving large-scale policies, changing bylaws and structures, and electing officers. Each congregation sends a delegation of lay leaders and ministers to an annual gathering of our continental association, the Unitarian Universalist Association, at which large-scale decisions about denominational issues are made, as well as electing denominational leaders. The Association provides resources for congregations, and district offices to facilitate this resource role, but has no ultimate authority over congregational life. Ministers are the spiritual leaders of congregations with only the authority of person and tradition. Having a congregational polity does not preclude working collectively with other UU congregations in regional, national, or international associations. While each congregation is free to call its own pastors, the Unitarian Universalist Association oversees the credentialing of its clergy.

How does one become a member of your church?
Many of our religious societies offer introductory sessions, study groups, videotapes, and increasingly, a World Wide Web homepage to acquaint those interested in membership with our history, principles, and programs. Individual appointments with ministers and members are encouraged. Many pamphlets are available through the UUA Bookstore. Usually, these are readily accessible in a church's foyer, and even small fellowships may have a good library of Unitarian Universalist writings. The last act of joining the con-

gregation is simple, but significant: You write your name on a membership card or in the membership book or parish register. We have no creedal requirements. With your signature you affirm your pledge to enter and to remain in a continuing and tolerant dialogue concerning the ways of truth and love, a dialogue within which free persuasion may occur; to share in our fellowship and in our corporate decision-making; and to support with your gifts of energy and money our common work for the common good.

What is your understanding of sacraments, especially Baptism and the Lord's Supper (or Holy Communion or Eucharist)?
If we use the term "sacrament" at all, it is not in the same sense that most Christians would understand it (i.e., outward, visible signs of an inward, spiritual, divine act). Unitarian Universalists celebrate marriages, births, and deaths in ceremonial ways that represent milestones in a person's spiritual bonding with a religious community. Unitarian Universalism has a small number of congregations that emphasize their ongoing ties to Christianity. Like many liberal Christian denominations, such congregations celebrate a Eucharist as a memorial ritual rather than as a sacrament.

Outline the structure of your liturgy or worship service
Generally speaking, our liturgy is similar to those found in liberal Protestant denominations. While there would be considerable variation in the orders of service found among Unitarian Universalist congregations, this might be a typical Sunday service in a New England Unitarian Universalist church:

Entrance Voluntary
Welcome and Announcements
Musical prelude
Invocation
Chalice Lighting
Unison Affirmation

Hymn
Children's Story
Hand of Friendship
Responsive Reading
Offertory Anthem
Prayer or Meditation
First Reading (sacred or secular)
Anthem
Second Reading (sacred or secular)
Hymn
Offertory (special music)
Sermon or Homily
Hymn
Benediction
Choral response
Musical postlude

How do you distinguish your denomination from other Protestant denominations and from Roman Catholicism?

Historically, Unitarian Universalism is descended from the liberal wing of the Protestant Reformation. Unitarianism distinguished itself from orthodox Protestantism by its rejection of Trinitarianism; Universalism, by its rejection of the Calvinistic doctrine of Predestination. Modern Unitarian Universalism differs from Roman Catholicism in ways too numerous to describe here; however, the most important distinctions would have to be unitarian vs. trinitarian theology, congregational vs. episcopal polity, and a theological inclusiveness vs. exclusiveness.

What distinguishes clergy from laypersons?

Unitarian Universalist clergy receive their ordination from congregations of laypersons rather than at the hands of other ordained clergy. They are ordained as religious teachers, counselors, and spiritual leaders. Their authority derives from a recognition of the gifts and wisdom of them as people, as well as the tradition of liberal religious leadership, which offers freedom of the pulpit. Clergy are extensively trained in the Judaeo-Christian tradition and scripture, world religions, arts of ministry, social and cultural understandings of religious history, and the history of Unitarian Universalism. They are received into fellowship as a Unitarian Universalist minister when they have demonstrated competence in these areas, completed a ministerial internship, undergone psychological assessment, completed a Clinical Pastoral Education unit, and successful examination before our denominational Ministerial Fellowship Committee. As noted above, congregations may ordain persons to be clergy without fulfilling the above requirements, but this ordination would be recognized only by that particular congregation, not by the Association as a whole.

What is your denomination's view of Judaism?

Most Unitarian Universalists would agree that we are spiritually indebted to Judaism, since like our Christian forebears we have also inherited much of its moral and ethical legacy. None would dispute that doctrinal and cultural differences continue to distinguish us from Judaism, yet among nominally Christian bodies, Unitarian Universalism generally enjoys a warm relationship with Judaism, especially with its Reform and some Conservative congregations. Many Jews who no longer feel religiously connected to Judaism are comfortable joining Unitarian Universalist congregations, since there is a certain familiarity with its rituals and a shared value system.

What is your denomination's position concerning the State of Israel as the eternal home of the Jewish people, and the Second Coming of Christ?

We have consistently maintained Israel's right to exist within secure borders, while simultaneously urging the formation of a Palestinian state to co-exist harmoniously alongside the State of Israel. As to the Second Coming of Christ, Unitarian Universalism, as a creed-less religion, has no official position concerning questions of Christian eschatology.

Chapter 9

ANGLICANISM

Rev. Robert W. Cudworth

Let us begin with a standard definition of the term Anglicianism:

> It properly denotes the system of doctrine and practice of those Christians who are in communion with the see of Canterbury [i.e., the archbishop of Canterbury] but it has come to be used especially in a more restricted sense of that system in so far as it claims to possess a religious and theological outlook distinguishable from that of other Christian communions, whether Catholic, Orthodox, or Protestant. The original formulation of Anglican principles is to be sought in the reign of Elizabeth I rather than Henry VIII or Edward VI, for it was under her that a *via media* between the opposing factions of Rome and Geneva (later called the "Elizabethan Settlement") became a political necessity and Anglicanism as a doctrinal system took shape.[1]

There are at least three ways to define anything: One can say what it is; one can say what it is not; or one can tell its story, its historical development. To some extent both Judaism and Christianity define who they are in that way. They are both very much historical religions.

The Episcopal Church is one of the churches in the Anglican Communion, all of which are in communion with the archbishop of

---

[1] Quoted from *The Oxford Dictionary of the Christian Church*, 3rd ed. (Oxford, 1997).

Canterbury. The bishops of the Anglican Communion gather once every ten years in England to dialogue about their faith. They used to meet at Lambeth Palace in London, which is the home of the archbishop of Canterbury, and so the convocation is known as the Lambeth Conference. It consists of more than thirty-three autonomous Christian churches. Today there are more Anglicans in Africa than on any other continent outside of the British Isles.[2] There is even a small Anglican community in Poland made up of converts from Judaism some nine or ten generations back. I once heard a priest from among them, Father Goldberg, preach in a church in Evanston, Illinois.

We are Catholic, but not Roman Catholic. There are basically three movements in the (American) Episcopal Church: Anglo-Catholic, evangelical, and charismatic. We are Protestant, or perhaps more accurately "Reformed" in that we do not acknowledge the bishop of Rome to be head of the Holy Catholic Church. Nor do we accept the two major doctrines of the Roman Catholic Church: that the Blessed Virgin Mary was conceived without sin (the Immaculate Conception), proclaimed by Pius IX in 1854, or of the bodily assumption of Mary into heaven; Pius XII defined the doctrine, in 1950.

It should be said that the Christian church began in what is now Israel. The lingua franca of Jews at the time that Jesus lived on this earth was Greek. The New Testament was written first in Greek. The Scriptures spoken of in that document were not the New Testament but the Septuagint version of the Tanakh (we call it the Old Testament). Jews in the time of Christ probably did not speak Hebrew, but Aramaic, a cognate language. This means that early Christians spoke Aramaic and understood Greek.

Those in the Eastern Mediterranean basin and far into the East understood Greek. The Western Mediterranean and the British Isles came to have Latin as its lingua franca.

---

[2] There are more Anglicans in the British Isles than on any Continent, however.

In the eleventh century there was a great deal of corruption in the Christian church. Some very intelligent church leaders in the West dialogued about what might be done about it, and out of those dialogues came the Hildebrandine Reform. It was named for one of these leaders whose name was Hildebrand, who later became Pope Gregory VII. There were four main points to the Reform. One of them was that the pope was the head of the Christian church. Another point was that clergy would no longer be allowed to marry. The purpose of this was to prevent nepotism. If a man were bishop of Mainz or wherever, he might want to have a patrimony or position for his son. If a clergyman could not marry, he could not pass title to his offspring. *Mortmain* ("dead hand") was the legal term. It would cut out one common source of corruption. The patriarch of Constantinople (this meant the Christians in the Eastern Mediterranean) did not accept the reforms. In fact, he excommunicated the pope of Rome, whereupon the pope excommunicated the patriarch. That was in 1054.

The (American) Episcopal Church, which grew out of the Church of England, began after the American Revolutionary War. Its first bishop was Samuel Seabury (the place where I live was named for him), and he was consecrated (made a bishop in Christ's holy Catholic Church) in 1784, in Scotland.

The (American) Episcopal Church is governed by a General Convention made up of a House of Bishops and a House of Deputies, which in turn is made up of lay (nonordained) delegates, and clerical (ordained) delegates, and they may under certain conditions vote separately, in which case to pass a measure both orders must agree by a majority.

All baptized persons are ministers in the Episcopal Church, and there are four kinds of ministers: lay people, bishops, priests, and deacons. All of the latter three sorts are ordained. There is a presiding bishop, who heads up and administers the church. Actually, his power is very circumscribed. The General Convention, which rules the church, meets every three years. The bishop and his (her) diocese is the basic unit of the church, not the parish. The House of Bishops gathers more frequently.

Permanent deacons ceased to be ordained in the Western church about the twelfth century, but in the Eastern Orthodox Church they have always had such deacons, and they have always allowed their clergy to marry. The way it works there is that a man is married before he is ordained. Once ordained, he cannot marry. Even in the Eastern Rite of the Roman Catholic Church until rather recently the same rule was followed regarding marriage.

It has been said, I think very wisely, that Orthodox and Anglican Christians tend to be paratactic, which means "both-and"; whereas the Roman Church tends to use hypotactic thinking, that is, "either-or." There is considerable diversity in the Episcopal Church.

The principal sacraments in the Anglican church are two in number: baptism and holy eucharist (also called holy communion or the Mass). Dom Gregory Dix thinks that this rite grew out of a rite still extant in Judaism, namely *havurah*, and not out of the Passover, as many maintain.

There are five minor sacraments in the Anglican church, or as the 1979 *Book of Common Prayer* calls them, "other sacramental rites." None of them is necessary to every person in the way that the two Dominical sacraments are. These five are:

Confirmation: a mature commitment to Christ, which is made by a person, or by sponsors on the person's behalf, at baptism. The bishop lays his hands on the confirmed in the ceremony.

Ordination: a rite in which a deacon, priest, or bishop is given authority by God and grace of the Holy Spirit. In each case this is done through the laying on of hands by a bishop, in the case of a deacon, by a bishop, and priests in the case of a priest, and by bishops (at least three) in the case of a bishop.

Holy matrimony: a rite in which each party makes a covenant with the other, and to which a priest gives a blessing.

Reconciliation of a penitent (formerly referred to as confession and absolution): in this rite a penitent confesses his or her sins to God before and in the hearing of a priest. And the priest assures pardon and the grace of absolution.

Unction: the rite of anointing the sick with oil which has been blessed by a bishop or priest, along with, or only by, the laying on of hands by a priest, with the laying on of hands by others in some cases.

God does not limit himself to these ways of imparting his grace, but these five rites have arisen under the direction of the Holy Spirit. Sacraments sustain our present hope and anticipate future fulfillment.

Jesus was once asked what the most important commandment in the law was, and He replied, "You shall love the Lord your God with all your heart, with all your soul, with all your strength," which is the verse following immediately after the *Shema*, and he went on to say, "and your neighbor as yourself" (Leviticus 19:18).

Chapter 10

THE CHURCH OF JESUS CHRIST OF LATTER-DAY SAINTS

Bishop David Williams

Articles of Faith of the Church of Jesus Christ of Latter-day Saints

We believe in God, the Eternal Father, and in His Son, Jesus Christ, and in the Holy Ghost.

We believe that men will be punished for their own sins, and not for Adam's transgression.

We believe that through the Atonement of Christ, all mankind may be saved, by obedience to the laws and ordinances of the Gospel.

We believe that the first principles and ordinances of the Gospel are: first, Faith in the Lord Jesus Christ; second, Repentance; third, Baptism by immersion for the remission of sins; fourth, laying on of hands for the gift of the Holy Ghost.

We believe that a man must be called of God, by prophecy, and by the laying on of hands, by those who are in authority to preach the Gospel and administer in the ordinances thereof.

We believe in the same organization that existed in the Primitive Church, viz., apostles, prophets, pastors, teachers, evangelists, etc.

We believe in the gift of tongues, prophecy, revelation, visions, healing, interpretation of tongues, etc.

We believe the Bible to be the word of God as far as it is translated correctly; we also believe the Book of Mormon to be the word of God.

We believe all that God has revealed, all that He does now reveal, and we believe that He will yet reveal many great and important things pertaining to the Kingdom of God.

We believe in the literal gathering of Israel and in the restoration of the Ten Tribes; that Zion will be built upon this [the American] continent; that Christ will reign personally upon the earth; and, that the earth will be renewed and receive its paradisiacal glory.

We claim the privilege of worshiping Almighty God according to the dictates of our own conscience, and allow all men the same privilege, let them worship how, where, or what they may.

We believe in being subject to kings, presidents, rulers, and magistrates, in obeying, honoring, and sustaining the law.

We believe in being honest, true, chaste, benevolent, virtuous, and in doing good to all men; indeed, we may say that we follow the admonition of Paul—We believe all things, we hope all things, we have endured many things, and hope to be able to endure all things. If there is anything virtuous, lovely, or of good report or praiseworthy, we seek after these things.

—*Joseph Smith*

Origin of the Church of Jesus Christ of Latter-day Saints

Joseph Smith was born December 23, 1805, at Sharon, Windsor County, Vermont. When the boy Joseph was ten years old, the family left Vermont and settled in the state of New York, first at Palmyra and later at Manchester.

In their religious inclinations the family favored the Presbyterian church; but Joseph, while at one time favorably impressed by the Methodists, kept himself free from all sectarian membership, being greatly perplexed over the strife and dissensions manifest among the churches of the time. When Joseph was in his fifteenth year the region of his home was visited by a storm of fierce religious excitement, which, beginning with the Methodists, soon became general among all the sects; there were revivals and protracted meetings, and discreditable exhibitions of sectarian rivalry were many and varied.

Here is Joseph's own account of his course of action:

In the midst of this war of words and tumult of opinions, I often said to myself: What is to be done? Who of all these parties is right; or, are they all wrong together? If any one of them be right, which is it, and how shall I know it?

While I was laboring under the extreme difficulties caused by the contests of these parties of religionists, I was one day reading the Epistle of James, first chapter and fifth verse, which reads: *If any of you lack wisdom, let him ask of God, that giveth to all men liberally, and upbraideth not; and it shall be given him.*

Never did any passage of scripture come with more power to the heart of man than this did at this time to mine. It seemed to enter with great force into every feeling of my heart. I reflected on it again and again, knowing that if any person needed wisdom from God, I did; for how to act I did not know, and unless I could get more wisdom than I then had, I would never know; for the teachers of religion of the different sects understood the same passages of scripture so differently as to destroy all confidence in settling the question by an appeal to the Bible.

At length I came to the conclusion that I must either remain in darkness and confusion, or else I must do as James directs, that is, ask of God. I at length came to the determination to "ask of God," concluding that if he gave wisdom to them that lacked wisdom, and would give liberally, and not upbraid, I might venture.

So, in accordance with this, my determination to ask of God, I retired to the woods to make the attempt. It was on the morning of a beautiful, clear day, early in the spring of eighteen hundred and twenty. It was the first time in my life that I had made such an attempt, for amidst all my anxieties I had never as yet made the attempt to pray vocally.

After I had retired to the place where I had previously designed to go, having looked around me, and finding myself alone, I kneeled down and began to offer up the desires of my heart to God. I had scarcely done so, when immediately I was seized upon by some power which entirely overcame me, and had such an astonishing influence over me as to bind my tongue so that I could not speak. Thick darkness gathered around me, and it seemed to me for a time as if I were doomed to sudden destruction.

But, exerting all my powers to call upon God to deliver me out of the power of this enemy which had seized upon me, and at the very moment when I was ready to sink into despair and abandon myself to destruction—not to an imaginary ruin, but to the power of some actual being from the unseen world, who had such marvelous power as I had never before felt in any being—just at this moment of great alarm, I saw a pillar of light exactly over my head, above the brightness of the sun, which descended gradually until it fell upon me.

It no sooner appeared than I found myself delivered from the enemy which held me bound. When the light rested upon me I saw two Personages, whose brightness and glory defy all description, standing above me in the air. One of them spoke unto me, calling me by name, and said, pointing to the other—*This is My Beloved Son. Hear Him!*

My object in going to inquire of the Lord was to know which of all the sects was right, that I might know which to join. No sooner, therefore, did I get possession of myself, so as to be able to speak, than I asked the Personages who stood above me in the light, which of all the sects was right—and which I should join.

I was answered that I must join none of them, for they were all wrong; and the Personage who addressed me said that all their creeds were an abomination in his sight; that those professors were all corrupt; that: "they draw near to me with their lips, but their hearts are far from me; they teach for doctrines the commandments of men, having a form of godliness, but they deny the power thereof."

On the night of September 21, 1823, while praying for forgiveness of sins and for guidance as to his future course, he was blessed with another heavenly manifestation. There appeared in his room a brilliant light, in the midst of which stood a personage clothed in white, and with a countenance of radiant purity. The heavenly visitant announced himself as Moroni, a messenger sent from the presence of God; and he proceeded to instruct the youth as to some of the divine purposes in which his instrumentality would be of great import. The angel said that God had a work for Joseph to do, and that his name "should be had for good and evil among all nations, kindreds, and tongues, or that it should be both good and evil spoken of among all people." He said there was a book deposited, written upon gold plates, giving an account of the former inhabitants of this continent, and the source from whence they sprang. He also said that the fullness of the everlasting Gospel was contained in it, as delivered by the Savior to the ancient inhabitants; also, that there were two stones in silver bows—and these stones, fastened to a breastplate, constituted what is called the Urim and Thummim—deposited with the plates; and the possession and use of these stones were what constituted "seers" in ancient or former times; and that God had prepared them for the purpose of translating the book.

The visiting angel, Moroni, then repeated several prophecies which are recorded in the ancient scriptures; some of the quotations were given with variations from the readings in the Bible. Of the words of Malachi the following were given, presenting small but significant variations from the biblical version: "For behold, the day cometh that shall burn as an oven, and all the proud, yea, and all that do wickedly shall burn as stubble; for they that come shall burn them, saith the Lord of Hosts, that it shall leave them neither root nor branch." Further: "Behold, I will reveal unto you the Priesthood, by the hand of Elijah the prophet, before the coming of the great and dreadful day of the Lord." He also quoted the next verse differently: "And he shall plant in the hearts of the children the promises made to the fathers, and the hearts of the children shall turn to their fathers. If it were not so, the whole earth would be utterly wasted at his coming." Among other scriptures, Moroni cited the prophecies of Isaiah relating to the restoration of scattered Israel, and the promised reign of righteousness on earth, saying that the predictions were about to be fulfilled; also the words of Peter to the Jews, concerning the prophet who Moses said would be raised up, explaining that the prophet referred to was Jesus Christ, and that the day was near at hand when all who rejected the words of the Savior would be cut off from among the people.

Having delivered his message the angel departed, the light in the room seeming to condense about his person and disappearing with him. But during the night he returned twice, and at each visit repeated what he had said at the first, with admonitions to which were added warnings as to the temptations that would assail the youth in the fulfillment of his mission. On the following day Moroni appeared to Joseph again, reciting anew the instructions and cautions of the preceding night, and telling him to acquaint his father with all he had heard and seen. This the boy did, and the father promptly testified that the communications were from God.

Joseph then went to the hill described to him in the vision. He recognized the spot indicated by the angel, and with some labor laid bare a stone box containing the plates and other things spoken of by Moroni. The messenger again stood beside him, and forbade the removal of the contents at that time, saying that four years were to elapse before the plates would be committed to his care, and that it would be his duty to visit the spot at yearly intervals. On the occasion of each of these visits the angel instructed the young man more fully regarding the great work awaiting him.

The organization of the Church as a body corporate was effected on the sixth day of April, A.D., 1830, at Fayette in the State of New York, and the names of but six persons are of record as those of active participants.

Malachi predicted the coming of Elijah especially commissioned with power to inaugurate the work of cooperation between the fathers and the children, and announced this mission as a necessary preliminary to "the great and dreadful day of the Lord."

The ancient scriptures teem with prophecies concerning the restoration of Israel in the last days, and the gathering of the people from among the nations and from the lands into which they have been led or driven as a penalty for their waywardness. In the predictions of olden times such prominence and importance are attached to this work of gathering that, from the days of Israel's exodus, the last days have been characterized in sacred writ as distinctively a gathering dispensation. The return of the tribes after their long and wide dispersion is made a preliminary work to the establishment of the predicted reign of righteousness with Christ upon the earth as Lord and King; and its accomplishment is given as a sure precursor of the Millennium. Jerusalem is to be reestablished as the City of the Great King on the eastern hemisphere; and Zion, or the New Jerusalem, is to be built on the western continent; the Lost Tribes are to be brought from their place of exile in the north; and the curse is to be removed from Israel.

Of the record of Joseph and its coming forth as a parallel testimony to that of Judah, or the Bible in part, the Lord thus spoke through the prophet Ezekiel: "Moreover, thou son of man, take thee one stick, and write upon it, For Judah, and for the children of Israel his companions: then take another stick, and write upon it, For

Joseph, the stick of Ephraim, and for all the house of Israel his companions: And join them one to another into one stick; and they shall become one in thine hand. And when the children of thy people shall speak unto thee, saying, Wilt thou not show us what thou meanest by these? Say unto them, Thus saith the Lord God; Behold, I will take the stick of Joseph, which is in the hand of Ephraim, and the tribes of Israel his fellows, and will put them with him, even with the stick of Judah, and make them one stick, and they shall be one in mine hand."

Joseph Smith's Authority was conferred upon him by direct ministrations of heavenly beings, each of whom had once exercised the same power upon the earth. On the fifteenth of May, 1829, the lesser or Aaronic Priesthood was conferred upon Joseph Smith and Oliver Cowdery under the hands of John the Baptist, who came in his immortalized state with that particular order of Priesthood, which comprises the keys of the ministrations of angels, the doctrine of repentance and of baptism for the remission of sins. This was the same John who, as the voice of one crying in the wilderness, had preached the same doctrine and administered the same ordinance in Judea, as the immediate forerunner of the Messiah. In delivering his message John the Baptist stated that he was acting under the direction of Peter, James, and John, apostles of the Lord, in whose hands reposed the keys of the higher or Melchizedek Priesthood, which in time would also be given. This promise was fulfilled a month or so later, when the apostles named visited in person Joseph Smith and Oliver Cowdery, ordaining them to the apostleship, which comprises all the offices of the higher order of Priesthood and which carries authority to minister in all the established ordinances of the Gospel.

Then, some time after the Church had been duly organized, commission for certain special functions was given, the appointing messenger in each case being the one whose right it was so to officiate by virtue of the authority he had held in the days of his mortality.

Thus, as has been seen, Moses conferred the authority to prosecute the work of gathering; and Elijah, who, not having tasted death, held a peculiar relation to both the living and the dead, delivered the appointment of vicarious ministry for the departed. To these divine commissions is added that given by Elias, who appeared to Joseph Smith and Oliver Cowdery and "committed the dispensation of the gospel of Abraham," saying as was said of the patriarch named and his descendants in olden times, that in them and in their seed should all succeeding generations be blessed.

It is evident, then, that the claims made by the Church with respect to its authority are complete and consistent as to the source of the powers professed and the channels through which such have been delivered again to earth. Scripture and revelation, both ancient and modern, support as an unalterable law the principle that no one can delegate to another an authority which the giver does not possess.

—*Articles of Faith*, 25.

We believe in God, the Eternal Father, and in His Son, Jesus Christ, and in the Holy Ghost.
The Holy Bible names God as the Creator of all things, and moreover, declares that He revealed Himself to our first earthly parents and to many other holy personages in the early days of the world. Adam and Eve heard His voice in the garden, and even after their transgression they continued to call upon God and to sacrifice to Him. After their expulsion they heard "the voice of the Lord from the way toward the Garden of Eden," though they saw Him not; and He gave unto them commandments, which they obeyed. Then came to Adam an angel, and the Holy Ghost inspired the man and bare record of the Father and the Son.

Of Moses we read that he heard the voice of God, who spoke to him from the midst of the burning bush in Mount Horeb, saying: "I am the God of thy father, the God of Abraham, the God of Isaac, and the God of Jacob. And Moses hid his face; for he was afraid to look upon God." Unto Moses and assembled Israel God appeared in a cloud, with the terrifying accompaniment of thunders and lightnings, on Sinai: "Thus thou shalt say unto the children of Israel, Ye have seen that I have talked with you from heaven." Of a later manifestation we are told: "Then went up Moses, and Aaron, Nadab, and Abihu, and seventy of the elders of Israel: And they saw the God of Israel: and there was under his feet as it were a paved work of a sapphire stone, and as it were the body of heaven in his clearness."

The Book of Mormon is replete with instances of communication between God and His people, mostly through vision and by the ministration of angels, but also through direct manifestation of the divine presence. Thus, we read of a colony of people leaving the Tower of Babel and journeying to the western hemisphere, under the leadership of one who is known in the record as the brother of Jared. In preparing for the ocean voyage, the man prayed that the Lord would touch with His finger, and thereby make luminous, certain stones, so that the voyagers might have light in the ships. In answer to this petition, the Lord stretched forth His hand and touched the stones, revealing His finger, which the man was surprised to see resembled the finger of a human being. Then the Lord, pleased with the man's faith, made Himself visible, and demonstrated to the brother of Jared that man was formed literally after the image of the Creator. To the Nephites who inhabited the western continent, Christ revealed Himself after His resurrection and ascension. To these sheep of the western fold, He testified of His commission received from the Father, showed the wounds in His hands, feet, and side, and ministered unto the believing multitudes in many ways. The pre-mortal Christ is Jehovah. (*Articles of Faith*, 26.)

Three personages composing the great presiding council of the universe have revealed themselves to man: (1) God the Eternal

Father; (2) His Son, Jesus Christ; and (3) the Holy Ghost. That these three are separate individuals, physically distinct from each other, is demonstrated by the accepted records of divine dealings with man.

The Godhead is a type of unity in the attributes, powers, and purposes of its members. Jesus, while on earth and in manifesting Himself to His Nephite servants, repeatedly testified of the unity existing between Himself and the Father, and between them both and the Holy Ghost. This cannot rationally be construed to mean that the Father, the Son, and the Holy Ghost are one in substance and in person, nor that the names represent the same individual under different aspects. A single reference to prove the error of any such view may suffice: Immediately before His betrayal, Christ prayed for His disciples, the Twelve, and other converts, that they should be preserved in unity, "that they all may be one" as the Father and the Son are one. We cannot assume that Christ prayed that His followers lose their individuality and become one person, even if a change so directly opposed to nature were possible. Christ desired that all should be united in heart, spirit, and purpose; for such is the unity between His Father and Himself, and between them and the Holy Ghost.

In the year 325, the Council of Nicea was convened by the emperor Constantine, who sought through this body to secure a declaration of Christian belief that would be received as authoritative, and be the means of arresting the increasing dissension incident to the prevalent disagreement regarding the nature of the Godhead and other theological subjects. The Council condemned some of the theories then current, including that of Arius, which asserted that the Son was created by the Father, and therefore could not be coeternal with the Father. The Council promulgated what is known as the Nicene Creed; and this was followed in time by the Athanasian Creed over which, however, controversy has arisen as to authorship. The creed follows:

We worship one God in Trinity, and Trinity in Unity, neither confounding the persons, nor dividing the substance. For there is one person of the Father, another of the Son, and another of the Holy Ghost. But the Godhead of the Father, Son, and Holy Ghost, is all one; the glory equal, the majesty coeternal. Such as the Father is, such is the Son, and such is the Holy Ghost. The Father uncreate, the Son uncreate, and the Holy Ghost uncreate. The Father incomprehensible, the Son incomprehensible, and the Holy Ghost incomprehensible. The Father eternal, the Son eternal, and the Holy Ghost eternal. And yet there are not three eternals, but one eternal. As also there are not three incomprehensibles, nor three uncreated; but one uncreated, and one incomprehensible. So likewise the Father is Almighty, the Son Almighty, and the Holy Ghost Almighty; and yet there are not three Almighties, but one Almighty. So the Father is God, the Son is God and the Holy Ghost is God, and yet there are not three Gods but one God.

It would be difficult to conceive of a greater number of inconsistencies and contradictions expressed in words as few.

The Church of England teaches the present orthodox view of God as follows: "There is but one living and true God, everlasting, without body, parts, or passions; of infinite power, wisdom, and goodness." The immateriality of God as asserted in these declarations of sectarian faith is entirely at variance with the scriptures, and absolutely contradicted by the revelations of God's person and attributes, as shown by the citations already made.

We affirm that to deny the materiality of God's person is to deny God; for a thing without parts has no whole, and an immaterial body cannot exist. The Church of Jesus Christ of Latter-day Saints proclaims against the incomprehensible God, devoid of "body, parts, or passions," as a thing impossible of existence, and asserts its belief in and allegiance to the true and living God of scripture and revelation.

—Articles of Faith, 44.

We believe that men will be punished for their own sins, and not for Adam's transgression.

Man has inherited, among the inalienable rights conferred upon him by his divine Father, freedom to choose the good or the evil in life, to obey or disobey the Lord's commandments, as he may elect. The Lord has given commandments and has established statutes, with promises of blessings for compliance and penalties for infraction; but in the choice of these, men are untrammeled.

It is no more a part of God's plan to compel men to work righteousness than it is His purpose to permit evil powers to force His children into sin. In the days of Eden, the first man had placed before him commandment and law with an explanation of the penalty to follow violation of that law. No law could have been given him in righteousness had he not been free to act for himself. "Nevertheless, thou mayest choose for thyself, for it is given unto thee; but remember that I forbid it" said the Lord God to Adam. Concerning His dealings with the first patriarch of the race, God has declared in this day: "Behold, I gave unto him that he should be an agent unto himself."

A knowledge of good and evil is essential to the advancement that God has made possible for His children to achieve; and this knowledge can be best gained by actual experience, with the contrasts of good and its opposite plainly discernible. Therefore has man been placed upon earth subject to the influence of good and wicked powers, with a knowledge of the conditions surrounding him, and the heaven-born right to choose for himself. The words of the prophet Lehi are explicit: "Wherefore, the Lord God gave unto man that he should act for himself. Wherefore, man could not act for himself save it should be that he was enticed by the one or the other. Wherefore, men are free according to the flesh; and all things are given them which are expedient unto man. And they are free to choose liberty and eternal life, through the great mediation of all men, or to choose captivity and death, according to the captivity and power of the devil; for he seeketh that all men might be miserable like unto himself."

Another of the Nephite prophets, in speaking of those who had died, said they had gone "that they might reap their rewards according to their works, whether they were good or whether they were bad, to reap eternal happiness or eternal misery, according to the spirit which they listed to obey, whether it be a good spirit or a bad one. For every man receiveth wages of him whom he listeth to obey, and this according to the words of the spirit of prophecy."

Samuel, a converted Lamanite upon whom the spirit of the prophets had fallen, admonished his fellows in this wise: "And now remember, remember, my brethren, that whosoever perisheth, perisheth unto himself; and whosoever doeth iniquity, doeth it unto himself; for behold, ye are free; ye are permitted to act for yourselves; for behold, God hath given unto you a knowledge and he hath made you free. He hath given unto you that ye might know good from evil, and he hath given unto you that ye might choose life or death."

When the plans for creating and peopling the earth were under discussion in heaven, Lucifer sought to destroy the free agency of man by obtaining power to force the human family to do his will, promising the Father that by such means he would redeem all mankind so that not one of them should be lost. This proposition was rejected, while the original purpose of the Father—to use persuasive influences of wholesome precept and sacrificing example with the inhabitants of the earth, then to leave them free to choose for themselves—was agreed upon; and the one to be known as the Only Begotten Son was chosen as the chief instrument in carrying the purpose into effect.

—*Articles of Faith*, 49.

We believe that through the Atonement of Christ, all mankind may be saved, by obedience to the laws and ordinances of the Gospel.

The Atonement of Christ is taught as a leading doctrine by all sects professing Christianity. The expression is so common a one, and the essential point of its signification is so generally admitted, that definitions may appear to be superfluous; nevertheless, there is a peculiar importance attached to the use of the word "atonement" in a theological sense. The doctrine of the atonement comprises proof of the divinity of Christ's earthly ministry, and the vicarious nature of His death as a foreordained and voluntary sacrifice, intended for and efficacious as a propitiation for the sins of mankind, thus becoming the means whereby salvation may be secured.

The New Testament, which is properly regarded as the scripture of Christ's mission among men, is imbued throughout with the doctrine of salvation through the work of atonement wrought by the Savior; and yet the word "atonement" occurs but once in the record; and in that single instance, according to the opinion of most biblical authorities, it is misused. The instance referred to is found in the words of Paul addressed to the saints at Rome: "But we also joy in God through our Lord Jesus Christ, by whom we have now received the atonement." The marginal rendering gives, instead of atonement, "reconciliation," and of this word a related form is used in the preceding verse. A consistent translation, giving a full agreement between the English and the Greek, would make the verse quoted, and that immediately preceding it, read in this way: For if, when we were enemies, we were reconciled to God by the death of his Son, much more, being reconciled, we shall be saved by his life. And not only so, but we also joy in God through our Lord Jesus Christ, by whom we have now received the reconciliation. The term "atonement" occurs repeatedly in the Old Testament, with marked frequency in three of the books of the Pentateuch, Exodus, Leviticus, and Numbers; and the sense in which it is employed is that of a sacrifice of propitiation, usually associated with the death of an acceptable victim, whereby reconciliation was to be effected between God and men.

The structure of the word in its present form is suggestive of the true meaning; it is literally *at-one-ment*, "denoting reconciliation, or the bringing into agreement of those who have been estranged." And such is the significance of the saving sacrifice of the Redeemer, whereby He expiated the transgression of the fall, through which death came into the world, and provided ready and efficient means for man's attainment of immortality through reconciliation with God.

—*Articles of Faith*, 68.

The atonement is a necessary sequel of the transgression of Adam; and, as the infinite foreknowledge of God made clear to Him the one even before Adam was placed upon the earth, so the Father's mercy prepared a Savior for mankind before the world was framed. Through the fall Adam and Eve have entailed the conditions of mortality upon their descendants; therefore all beings born of earthly parents are subject to bodily death. The sentence of banishment from the presence of God was in the nature of a spiritual death; and that penalty, which was visited upon our first parents in the day of their transgression, has likewise followed as the common heritage of humanity. As this penalty came into the world through an individual act, it would be manifestly unjust to cause all to eternally suffer there from without means of deliverance. Therefore was the promised sacrifice of Jesus Christ ordained as a propitiation for broken law, whereby Justice could be fully satisfied, and Mercy be left free to exercise her beneficent influence over the souls of mankind. All the details of the glorious plan, by which the salvation of the human family is assured, may not lie within the understanding of man; but man has learned, even from his futile attempts to fathom the primary causes of the phenomena of nature, that his powers of comprehension are limited; and he will admit, that to deny an effect because of his inability to elucidate its cause would be to forfeit his claims as an observing and reasoning being.

—Articles of Faith, 68.

Resurrection

Resurrection is the reunion of the spirit with an immortal physical body. The body laid in the grave is mortal; the resurrected physical body is immortal. The whole of man, the united spirit and body, is defined in modern scripture as the "soul" of man. Resurrection from the dead constitutes the redemption of the soul (Doctrine and Covenants 88:15–16).

Although the idea of resurrection is not extensively delineated in the Old Testament, there are some definite allusions to it (e.g., 1 Samuel 2:6; Job 14:14, 19:26; Isaiah 26:19; Daniel 12:2). And in the New Testament, the resurrection of Jesus Christ, as the prototype of all resurrections, is an essential and central message: "I am the resurrection and the life" (John 11:25).

The evidence of Christ's resurrection is measurably strengthened for Latter-day Saints by other records of post-Resurrection visitations of the Christ (see Jesus Christ: Forty-day Ministry and Other Post-Resurrection Appearances). For example, in the 3 Nephi account in the Book of Mormon, an entire multitude saw, heard, and touched him as he appeared in transcendent resurrected glory. This is accepted by Latter-day Saints as an ancient sacred text. The tendency of some recent scholarship outside the Church to radically separate the "Jesus of history" and the "Christ of faith" and to ascribe the resurrection faith to later interpreters is challenged by these later documents and by modern revelation.[1]

In the theology of Judaism and some Christian denominations resurrection has often been spiritualized—that is, redefined as a

---

[1] Daniel H. Ludlow, ed., *Encyclopedia of Mormonism*, 4 vols. (New York: Macmillan, 1992), p. 1222.

symbol for immortality of some aspect of man, such as the active intellect, or of the soul considered to be an immaterial entity. In contrast, scientific naturalism tends to reject both the concept of the soul and of bodily resurrection. Latter-day Saints share few of the assumptions that underlie these dogmas. In LDS understanding, the spirit of each individual is not immaterial, but consists of pure, refined matter: "It existed before the body, can exist in the body; and will exist separate from the body, when the body will be moldering in the dust; and will in the resurrection, be again united with it", p. 207). Identity and personality persist with the spirit, and after the resurrection the spirit will dwell forever in a physical body.

Platonism and Gnosticism hold that embodiment is imprisonment, descent, or association with what is intrinsically evil. In contrast, the scriptures teach that the physical body is a step upward in the progression and perfection of all. The body is sacred, a temple (1 Corinthians 3:16; Doctrine and Covenants 93:35). Redemption is not escape from the flesh but its dedication and transformation. Joseph Smith taught, "We came into this earth that we might have a body and present it pure before God in the Celestial Kingdom" (*TPJS*, p. 181). On the other hand, if defiled, distorted, and abused, the body may be an instrument of degradation, an enemy of genuine spirituality.[2]

In a general sense, the Resurrection may be divided into the resurrection of the just, also called the first resurrection, and the resurrection of the unjust, or the last resurrection. The first resurrection commenced with the resurrection of Christ and with those who immediately thereafter came forth from their graves. In much larger numbers, it will precede the thousand-year millennial reign, inaugurated by the "second coming" of the Savior (Doctrine and Covenants 45:44–45; cf. 1 Thessalonians 4:16–17). At that time, some will be brought forth to meet him, as he descends in glory.

[2] Ibid.

This first resurrection will continue in proper order through the Millennium. The righteous who live on earth and die during the Millennium will experience immediate resurrection. Their transformation will take place in the "twinkling of an eye" (Doctrine and Covenants 63:51). The first resurrection includes the celestial and terrestrial glories.

The final resurrection, or resurrection of the unjust, will occur at the end of the Millennium. In the words of the apocalypse, "the rest of the dead lived not again until the thousand years were finished" (Revelation 20:5). This last resurrection will include those destined for the telestial glory and perdition.[3]

We believe that the first principles and ordinances of the Gospel are: first, Faith in the Lord Jesus Christ; second, Repentance; third, Baptism by immersion for the remission of sins; fourth, Laying on of hands for the gift of the Holy Ghost.

Faith

One who has this faith believes him to be the living Son of God, trusts in his goodness and power, repents of one's sins, and follows his guidance. Faith in the Lord Jesus Christ is awakened as individuals hear his gospel (Romans 10:17). By faith they enter the gate of repentance and baptism, and receive the gift of the Holy Ghost, which leads to the way of life ordained by Christ (2 Nephi 31:9, 17–18). Those who respond are "alive in Christ because of [their] faith" (2 Nephi 25:25). Because God's way is the only way that leads to salvation, "it is impossible to please him" without faith (Hebrews 11:6). Faith must precede miracles, signs, gifts of the Spirit, and righteousness, for "if there be no faith . . . God can do no miracle" (Ether 12:12). The Book of Mormon prophet Moroni summarized these points:

---

[3] Ibid., p. 1223.

The Lord God prepareth the way that the residue of men may have faith in Christ, that the Holy Ghost may have place in their hearts, according to the power thereof; and after this manner bringeth to pass the Father, the covenants which he hath made unto the children of men. And Christ hath said: If ye will have faith in me ye shall have power to do whatsoever thing is expedient in me. And he hath said: Repent all ye ends of the earth, and come unto me, and be baptized in my name, and have faith in me, that ye may be saved (Moroni 7:32–34).[4]

Repentance

Repentance is the process by which humans set aside or overcome sins by changing hearts, attitudes, and actions that are out of harmony with God's teachings, thereby conforming their lives more completely to his will. In the words of one latter-day prophet, repentance is "to change one's mind in regard to past or intended actions or conduct."[5] Paul observes that "all have sinned, and come short of the glory of God" (Romans 3:23). For this reason, the Lord "gave commandment that all men must repent" (2 Nephi 2:21; Moses 6:57). This means that repentance is required of every soul who has not reached perfection.[6]

True repentance, while seldom easy, is essential to personal happiness, emotional and spiritual growth, and eternal salvation. It is the only efficacious way for mortals to free themselves of the permanent effects of sin and the inevitable attendant burden of guilt. To achieve it, several specific changes must occur. One must first recognize that an attitude or action is out of harmony with God's teachings and feel genuine sorrow or remorse for it. Paul calls this "godly sorrow" (2 Corinthians 7:10). Other scriptures describe this

---

[4] Ibid., p. 483.
[5] McKay, p. 14.
[6] Ludlow, *Encyclopedia of Mormonism*, p. 1216.

state of mind as "a broken heart and a contrite spirit" (Psalms 51:17; 2 Nephi 2:7; 3 Nephi 9:20). This recognition must produce an inward change of attitude. The prophet Joel exhorted Israel to "rend your heart, and not your garments" (Joel 2:12–13), thereby bringing the inner transformation necessary to begin the process of repentance.

Some form of confession is also necessary in repentance. In some cases, the transgressor may need to confess to the person or persons wronged or injured and ask forgiveness; in other cases, it may be necessary to confess sins to a Church leader authorized to receive such confessions; in still other cases, a confession to God alone may be sufficient; and sometimes all three forms of confession may be necessary.

In addition, repentance requires restitution to others who have suffered because of the sin. Whenever possible, this should be done by making good any physical or material losses or injury. Even when this is not possible, repentance requires other, equally significant actions, such as apologies, increased acts of kindness and service toward offended persons, intensified commitment to, and activity in, the Lord's work, or all of these in concert.

Finally, for repentance to be complete, one must abandon the sinful behavior. A change of heart begins the process; a visible outward change of direction, reflected in new patterns of behavior, must complete it (Mosiah 5:2). Failure to alter outward actions means that the sinner has not repented, and the weight of the former sin returns (Doctrine and Covenants 82:7; cf. Matthew 18:32–34).[7]

Baptism

Baptism is an essential initiatory ordinance for all persons who are joining the Church, as it admits them to Christ's church on earth (John 3:3–5; Doctrine and Covenants 20:37, 68–74). It is a prima-

---

[7] Ibid., p. 1217.

ry step in the process, which includes faith, repentance, baptism of fire and of the Holy Ghost, and enduring to the end, whereby members may receive remission of their sins and gain access to the Celestial Kingdom and eternal life (e.g., Mark 16:15–16; 2 Nephi 31:13–21; Doctrine and Covenants 22:1–4, 84:64, 74; *MD*, pp. 69–72).

Latter-day Saint baptisms are performed for converts who have been properly instructed, and are at least eight years of age (the age of accountability). Baptism must be performed by one who has proper priesthood authority. The major features of the ordinance include the raising of the right hand, the reciting of the prescribed baptismal prayer by the one performing the baptism, and the complete immersion of the candidate (3 Nephi 11:23–26; Doctrine and Covenants 20:71–74, 68:27). Baptism symbolizes the covenant by which people promise to come into the fold of God, to take upon themselves the name of Christ, to stand as a witness for God, to keep his commandments, and to bear one another's burdens, manifesting a determination to serve him to the end, and to prepare to receive the spirit of Christ for the remission of sins. The Lord, as his part of the covenant, is to pour out his spirit upon them, redeem them from their sins, raise them in the first resurrection, and give them eternal life (Mosiah 18:7–10; Doctrine and Covenants 20:37).

The rich symbolism of the ordinance invites candidates and observers to reflect on its meanings. Burial in the water and arising out of the water symbolize the candidate's faith in the death, burial, and resurrection of Jesus Christ, as well as the future resurrection of all people. It also represents the candidate's new birth to a life in Christ, being born of God, thus born again of the water and of the spirit (Romans 6:3–6, Mosiah 18:13–14; Moses 6:59–60; Doctrine and Covenants 128:12–13).[8]

---

[8] Ibid., p. 93.

Laying on of hands for the gift of the Holy Ghost

The gift of the Holy Ghost is the right or privilege of receiving divine manifestations, spiritual gifts, and direction from the Holy Ghost. This gift is conferred upon members of the Church by the laying on of hands following baptism. It is considered one of the essential ordinances of the gospel of Jesus Christ and an absolute prerequisite of salvation.

The Holy Ghost is the third member of the Godhead, while the gift of the Holy Ghost consists of the privilege to receive inspiration, manifestations, and other spiritual gifts and blessings from that member of the Godhead (*TPJS*, p. 199). Among the most important spiritual blessings associated with the gift of the Holy Ghost is the sanctifying or cleansing power of the Holy Ghost, whereby men and women are born of God. Through this baptism of fire and of the Holy Ghost, individual hearts and desires are cleansed and spirits made pure as the culmination of the process of repentance and baptism (2 Nephi 31:13, 17; 3 Nephi 27:20). Other important manifestations of the Holy Ghost include bearing witness of Jesus Christ and of divine truths, providing spiritual guidance and warning as appropriate, and enabling discernment of right and wrong.

The gift of the Holy Ghost is understood to be the key to all of the "spiritual gifts" found in the Church, including the gifts of prophecy and revelation, of healing, of speaking in tongues, and of the translation and interpretation of tongues. These distinctive gifts of the spirit normally are manifested only among those who have received the gift of the Holy Ghost and who qualify by their needs and their worthiness for such divine assistance, even as the original apostles of Christ received these gifts only after the Holy Ghost came upon them on the Day of Pentecost (Acts 2:1–17).

In LDS practice, the gift of the Holy Ghost is given by the laying-on of hands as indicated in the New Testament (see Acts 8:17–18, 19:2–6; 2 Timothy 1:6; Hebrews 6:2), normally immediately following or within a few days of the baptism by water. A bearer of the Melchizedek Priesthood (usually joined by a few others holding the same priesthood) lays his hands upon the head of the newly baptized member, calls the person by name, confirms him or her a member of the Church, and says, "Receive the Holy Ghost." The exact wording of this ordinance is not prescribed, but it always involves the confirmation of membership, the bestowal of the gift of the Holy Ghost, and a reference to the priesthood authority by which the ordinance is performed. These basic components of the ordinance often are followed by a verbal blessing that offers counsel and direction to the new member. In proxy temple ordinance work for deceased persons, the same basic confirmation follows the ordinance of baptism for the dead.[9]

We believe that a man must be called of God, by prophecy, and by the laying on of hands, by those who are in authority to preach the Gospel and administer in the ordinances thereof.
Today, the authority of the church resides in the living prophet, individually, and by the Quorum of Twelve Apostles collectively. Succession is determined at the time of death of the current prophet by virtue of being the Senior member of the Quorum of the Twelve, whereby the Twelve collectively lay their hands on the head of the new prophet and ordain him prophet, seer, and revelator. The general church membership sustains the prophet by the raise of their right hand during general meetings of the church. The living prophet today is President Gordon B. Hinckley.

We believe in the same organization that existed in the Primitive Church, viz., apostles, prophets, pastors, teachers, evangelists, etc.

The Foundation
Joseph Smith and Oliver Cowdery received priesthood ordination and baptism under the direction of heavenly messengers in 1829.

---

[9] Ibid., p. 543.

They then baptized others. This cluster of believers gathered on April 6, 1830, for the formal organization of the church, with Joseph Smith as First Elder and Oliver as Second Elder. Two months later the Church held its first conference and soon established a tradition of semiannual general conferences. From the beginning, Church officers were sustained by conference vote, and members and officials received certificates of membership or ordination from conferences.

During the first two years of the Church, deacons, teachers, priests, and elders constituted the local ministry. The *Articles and Covenants* served as a handbook explaining the duties of these officers (see Doctrine and Covenants, sec. 20).

A revelation in 1831 instituted the office of bishop, initially one for Missouri and another for Ohio. Temporal affairs were their primary stewardship at first; they received consecrations of property in the 1830s, tithes afterward, and cared for the poor. Soon bishops also received responsibility for disciplinary procedures and for the Aaronic Priesthood. Not until 1839, in Nauvoo, Illinois, did the Church have bishops assigned to local geographical subdivisions called wards, under the jurisdiction of the bishop responsible for the larger region.

The office of high priest was instituted in 1831, with Joseph Smith as the presiding high priest over the Church. In 1832 he chose counselors to assist him, initiating what became the First Presidency. Revelation in March 1833 (Doctrine and Covenants 90) gave the presidency supreme authority over all affairs of the Church; their roles at the head of the hierarchy remain essentially unchanged. Late in 1833 a second general officer, the patriarch to the church, was called and ordained.

In 1834 two stakes—geographic entities—were formed (one in Ohio and the second in Missouri) to direct the operation of branches (congregations) and local officers. Stakes were led by a three-man stake presidency and a twelve-member high council (Doctrine and Covenants 102). High councils arbitrated disputes, investigated and tried charges of misconduct, and generally oversaw local ecclesiastical operations. Outside stake boundaries, members clustered into isolated branches led by elders or priests.

In 1835 the Quorum of the Twelve Apostles and the quorum of the seventy were organized. The Twelve, subordinate to the First Presidency, were assigned by revelation to preside outside organized stakes as a traveling high council. This included ordaining and supervising other officers of the Church outside stakes, including Patriarchs. They were also to direct proselytizing in all lands, assisted by the seventy. The Seventy's presidency of seven, called the first council of the seventy, were sustained with other General Authorities in August 1835.

By 1835 revelations defined two orders of priesthood: the higher, or Melchizedek Priesthood, including the offices of high priest, seventy, and elder; and the lesser, or Aaronic Priesthood, comprising priests, teachers, and deacons. Priesthood quorums in the stakes consisted of up to ninety-six elders, forty-eight priests, twenty-four teachers, and twelve deacons, each with its own presidency except the priests, whose president is a bishop.

In the fall of 1835 the Church published the first edition of the Doctrine and Covenants. The three revelations placed first (now secs. 20, 107, and 84) described priesthood and its organization.

Visitations by Moses, Elias, and Elijah in 1836 restored the keys of the priesthood and responsibility to gather scattered Israel and the sealing powers by which families could be linked for eternity in temples (see Doctrine and Covenants, secs. 109–110). These keys are still the basis for LDS missionary, family history/genealogy, and temple work.

After a mission to Great Britain, in 1839–1841, the Twelve received broadened responsibility, under the First Presidency, for Church government within the stakes as well as outside them, a responsibility they have carried since. In Nauvoo they received temple ordinances and the keys necessary to govern the Church if there were no First Presidency.

To complete Church organization and prepare the women, along with the men, for the temple, in 1842 Joseph Smith organized the women's Relief Society in Nauvoo. A counterpart of priesthood organization for men, the Relief Society was seen as a more integral part of Church organization than were later auxiliary organizations.

The First Presidency, Twelve, Seventy, and Presiding Bishopric—all dating from this first generation—continue to be the main administrative officers of the Church. These General Authority offices are generally life-tenured callings except in cases of calls to a higher position or removal for cause or health problems, though emeritus status has recently been introduced. The Second Quorum of the Seventy is comprised of men called to serve a five-year period.

After Joseph Smith's death in 1844, the Twelve Apostles led the Church under the direction of senior apostle and quorum president Brigham Young. In 1847 he was sustained as President in a new First Presidency. Succession in the presidency continues to adhere to that basic pattern.

Members of The Church of Jesus Christ of Latter-day Saints believe that certain organizational principles, laws, and arrangements are divinely inspired. As evidence of this they point to callings and offices in the contemporary organization of the Church (e.g., prophet, apostle, the seventy, and evangelist or patriarch) that were also present in the early Christian church. Several early revelations, including the original articles of Church organization and government (Doctrine and Covenants 20) and the revelation on priesthood (Doctrine and Covenants 107), are seen by members of the Church as sources of a divinely inspired organizational pattern. All offices and callings are filled by lay leaders, as the Church has no professional clergy. Even full-time missionaries and General Authorities are drawn from the laity.

Principles of Organization

Six basic principles that can be inferred from the revelations have shaped the historical and contemporary organization of the Church.

First is the guiding principle that the Church functions in the context of God's eternal plan. Latter-day Saints believe that God's work and glory is to "bring to pass the immortality and eternal life" of mankind (Moses 1:39). To further this plan, the Church pursues a complex mission that can be described as threefold: (1) proclaiming the gospel of Jesus Christ to every nation, kindred, tongue, and people; (2) perfecting the Saints by preparing them to receive the ordinances of the gospel and, by instruction and discipline, to gain exaltation; and, (3) redeeming the dead by performing vicarious ordinances in the temple for those who have lived on the earth.[10] The structures, programs, and processes of the contemporary organization of the Church are designed to fulfill one or more dimensions of the Church mission.

The second principle establishes the priesthood of God as the organizing authority of the Church. Structurally, the Church follows a strict hierarchical form, and authority is exercised through priesthood keys, which determine who presides over the Church and who directs its affairs at each organizational level. The president of the church is the only person on earth authorized to exercise all priesthood keys. But through his authority different keys are delegated to individuals when they are called and "set apart" to specific positions of priesthood leadership and responsibility.

Third is the principle of presidencies and councils. Presidents, because they hold priesthood keys and are entitled to the powers of presidency, possess the ultimate decision-making authority for their assigned stewardships. Nevertheless, all presidents are instructed to meet in presidencies and councils to hear various points of view. For example, it is the responsibility of counselors to

---

[10] Kimball, p. 5.

presidents to give counsel; in Church disciplinary councils, council members may even be assigned to represent competing points of view. The same patterns are observed in the presidencies of the auxiliary organizations, even though no priesthood keys may be involved.

Fourth is the law of common consent. Church leaders are selected through revelation by those in authority. Before new leaders may serve, they must receive a formal sustaining vote from the members whom they will serve or over whom they will preside. When members of the Church sustain leaders, they commit themselves to support these leaders in fulfilling their various stewardships.

Fifth is the principle of orderly administration. The organization of the Church follows prescribed policies and procedures that in the contemporary Church are defined in the general handbook of instructions, the *Melchizedek Priesthood Handbook*, and other handbooks and manuals for specific programs. An order or pattern is indicated for such procedures as ordinations, ordinances, and blessings; conducting meetings; extending callings and releases to members in various callings in the Church; keeping records and reports; controlling finances; and exercising Church discipline.

Sixth, the contemporary organization of the Church continues to change in response to the demands of rapid international growth. New auxiliary organizations and new levels of geographic representation (e.g., region and area) have been added since the original revelations were received. Nevertheless, the influence of the first five organizing principles can still be seen at every organizational level, in both the ecclesiastical order and the administrative support system of the Church. In this respect, the contemporary organization of the Church is a product of both constancy and change.

Most people experience the organization of the LDS Church principally at the local level, where congregations are organized into wards. Although the local ward organization meets most of the religious needs of the members within its boundaries, many specialized services are provided at a higher level. In addition, ward officers are in continuing contact with a hierarchy of priesthood leaders linking them directly to the central authorities in Salt Lake City. Wards are organized into stakes, stakes into regions, and regions into areas, which constitute the major international divisions of the Church organization. The present article will describe the organization beginning with the most general level and ending with the local wards.

A body of priesthood leaders called the General Authorities heads the organization of the Church. They are full-time ecclesiastical leaders drawn from the laity, and they receive modest living allowances from returns on investments made by the Church, not from the tithes and offerings paid by members of the Church. The General Authorities consist of the First Presidency of the Church, the Quorum of the Twelve Apostles or Council of the Twelve, the quorums of the seventy, and the Presiding Bishopric.

These General Authorities preside over the entire ecclesiastical organization of the Church, from the central headquarters in Salt Lake City, and its area offices in major cities in different parts of the world. They also manage the departments of the central office, which are composed largely of full-time employees who serve the administrative needs of the Church from offices in Salt Lake City and other locations as needed. This administrative support system functions in cooperation with the normal ecclesiastical channels, maintaining clear and direct lines of authority and responsibility between local and general officers of the Church.[11]

We believe in the gift of tongues, prophecy, revelation, visions, healing, interpretation of tongues, etc.
All such heavenly endowments come as gifts of the Spirit—that is, through the grace of God and the operation and power of the Holy Ghost. As prerequisites to obtaining such gifts, a person must

---

[11] Ludlow, *Encyclopedia of Mormonism*, p. 1035.

receive the ordinances of baptism and the bestowal of the gift of the Holy Ghost from an authorized priesthood holder, must earnestly seek to obtain the gift or gifts, and must make sincere efforts to keep the Lord's commandments.

Clearly the Spirit can grant any gift that would fill a particular need; hence, no exhaustive list is possible, but many gifts have been promised the Church. Through the New Testament, readers are familiar with the six specified above: the two related to the gifts of tongues and their interpretation, or the power to speak in a language not previously learned and the ability to interpret such speech; the gift of prophecy, exhibited sometimes in the predictive sense but more often in the sense that "the testimony of Jesus is the spirit of prophecy" (Revelation 19:10); revelation, or the heaven-inspired receipt of knowledge, wisdom, or direction; visions, or visual spiritual manifestations such as prophets have received in all ages and as Joel predicted for many others in the latter days (Joel 2:28–29); healing, or the power to "lay hands on the sick" that they may recover (Mark 16:18).[12]

We believe the Bible to be the word of God as far as it is translated correctly; we also believe the Book of Mormon to be the word of God.

The Church of Jesus Christ of Latter-day Saints reveres the Bible as the word of God given through ancient prophets and apostles, though it recognizes that the current text is not identical with the original. The Church has consistently used the King James Version (KJV) for formal classes, missionary work, and personal study among English-speaking peoples, utilizing KJV editions issued by the major Bible publishing houses. However, because latter-day revelation offers insight, interpretation, and supplemental material to thousands of biblical passages and in order to make the message of the Bible more readily accessible to LDS readers, the Church

---

[12] Ibid., p. 544.

published in 1979 an edition of the KJV with multiple study helps. These include chapter headings, cross-references to other LDS scriptural works, explanatory footnotes, clarification of Greek and Hebrew terms and idioms, a subject-matter guide, a dictionary, maps, and excerpts from an inspired translation of the Bible by the Prophet Joseph Smith.

The origins of the Book of Mormon are mentioned above.

We believe all that God has revealed, all that He does now reveal, and we believe that He will yet reveal many great and important things pertaining to the Kingdom of God.

Receiving personal revelation is a vital and distinctive part of the LDS religious experience. Response to personal revelation is seen as the basis for true faith in Christ, and the strength of the Church consists of that faithful response by members to their own personal revelations. The purpose of both revelation and the response of faith is to assist the children of men to come to Christ and learn to love one another with that same pure love with which Christ loves them.[13]

We believe in the literal gathering of Israel and in the restoration of the Ten Tribes; that Zion will be built upon this (the American) continent; that Christ will reign personally upon the earth; and, that the earth will be renewed and receive its paradisiacal glory.

For Latter-day Saints, the gathering of Israel involves bringing together the heirs of the covenant to designated places where they can enjoy the blessings of temples. Latter-day Saints believe in "the literal gathering of Israel" and hold that, along with a vital future role for the Old World Jerusalem, "Zion" (the New Jerusalem) will be built upon the American continent." Church members still look

---

[13] Ibid., p. 1225.

for an eventual temple and permanent headquarters to be built in Zion, a New Jerusalem in Missouri.

Early Latter-day Saints first encountered the concept of a New Jerusalem separate from the Old World Jerusalem in Book of Mormon prophecies that the land of America was to be "the place of the New Jerusalem" (3 Nephi 20:22; Ether 13:3). More information came in September 1830, soon after the Church was organized, when a revelation mentioned building a New Jerusalem near the Missouri River at a location soon to be revealed (Doctrine and Covenants 28:9). Another revelation that same month enjoined the Saints to "bring to pass the gathering of [the Lord's] elect," suggesting both the work of missionaries and the physical gathering of the faithful to a designated location. It also stressed that the Saints should be "gathered in unto one place" (Doctrine and Covenants 29:7–8).

In Nauvoo, Joseph Smith taught that "in any age of the world" the object of gathering the people of God was the same—"to build unto the Lord an house whereby he could reveal unto his people the ordinances" of his temple. The gathering was necessary to build a temple, and a temple was a prerequisite for the establishment of Zion. Consequently, at each of the Saints' headquarters gathering places, a temple site was designated, and in Kirtland, Nauvoo, and Salt Lake City, temples were constructed. Gathering also provided a refuge, a place for mutual protection and spiritual reinforcement and instruction. It strengthened LDS communities and brought economic and political benefits as well.

Although the major current purposes for gathering the faithful into a single place have been accomplished, belief in the necessity of gathering the elect continues. Members in all parts of the world are now encouraged to remain in their own communities and "build Zion" in their own wards and stakes. Temples have now been built in many countries, and missionaries further the establishment of

Zion by gathering "the pure in heart" (Doctrine and Covenants 97:21) to the stakes of Zion throughout the world.[14]

We claim the privilege of worshiping Almighty God according to the dictates of our own conscience, and allow all men the same privilege, let them worship how, where, or what they may.
The gospel of Jesus Christ does not represent freedom merely as a philosophic concept or abstract possibility, but establishes it at the foundations of the creation of the world and as the fundamental condition of God's dealings with his children. As a general expression the word "freedom" refers to agency, liberty, independence, and autonomy. Freedom, or the genuine possibility of choosing, necessarily defines the most basic condition of human beings in the temporal world.

Latter-day Saint scriptures teach that the premortal life was an environment of choice in which God proposed to his spirit children a Plan of Salvation for their growth and advancement (see Job 38:6–7; 2 Nephi 2:17; Doctrine and Covenants 29:36; Abraham 3:22–28). In earth life, with bodies of flesh and bone and vast new possibilities of action, God's children would be free to make choices within the whole spectrum of good and evil. They would also experience the necessary consequences of those choices. "And we will take of these materials, and we will make an earth whereon these may dwell; And we will prove them herewith, to see if they will do all things whatsoever the Lord their God shall command them" (Abraham 3:24–25).

God promised those who would do his will that they would be redeemed from their errors and sins and gain eternal life. Satan opposed the Father's plan, aware that this more extensive freedom involved the risk of spiritual death, where some would be separated from the Father by their sins, would not repent, and thus could not return to dwell in his kingdom. To avert such a separation, Satan

---

[14] Ibid., p. 537.

proposed an environment without freedom and hence without sin. Consequently, all would return to the Father, but without moral improvement or advancement. The "honor" for their return would belong to Satan (Isaiah 14:13; Moses 4:1).[15]

We believe in being subject to kings, presidents, rulers, and magistrates, in obeying, honoring, and sustaining the law.

Three types of laws exist: spiritual or divine laws, laws of nature, and civil laws. Latter-day Saints are deeply and consistently law-oriented, because laws, whether spiritual, physical, or civil, are rules defining existence and guiding action. Through the observance of laws, blessings and rewards are expected, and by the violation of laws, suffering, deprivation, and even punishment will result.

Basic LDS attitudes toward law and jurisprudence are shaped primarily by revelations contained in the Doctrine and Covenants, and by explanations given by the Presidents of the Church. God is, by definition, a God of order: "Behold, mine house is a house of order, saith the Lord God, and not a house of confusion" (Doctrine and Covenants 132:8). God and law are inseparable, for if there is no law, there is no sin; and if there is no sin, there is no righteousness, "and if these things are not there is no God" (2 Nephi 2:13). Law emanates from God through Christ. Jesus said, "I am the law, and the light" (3 Nephi 15:9), and God's word is his law (Doctrine and Covenants 132:12).

In an 1832 revelation, Joseph Smith learned that law is a pervasive manifestation of God's light and power: "The light which is in all things . . . is the law by which all things are governed" (Doctrine and Covenants 88:12–13). In connection with both spiritual law and natural law, no space or relationship occurs in which law is nonexistent. "There are many kingdoms; for there is no space in which there is no kingdom; . . . and unto every kingdom is given a

---

[15] Ibid., p. 525.

law; and unto every law there are certain bounds also and condi-tions" (Doctrine and Covenants 88:37–38).

Existence is a process of progressively learning to obey higher law. Obeying and conforming to law are understood as a sign of growth, maturity, and understanding, and greater obedience to law produces greater freedom (Doctrine and Covenants 98:5) and asso-ciated blessings (Doctrine and Covenants 130:20–21).

At all levels, the principles of agency and accountability are in effect: People may choose which laws to obey or to ignore, but God will hold them accountable and reward them accordingly (Doctrine and Covenants 82:4). This is not viewed as a threat; law's purpose is not to force or punish but to guide and provide structure.

In the divine or spiritual sphere, law is not the product of a philo-sophical or theoretical search for what is right or good. It emanates from deity and is revealed through Jesus Christ and his prophets.

Spiritual laws given by God to mankind are commonly called commandments, which consist variously of prohibitions ("thou shalt not"), requirements ("thou shalt"), and prescriptions ("if a man"). The commandments are uniformly coupled with promised blessings for faithful compliance. Thus, Latter-day Saints describe themselves as covenant people who may be rewarded now, and in the hereafter, for their faithfulness. Many such covenants are bilat-eral in character; that is, members make personal commitments in a variety of formal ordinances to keep in accord with certain com-mandments.

Spiritual laws, or God's commandments, are generally under-stood to have been purposefully decreed by a loving Heavenly Father, who desires to bring to pass the exaltation of his spirit chil-dren. Thus, "there is a law, irrevocably decreed in heaven before the foundations of this world, upon which all blessings are predicated" (Doctrine and Covenants 130:20). Latter-day Saints believe that God knows or stipulates all types of acts and forbearances required by all individuals in order for them to attain that blessed eternal state of exaltation and that he has revealed these requirements to humankind through his servants. No law given of God is temporal (Doctrine and Covenants 29:34).

In accordance with the principle of agency, God commands, but he does not compel. No earthly mechanism exists for the enforcement of God's laws. The prophet teaches the members correct principles, and they are expected to govern themselves. Missionary work and education of Church members are carried out so that people may make informed choices. They are taught that making an informed choice results either in a blessing (current or deferred) or an undesirable consequence (current or deferred). Ignorance of the law is considered a legitimate excuse. Because of the Atonement of Jesus Christ, repentance is not required of those "who have ignorantly sinned" or "who have died not knowing the will of God concerning them" (Mosiah 3:11), even though failure to abide by the commandment may result in the loss of blessings that would flow from proper conduct. In most cases, violators of divine law can escape the punishment connected with the offense by repentance, the demands of justice having been satisfied by the Atonement of Christ in the interest of all.[16]

The scriptures teach that God instituted governments to bless humankind on the earth. Good government must do more than preserve order; it must protect freedom, ensure justice, and secure the general welfare. "And the law of the land which is constitutional, supporting that principle of freedom in maintaining rights and privileges, belongs to all mankind, and is justifiable before me" (Doctrine and Covenants 98:5). God proclaims, "I, the Lord God, make you free, therefore ye are free indeed; and the law also maketh you free" (Doctrine and Covenants 98:8). The law protects individuals and their liberties from the arbitrary and deleterious acts of others. The genuine rule of law requires that all be equally subject to rules that are prospective, widely known, and publicly

---

[16] Ibid., p. 808.

arrived at through mechanisms of government that have been and continue to be consensually agreed upon. The law secures peace by proscribing choices injurious to others, ensures justice by holding all accountable to the law in accordance with fair procedures, and secures the general welfare through the passage of laws that regulate and coordinate social intercourse to the benefit of all. In exchange for these advantages, citizens must fulfill their obligations to sustain and support the government. In the end, the environment of freedom is enhanced and expanded through good government.

Nevertheless, governments are often oppressive and act to restrict freedom and establish privileges for the few by arbitrarily setting up public rules and applying them unevenly without proper safeguards. The abuse of political power is most offensive and bondage nearly complete when freedom of conscience and its expression in free speech are restricted and the right to worship God openly according to one's own beliefs is abridged. In the end, Latter-day Saints believe that the claims of government should be limited to its own proper domain and not allowed to encroach upon the province of freedom to act according to moral conscience. To avoid such political evil, Latter-day Saints are encouraged not only to support constitutional government and the processes it establishes but also to work for laws that bring about freedom and encourage virtue. In this larger sense, the scriptures summon those who follow Jesus to go the extra mile, to give more than they receive, to do good without thought of what they might gain in return. Thus, as citizens, Latter-day Saints are obligated to go beyond the pursuit of self-interest; they are committed to serve others, to bring about the common good, and to secure the general welfare of the people.[17]

---

[17] Ibid., p. 526.

We believe in being honest, true, chaste, benevolent, virtuous, and in doing good to all men; indeed, we may say that we follow the admonition of Paul—we believe all things, we hope all things, we have endured many things, and hope to be able to endure all things. If there is anything virtuous, lovely, or of good report or praiseworthy, we seek after these things.

In this article of their faith, the Latter-day Saints declare their acceptance of a practical religion; a religion that shall consist, not alone of professions in spiritual matters, and belief as to the conditions of the hereafter, of the doctrine of original sin and the actuality of a future heaven and hell, but also, and more particularly, of present and every-day duties, in which proper respect for self, love for fellow men, and devotion to God are the guiding principles. Religion without morality, professions of godliness without charity, church-membership without adequate responsibility as to individual conduct in daily life, are but as sounding brass and tinkling cymbals—noise without music, the words without the spirit of prayer. "Pure religion and undefiled before God and the Father is this, To visit the fatherless and widows in their affliction, and to keep himself unspotted from the world." Honesty of purpose, integrity of soul, individual purity, freedom of conscience, willingness to do good to all men even enemies, pure benevolence—these are some of the fruits by which the religion of Christ may be known, far exceeding in importance and value the promulgation of dogmas and the enunciation of theories. Yet a knowledge of things more than temporal, doctrines of spiritual matters, founded on revelation and not resting on the sands of man's frail hypotheses, are likewise characteristic of the true Church.[18]

Sacrament meeting

Sacrament meeting is the principal LDS worship service held on the Sabbath and is based on the commandment "Thou shalt go to

---

[18] James E. Talmage, *Articles of Faith* (Salt Lake City: Deseret Book Co., 1981), p. 389.

the house of prayer and offer up thy sacraments upon my holy day" (Doctrine and Covenants 59:9). The entire ward membership, from infants to the elderly, attend the weekly Sacrament meeting as families, and partake of the Sacrament of the Lord's Supper together.

A Sacrament meeting was held on the day the Church was organized, April 6, 1830. It is recorded, "The Holy Ghost was poured out upon us to a very great degree—some prophesied, whilst we all praised the Lord, and rejoiced exceedingly" (History of the Church 1:78). In Church annals this primal worship service is called a "time of rejoicing," a time of "great solemnity," and "truly a refreshing season to spirit and body" (History of the Church 2:430, 433, 480). At the time of entering the new land of Zion (in Missouri), a revelation was given concerning the Sabbath with the admonition that all should come to this meeting in the spirit of thanksgiving and should offer up "a sacrifice of a broken heart and a contrite spirit" (Doctrine and Covenants 59:8). Hence, it is often referred to as a time for the renewing of covenants.

The Sacrament meeting is led by the bishop of the ward or one of his counselors. To enhance the spirit of worship and fellowship, there are other participants: the organist, music director, and members of the ward preassigned to give talks and the invocation and benediction. From the earliest days of the Church, music has been essential in the worship of Latter-day Saints. In the Sacrament meeting, music is manifest in the singing of hymns such as "He Died! The Great Redeemer Died," "While of These Emblems We Partake," "In Memory of the Crucified," and "Reverently and Meekly Now." Each ward is encouraged to maintain a choir to periodically perform hymns and anthems. The orientation of all music is toward the classical tradition.

The two Sacrament prayers—one on the bread, one on the water—are offered by priests, usually young men between the ages of sixteen and nineteen. They kneel in the presence of the congregation and ask that all present, by their partaking of the broken bread and the water, witness unto the Father their willingness "to take upon them the name of thy Son," Jesus Christ, to always remember him, to keep his commandments, and to seek his Spirit. These patterns are derived in part from the dramatic introduction of the Sacrament in the Book of Mormon, where the Master teaches a multitude of men, women, and children, "And if ye shall always do these things blessed are ye, for ye are built upon my rock" (3 Nephi 18:12). And he promises, "And if ye do always remember me ye shall have my Spirit to be with you" (3 Nephi 18:7, 11).

During the passing of the bread and water to the congregation, silence prevails. The communion aspired to is embodied in statements of modern leaders: Hyrum Smith spoke of the sacramental process as bestowing spiritual sustenance enough to "last a whole week." The ordinance was given, as President Brigham Young taught, "in order that the people may be sanctified" (*JD* 19:91–92). "I am a witness," said Elder Melvin J. Ballard, "that there is a spirit attending the administration of the Sacrament that warms the soul from head to foot; you feel the wounds of the spirit being healed."[19]

The typical Sacrament meeting is sixty to seventy minutes long and has the following components, with mild variations from week to week:

Organ prelude
Greeting by a member of the bishopric
Opening hymn sung by the congregation
Announcements and ward business
Invocation by a ward member
Sacramental hymn sung by the congregation
Administration and partaking of the sacrament
Musical selection
Speakers

---

[19] Hinckley, p. 133.

Closing hymn sung by the congregation
Benediction by ward member
Organ postlude

The spoken messages in Sacrament meetings are given by different members of the congregation each Sunday, or by visiting officers from the stake organization. All speak with the same purpose: to witness of Jesus Christ, to review gospel principles, to inspire, to uplift, to encourage, and to motivate the congregation to renewed efforts to live a Christ-like life. Speakers frequently quote from the scriptures, and members, young and old, are encouraged to bring their own book of scriptures and to follow the cited references. The time is usually shared by several speakers. Sometimes entire families are assigned to develop a gospel topic, and each member contributes to the chosen theme. Youth speakers are likewise regularly invited to give Sacrament meeting talks. Sometimes the bishop assigns topics, and sometimes he leaves the choice to the individual or family.

Sacrament meeting is periodically combined with the observance of special events such as Christmas, Easter, Mother's Day, and Father's Day. On such occasions, the meeting follows the usual pattern through the Sacrament and then proceeds around the commemoration program.

On one Sunday a month, usually the first, Sacrament meeting is a fast and testimony meeting. After the Sacrament, the final portion of the meeting is devoted to extemporaneous testimony bearing by members of the congregation.[20]

Relationship to other major religions: Christian
The Church has never existed in isolation or insulation from other Christian faiths. Its roots and its nurture are in, and remain in, the

---

[20] Ludlow, *Encyclopedia of Mormonism,* p. 1246.

Christian heritage. But its claim that the heavens have opened anew, that a restoration of the lost radiance and power of the full gospel of Jesus Christ is under way at divine initiative, and its rejection of many long-standing traditions have generated misunderstanding and ill will. In the first generation in the United States, the solidarity of the Latter-day Saints was thought to be inimical to pluralism and at the same time aroused the ire of sectarians. Missionary efforts through personal contact more than through mass media and image making sometimes compounded the problem. In certain times and circumstances, there has been no will, or at least no lasting resolve by either side, for outreach and cooperation.

In three ways these tensions are being reduced:

1. Institutionally. Church officers now participate with leaders of other faiths in Christian interchange. LDS leaders in many countries are welcomed to interfaith devotionals with their Protestant, Catholic, and Orthodox counterparts. This has been in keeping with the precept and example of early Church authorities. For mutual support, they likewise meet and organize, across varied lines and programs, for example, the chaplaincies of many nations of the free world, the Boy Scout movement, the National Council of Christians and Jews, and local and international service clubs concerned with social, ethical, and moral issues.

2. Educationally. The Church fosters the largest adult education curriculum in the world. Many of the courses are Bible-related, and some focus on Christian history and institutions. For high school and college-age students, who now exceed half a million, the Church provides similar courses in its seminaries and institutes adjacent to high schools and major universities. Teachers in the Church Educational System are given financial supplements to visit the Holy Land, to study the origins of the three great monotheistic religions, to become familiar with the vocabularies and worldviews of alternative Christian institutions, and to understand and recognize common ground in the lives of the youth they teach. LDS

scholars of many disciplines are increasingly involved in the religious studies programs of academic and professional organizations.

The Church has opened its extensive broadcasting facilities to representative programming across the spectrum of Christian groups. It has also been a major participant in religious broadcasts in the VISN Religious Interfaith Cable Television Network, which represents most major denominations in the United States.

To establish two-way interchange, the Richard L. Evans Chair of Christian Understanding was established at Brigham Young University. Funded and advised by a variety of Christian groups (the initial commitment came from a Presbyterian), this endowment fosters religious studies symposia, lectures, forums, exchange programs, and visiting professorships. It also sponsors interfaith meetings where common as well as controversial theological issues are presented by representatives of each tradition, and where workshops help resolve tensions in an atmosphere of goodwill.

The Religious Studies Center at Brigham Young University produces distinguished volumes utilizing scholars of many faiths who represent interdisciplinary and comparative expertise. Although a literature of disparagement continues both from the left and from the right, Church leaders continually remind the membership that whatever may be said of those who make a religion of anti-Mormonism, a retaliatory response is neither wise nor Christian.

3. Practically in Christian Humanitarianism. At its best the pattern of LDS life, institutionally and individually, has not been to demand rights but to merit them, not to clamor for fellowship and goodwill but to manifest them and to give energy and time beyond rhetoric. In a major address to regional Church leaders, former President Spencer W. Kimball set the tone:

We urge members to do their civic duty and to assume their responsibilities as individual citizens in seeking solutions to the problems which beset our cities and communities.

With our wide ranging mission, so far as mankind is concerned, Church members cannot ignore the many practical problems that require solution if our families are to live in an environment conducive to spirituality.

Where solutions to these practical problems require cooperative action with those not of our faith, members should not be reticent in doing their part in joining and leading in those efforts where they can make an individual contribution to those causes which are consistent with the standards of the Church.[21]

Examples of recent Church-encouraged projects that reach across different affiliations include cooperative emergency assistance, support for homeless shelters in many cities, and linkage with the work of the Salvation Army. At BYU, students of other faiths are often elected to student offices, and various service clubs strive against intolerance and clannishness. In the same spirit, the Church was among the first to give aid, with other Christian bodies, to disaster areas in such places as China, El Salvador, Nicaragua, Los Angeles, Peru, Armenia, Japan, Iran, Chile, and Greece. Through two special fasts, the Church raised $11 million for the hungry in Africa and Ethiopia, and utilized Catholic services as a delivery system.

Because so much in contemporary society is dissonant, centrifugal, and divisive, interfaith understanding and mutuality seem indispensable. LDS history suggests that what appear to be intractable political, social, and economic clashes are often, at root, religious. To overcome needless divisions and to heal the wounds of modern life, including the religious life, are not just the commission of Latter-day Saints but of all who take seriously the message and ministry of Jesus Christ. Unless in some there is Christ-like concern for all, there is little hope for any.

---

[21] Kimball, *Ensign* 8 (May 1978):100.

Bibliography

Arrington, Leonard. "Historical Development of International Mormonism." University of Alberta, *Religious Studies and Theology* 7, no. 1 (January 1987).

Keller, Roger R. *Reformed Christians and Mormon Christians: Let's Talk.* Ann Arbor, Mich., 1986.

Madsen, Truman G. "Are Christians Mormon?" *BYU Studies* 15 (autumn 1974): 73–94.

Relationship to other major religions: Jewish

The chief nexus for interfaith relationships between Jews and Latter-day Saints has been Salt Lake City, Utah. A certain amount of contact has also occurred in the State of Israel as well as in cities in the United States with large Jewish populations, such as Los Angeles and New York. Generally, relations between members of the two groups have been characterized by mutual respect and goodwill. Exceptions include sharp differences between Mormons and some Jews on the issue of the purpose of the Brigham Young University Center for Near Eastern Studies in Jerusalem (dedicated 1989). However, a workable relationship prevails.

One of the earliest direct contacts between communities was initiated by Orson Hyde, an LDS apostle, who in 1841 traveled through Europe to reach the Holy Land. With rare exceptions, instead of seeking audience with European Jewish leaders to proselytize them, he warned them of difficulties that they would experience, and urged them to emigrate to Palestine. Orson Hyde continued on to the Holy Land, where, on October 24, 1841, he prayed on the Mount of Olives to "dedicate and consecrate this land . . . for the gathering together of Judah's scattered remnants" (History of the Church 4:456–59).

Broader contacts began after 1853 with the arrival of the first Jewish family in Utah. While Jews tended to align themselves politically with non-Mormons, they enjoyed the goodwill of their LDS neighbors. Although some Jewish immigrants into Utah—particularly from eastern Europe and Russia—were ridiculed because of their language and their lack of acquaintance with frontier life, they found no cruelty, no restrictions of movement, and no ugly intolerance. While there were no handouts, charity, or dole, they discovered no restrictions on opportunity among the Latter-day Saints.

In 1900, when Utah Jewish leader Nathan Rosenblatt and his associates decided to build a synagogue for a second congregation, the principal help came from the LDS Church's First Presidency. When the building opened in 1903, Rosenblatt proclaimed his gratitude for the blessing and privilege of living in Utah with the tolerant, understanding men and women of the Mormon faith. He and his associates had always found them to be a people devoted to their own faith, yet a people who respected the Jewish Torah and knew what the noted teacher Hillel meant when he taught, "Do not do to your neighbor what you would not want done to yourself."

Brigham Young University in Provo, Utah, regularly offers courses that focus on the religion and history of Jews and Judaism. In addition, Jewish scholars have lectured and taught courses at the university, particularly in recent years. In 1921 President Heber J. Grant offered clear counsel to Latter-day Saints against anti-Semitism: "There should be no ill-will . . . in the heart of any true Latter-day Saint, toward the Jewish people."[22]

An indicator of the reciprocal respect that has existed between Utah Jews and Mormons is the number of Jewish public officials elected to serve the state. These include the state's fourth governor (Simon Bamberger, 1917–1921), a district judge (Herbert M. Schiller, 1933–1939), a mayor of Salt Lake City (Louis Marcus, 1931–1935), and several legislators.

Bibliography

Brooks, Juanita. *History of the Jews in Utah and Idaho*. Salt Lake City, 1973.

---

[22] *Gospel Standards* (Salt Lake City, 1941), p. 147.

Zucker, Louis C. *Mormon and Jew: A Meeting on the American Frontier.* Provo, Utah, 1961.

Zucker, Louis C. "Utah." *Encyclopaedia Judaica* (Jerusalem: Keter, 1972), vol. 16, cols. 33–34.

Zucker, Louis C. "A Jew in Zion." *Sunstone* 6 (September–October 1981): 35–44.

A documentary released in December, 2002, in the United States, pays homage to the anti-Nazi activities of three young Latter-day Saints who resisted the regime. Karl-Heinz Schnibbe states of his experience: "Nazi Germany was a time when good people were forced to make difficult decisions based on what information they had. For many of us, it was a time when patriotism and faith were at odds." Karl-Heinz lost his closest boyhood friend attempting to assist his Jewish friends. An article entitled "Documentary Reveals 'Truth and Conviction' " may be found in the Church News at www.ldschurchnews.com.

Other faiths

In August 1852, while the Church was still struggling to establish itself in the western United States, President Brigham Young issued a bold call for missionaries to go to China, India, Siam (Thailand), and Ceylon (Sri Lanka). The seventeen missionaries who were sent formed some of the earliest contacts that LDS members had with non-Christians. Because of civil wars, rejection, and language and cultural difficulties, the work in most countries lasted only months; however, work in India continued until 1856. Although some attempts were made in the early twentieth century, the Church did not undertake further significant efforts to establish itself in non-Christian nations, including Asia, until after World War II.

Stimulated by experiences of LDS servicemen in Asia during and after the war, the Church established missions in East Asia at the end of the 1940s. Since then, wards and stakes led by local members have been established in Japan, South Korea, Hong Kong,

Taiwan, and the Philippines; temples have been built in all these places, including Hong Kong.

In the 1970s and 1980s, the Church expanded into such Southeast Asian nations as Singapore, Thailand, Indonesia, and Malaysia, and in the South Asian nations of India and Sri Lanka. Although small beginnings have been made in some Muslim countries, Church growth in such countries has been limited.

LDS health services programs in the Philippines and refugee assistance in Thailand have been favorably received. High-level contacts with government officials in many countries have elicited a positive response to the values of the Church and its members. Overall, the Church has made consistent efforts to remain sensitive to and abide by local laws and customs, including regulations based on religious sentiment.

Church growth in Africa has principally taken place in the last quarter of the twentieth century, particularly following the 1978 revelation allowing all worthy males to hold the priesthood (see Doctrine and Covenants: Official Declaration 2). Congregations have been established in several countries, and Church membership is growing rapidly. In recent years, the Church has joined various charitable organizations in sending famine relief to stricken nations on the African continent.

In an educational vein, Missionary Training Centers teach many foreign languages and courses on the religions and cultures of non-Western countries, and for educational purposes "culturegrams" have been developed that are now used by U.S. government agencies. In addition, courses on world religions are regularly taught in institutions of higher learning. Moreover, symposia on Islam and on the religions of Africa have been hosted at Brigham Young University, with a number of distinguished religious leaders and scholars participating.

In many countries, the Church of Jesus Christ of Latter-day Saints is viewed as an American church. However, Church leaders have strongly emphasized that it is universal, a church for all people everywhere. A powerful presentation by President Spencer W. Kimball in 1974 stressed the responsibility of the Church to share the gospel with all of God's children.[23] Consequently, in the last half of the twentieth century the Church has made its most significant efforts to establish itself throughout the world.

Generally the LDS outreach to non-Christians has had a positive, invigorating effect on members of the Church, has strengthened Church membership significantly, and has brought about increased awareness of cultural differences as well as a willingness to work within those differences.[24]

Bibliography
Palmer, Spencer J. *The Expanding Church*. Salt Lake City, 1978.
Palmer, Spencer J., ed. *Mormons and Muslims*. Provo, Utah, 1983.

Family history
LDS interest in family history is based on the fundamental doctrines of salvation, agency, and exaltation. It is the plan of God that all persons shall have the opportunity to hear the gospel of Jesus Christ and receive the saving ordinances, regardless of when they lived on earth. If they do not hear the gospel preached through the Lord's authorized servants in this life, they will hear it in the spirit world after death. Latter-day Saints identify their ancestors and arrange for baptism and other ordinances to be performed by proxy—that is, with a living person standing in for the deceased person—in a temple. This is not an optional function of LDS belief; it is, rather, a commandment of God. As Elder Oaks explained, "We are not hobbyists in genealogy work. We do family history work in order to provide the ordinances of salvation for the living and the dead" (1989, p. 6).

---

[23] *Ensign* 4 (October 1974): 2–14.
[24] Ludlow, *Encyclopedia of Mormonism,* p. 696.

Members of the Church were instructed in the sacred role of family history work in 1894, when President Wilford Woodruff declared, "We want the Latter-day Saints from this time to trace their genealogies as far as they can, and to be sealed to their fathers and mothers. Have children sealed to their parents, and run this chain through as far as you can get it. . . . This is the will of the Lord to this people." The purpose of family history, President Woodruff explained, is to obtain names and statistical data so that temple ordinances can be performed in behalf of deceased ancestors who did not have the opportunity to hear the restored gospel during mortal life. He taught on another occasion that "we have got to enter into those temples and redeem our dead—not only the dead of our own family, but the dead of the whole spirit world" (*JD* 21:192).

Fundamental to the doctrine of the salvation of the dead is the exercise of agency. When persons die, their spirits continue living in the post-mortal spirit world and are capable of making choices. Latter-day Saints perform baptisms for the dead so that those who live as spirits may choose whether or not to accept baptism in the true Church of Jesus Christ in the spirit world. If they do not accept the baptism, it is of no effect. The same is true of the other saving ordinances that members perform in the temples in behalf of the dead.

Love is the central motivation for family history work. Identifying ancestors and performing saving ordinances for them are an expression of love. It is the spirit and power of Elijah, who gave the keys of this power to Joseph Smith in the Kirtland Temple in 1836, to "turn the hearts of the fathers to the children, and the children to the fathers" (Doctrine and Covenants 110:15; see also Malachi 4:5–6, Joseph Smith—History 1:39, Doctrine and Covenants 2:2). The desire to discover one's ancestors and complete temple ordinances for them is sometimes referred to as the Spirit of Elijah. President Joseph Fielding Smith associated family history and temple work with love for mankind, declaring that laboring on behalf of the dead is "a work that enlarges the soul of man, broadens his views regarding the welfare of his fellowman, and plants in his heart a love for all the children of our Heavenly Father. There is no work equal to that in the temple for the dead in teaching a man to love his neighbor as himself."

In response to President Woodruff's teaching regarding family history responsibilities, Latter-day Saints organized the genealogical society of Utah in Salt Lake City in 1894. Over the years, the society, through the Family History Library and its worldwide network of more than 1,500 family history centers, has become a major support of the Church's efforts to provide instruction in family history through research information (first in book form and later in microfilm and then in compact disc) and through making available a skilled staff to assist researchers to identify their ancestors.

Interest in family history is not limited to Latter-day Saints. There has been remarkable growth of interest in genealogy and family history dating from about 1836, when Elijah committed the keys to the Prophet Joseph Smith. In many countries, thousands of people have joined genealogical and historical societies, and more than half of the patrons of the Family History Library and its associated Family History Centers are members of other faiths. The Church has joined in cooperative efforts with hundreds of genealogical and family history societies, archives, and libraries in identifying family history records and preserving the information found in them.

Modern technology has played a significant role in the advance of family history in the second half of the twentieth century. The Church has developed an extensive worldwide microfilming program. Since 1938, it has done microfilming in more than a hundred countries, and has accumulated more than 1.3 billion exposures with approximately 8 billion names. Microfilm records have provided the basis for dramatic expansion of family history research.

They have enabled rapid growth of the collections of the Family History Library and has made possible both the distribution of family history information to the Church's Family History Centers and the name extraction programs that have allowed the extensive automation of family history information contained in the Family Search computer system.

As a result, doing family history research has never been easier than it now is. Through Family Search, patrons of the Family History Library and Family History Centers have access to the 147 million names in the International Genealogical Index and the growing 9.67-million-name lineage-linked Ancestral File™. As name extraction programs convert information from paper records (such as the 1880 U.S. Federal Census and the 1881 British Census), and as people from around the world contribute information to the Ancestral File, the computer resources associated with Family Search will make identifying one's ancestors a much simpler task.[25]

Celibacy

Celibacy, the deliberate renunciation of marriage, is foreign to LDS life. Like other forms of ascetic withdrawal, it may deprive the participant of crucial life experiences. Spiritual maturity and exaltation in the highest degree of the Celestial Kingdom require marriage (Doctrine and Covenants 131:2–3).

The norm of Latter-day Saint teaching and practice is for individuals to marry, procreate, and foster righteous living in their families as indicated in the scriptures: "Be fruitful, and multiply, and replenish the earth" (Genesis 1:28). "Marriage is honorable in all" (Hebrews 13:4). "Whoso forbiddeth to marry is not ordained of God, for marriage is ordained of God unto man" (Doctrine and Covenants 49:15). Those who are unable to marry in a temple in

---

[25] Ludlow, *Encyclopedia of Mormonism*, p. 493.

mortality through no fault of their own will receive compensatory blessings later (Doctrine and Covenants 137:5–8).

The practice of celibacy was not widespread among the Christian clergy until centuries after the death of the apostles. "Forbidding to marry" was, for Paul, a sign of apostasy (1 Timothy 4:3). Because ancient and modern revelation endorses marriage, and because most religious leaders in the Old and New Testaments were married, Latter-day Saints reject attempts to interpret the Bible as advocating celibacy.[26]

The Old Testament

The Old Testament is one of the standard works, or scriptures, accepted by the Church of Jesus Christ of Latter-day Saints, which values it for its prophetic, historical, doctrinal, and moral teachings. The Old Testament recounts an epochal series of ancient dispensations during which people received periodic guidance through divine covenants and commandments, many of which remain basic and timeless. In relation to the Old Testament, it is significant for Latter-day Saints that in September 1823 the angel Moroni quoted a series of Old Testament prophecies when he revealed the location of an ancient record written on gold plates to the Prophet Joseph Smith, whose translation yielded the Book of Mormon (Joseph Smith—History 1:36–41). Moreover, Joseph Smith's extensive labors on the Old Testament and the accompanying revelations to him (June 1830–July 1833), which led to the Joseph Smith Translation of the Bible (JST) and certain informative sections of the Doctrine and Covenants, underscore the importance of these scriptural texts. In addition, from the Book of Mormon it is clear that before 600 B.C.E. the prophet Lehi and his colony carried to the Western Hemisphere from Jerusalem a record on the plates of brass that included many Old Testament texts (1 Nephi 5:10–15), leading

---

[26] Ibid., p. 260.

Lehi and his descendants to look forward to a redeemer (1 Nephi 19:22–23) and giving them a guide for their moral and spiritual development (Mosiah 1:3, 5).

The Old Testament, even by the name Old Covenant, is thus not outmoded in the LDS view. It contains narrative, wisdom, and prophetic literature from ancient epochs; and even though some "plain and precious" parts have been lost, many of these have been restored in LDS scripture (1 Nephi 13:40). It frames a series of ancient covenants with Jehovah (Jesus Christ) as distinguished from the higher covenants in the New Testament (e.g., Matthew 26:28; Luke 22:20; 1 Corinthians 11:25; 2 Corinthians 3:6; Hebrews 7:22). Latter-day Saints view them all as elements in the same divine Plan of Salvation.[27]

---

[27] Ibid., p. 1027.

CONTRIBUTORS

Bishop LeRoy Bailey, Jr. is the Senior Pastor and Chief Executive Officer of The First Cathedral, Bloomfield, CT. Bishop Bailey received a B.A. from American Baptist College, Nashville, TN; a Master of Divinity from Howard University, Washington, DC; honorary Doctor of Divinity Degree from Tennessee Baptist School of Religion, Memphis, TN; a Doctor of Ministry from Hartford Seminary, Hartford, CT and a Honorary Doctorate Degree from Biblical Life College and Seminary, Marshville, MO. Bishop Bailey is the author of *A Solid Foundation*.

W. Robert Chapman is the author of *One God in One Person Only: Unitarianism Challenges the Connecticut Standing Order, 1800–1820* (1991) and other works about Unitarian Universalist history. A member of the Unitarian Society of Hartford, he was graduated with honors in history at Trinity College, where he was elected to the Phi Beta Kappa and Pi Gamma Mu honor societies. He is a reference librarian at the Hartford Public Library.

Rev. Robert W. Cudworth, Deacon served in the U.S. Navy 1943–1946; saw action Omaha Beach, Normandy, France, June 6, 1944. Graduated from Trinity College, class of 1945. He was ordained a deacon in the Episcopal Church, Christ Church Cathedral, Hartford, CT, December 1, 1990. Rev. Cudworth served as a deacon in the following parishes: Saint John the Evangelist, Yalesville, CT; Trinity, Portland, CT; Grace, Newington, CT and Saint John's, West Hartford, CT. He also served as chaplain, Institute of Living, February, 1990 and continuing.

Rev. Aidan N. Donahue, S.T.L., is a priest of the Archdiocese of Hartford, Connecticut. After completing studies for the licentiate in dogmatic theology at the Pontifical University of St. Thomas Aquinas in Rome in 1996, he served five years as President-Rector of St. Thomas Seminary in Bloomfield. He currently serves as pastor of Sacred Heart Parish in Bloomfield, Connecticut with additional duties as Ecumenical Officer, as Director of Continuing Formation of Priests, and as Director of Diaconate Formation for the Archdiocese of Hartford.

The Reverend Dr. Alvan Nathaniel Johnson, Jr., a native of Oklahoma was raised in Georgia and Boston, MA. He pastors Bethel African Methodist Episcopal Church in Bloomfield, CT. He is extensively involved in the spiritual, educational, and social concerns of the Greater Hartford, Connecticut area community. He also teaches as an adjunct professor at the Hartford Seminary and Yale University. In addition to his pastoral duties he presently serves as Chairman of the Greater Hartford Interfaith Coalition for Equity and Justice; a coalition comprised of 36 congregations from the Catholic, Protestant, Jewish, Muslim, Unitarian Universalist, Church of God in Christ, and First Church of the Living God faiths. He has traveled extensively throughout the United States, Europe, Canada, Israel, Africa, and the former Soviet Union spreading the message of God's love, lecturing, and teaching.

Frank G. Kirkpatrick is the Ellsworth Morton Tracy Lecturer in Religion and Professor of Religion at Trinity College, Hartford, where he has been on the faculty since 1969. He has published 5 books *Living Issues in Ethics* (Wadsworth, 1982), *Community: A Trinity of Models* (Georgetown University, 1986), *Together Bound: God, History, and the Religious Community* (Oxford University, 1994), *The Ethics of Community* (in the series "New Dimensions to Religious Ethics", Blackwell's 2001), *A Moral Ontology for A*

Theistic Ethic (for the Heythrop Studies in Contemporary Philosophy, Religion, and Theology, Ashgate, 2003). He received his BA from Trinity College in 1964, his MA from Union Theological Seminary and Columbia University in 1966 and his PhD in Religious Studies from Brown University in 1970.

Rabbi Dr. Philip Lazowski was born in Poland and is a Holocaust survivor. He received his BA from Brooklyn College, was ordained by the Academy of Higher Jewish Learning and received Doctorates from the Jewish Theological Seminary of America and the Jewish Teachers' Seminary and Peoples' University. He is Rabbi Emeritus of Beth Hillel Synagogue of Bloomfield, Connecticut which he served from 1969–2000. He has served as Chaplain at the Institute of Living, the Hartford Police Department and the Connecticut State Senate. *Understanding Your Neighbor's Faith* is his sixth published book.

Dr. Andrew Walsh is associate director of the Leonard E. Greenberg Center for the Study of Religion in Public Life at Trinity College in Hartford, Connecticut. His book, *Orthodox Christianity in America*, is scheduled to be published by Columbia University Press in 2004.

Terry W. Wiles is the Senior Pastor of Crossroads Community Cathedral, East Hartford, Connecticut, President of Crossroads Community International Fellowship and on the Chaplain Corps of the Hartford Police Department. Through his ministry over forty churches have been built in Africa and in Central and South America. During his tenure in the Hartford area Pastor Wiles has served two terms on the board of directors of the Connecticut Prison Association, five years on the executive board of Christian Advance International and fifteen years as an overseer of churches for the Southern New England Assemblies of God.

David Williams has served as the Bishop of the West Hartford Ward since 1999. He has served in various Church callings including the High Council, Ward and Stake Young Men's Presidencies, Seminary Teacher, and Bishop's Councilor. He is employed by Milliman USA as a Health Care Counsultant.

INDEX